Stephanie Gross

Banks and Shareholder Value

GABLER EDITION WISSENSCHAFT

Stephanie Gross

Banks and Shareholder Value

An Overview of Bank Valuation
and Empirical Evidence on
Shareholder Value for Banks

With a foreword by Prof. Dr. Andreas Hackethal

Deutscher Universitäts-Verlag

Bibliografische Information Der Deutschen Nationalbibliothek
Die Deutsche Nationalbibliothek verzeichnet diese Publikation in der
Deutschen Nationalbibliografie; detaillierte bibliografische Daten sind im Internet über
<http://dnb.d-nb.de> abrufbar.

Dissertation Universität Frankfurt am Main, 2006

1. Auflage Dezember 2006

Alle Rechte vorbehalten
© Deutscher Universitäts-Verlag I GWV Fachverlage GmbH, Wiesbaden 2006

Lektorat: Ute Wrasmann / Nicole Schweitzer

Der Deutsche Universitäts-Verlag ist ein Unternehmen von Springer Science+Business Media.
www.duv.de

Umschlaggestaltung: Regine Zimmer, Dipl.-Designerin, Frankfurt/Main
Druck und Buchbinder: Rosch-Buch, Scheßlitz
Gedruckt auf säurefreiem und chlorfrei gebleichtem Papier
Printed in Germany

ISBN 978-3-8350-0433-7

To my parents and Kim

Foreword

When CEO Joseph Ackermann set Deutsche Bank the target for 2005 of achieving at least 25% return on equity before tax, he was sending out a clear signal: Management in the German banking sector was finally realizing that it had to focus more on shareholder interests. Parallel to the discontinuation of German state guarantees, Gewährträgerhaftung and Anstaltslast, in 2005, there was a change in owner's requirements on members of the largest German banking group - the Landesbanks and savings banks. Some municipalities have been increasing pressure on their institutions to create greater financial value, which will then allow higher payouts. The increasing importance of shareholder value orientation in the banking sector poses at least three interesting sets of questions:

- How should one measure economic value creation (for shareholders) in banking? Does the banking sector possess any special features that have to be taken into consideration when measuring this?
- To what extent do banks' market values truly reflect expected shareholder value creation? Which factors are responsible for systematic deviations of a bank's intrinsic value from its market value?
- What are the key financial and operational levers that bank managers should focus on in order to increase shareholder value?

This dissertation by Ms. Gross focuses on precisely these three sets of questions. It provides a very good summary of the status of the relevant literature and uses high quality data and appropriate methodology to achieve groundbreaking results that are relevant both in terms of scientific value and in terms of practical application.

Prof. Dr. Andreas Hackethal

HCI Endowed Chair of Financial Services Sales and Distribution

European Business School, Oestrich-Winkel

Preface

This dissertation was written during my time as a doctoral student at the Faculty of Economics and Business Administration of the Johann Wolfgang Goethe University in Frankfurt am Main. Several people and institutions kindly supported me throughout the dissertation process and I would like to express my sincere thanks for this support.

I owe special thanks to my academic supervisor, Prof. Dr. Andreas Hackethal, who continually facilitated my research project and academic development. His constructive advice combined with his accessibility at any time and his openess for discussion were a great help in writing this dissertation. I would also like to thank my second advisor, Prof. Dr. Mark Wahrenburg, for his valuable and helpful suggestions. In addition, I would like to express my gratitude to the colleagues and friends who supported me in discussing the content and methodology as well as proofreading the dissertation. In particular, I would like to thank my sister for her relentless advice.

Most of all, I would like to express my deepest gratitude to my parents and Kim. This dissertation is dedicated to them.

Stephanie Gross

Summary of Contents

Table of Contents

List of Figures

List of Tables

List of Abbreviations

APT	Arbitrage Pricing Theory
APV	Adjusted present value
AR1	First-order autoregressive process
Bn	Billion
CAPM	Capital Asset Pricing Model
CIR	Cost-income ratio
DCF	Discounted cash flow
DNA	Deoxyribonucleic acid
DS	Datastream
DSGV	Deutscher Sparkassen- und Giroverband
EP	Economic profit
EPS	Earnings per share
EUR	Euro (currency)
EVA	Economic value added
EV/EBIT	Enterprise value to earnings before interest and taxes (multiple)
EV/EBITDA	Enterprise value to earnings before interest and taxes, depreciation and amortization (multiple)
HGB	Handelsgesetzbuch (German accounting standards)
HVB	HypoVereinsbank
IAS	International Accounting Standards
IFRS	International Financial Accounting Standards
IT	Information technology
IV	Intrinsic value
LLP	Loan loss provision
LM	Langrange Multiplier (test)
LSDV	Least squares dummy variable (model)
MA1	First-order moving average (autoregressive) process
M&A	Mergers and acquisitions
M/A	Market value to book assets (multiple)

M/B	Market value to book equity (multiple)
Mn	Million
MVA	Market value added
N	Number of observations
NOPAIT	Net operating profit after interest and taxes
OLS	Ordinary least squares
P/E	Price to earnings (multiple)
PV	Present value
P-value	Probability value (exact level of significance)
R^2	Coefficient of determination
R&D	Research and development (expense)
RAROC	Risk-adjusted return on capital
RI	Residual income
RIOE	Residual income on equity
ROE	Return on equity
ROIC	Return on invested capital
SDC	Securities Data Company (worldwide M&A database)
SIC	Standard Industrial Classification (industry code)
TMT	Telecommunication, media, and technology (sector)
TRS	Total return to shareholders
TV	Terminal value
UK	United Kingdom
US	United States (of America)
USD	US Dollar (currency)
US GAAP	United States Generally Accepted Accounting Principles
WACC	Weighted average cost of capital

List of Symbols

A	Assets (control variable)
α	Intercept coefficient (constant)
α_t	Intercept coefficient (time-variant)
α_{it}	Intercept coefficient (time- and unit-variant)
b	Subscript denoting business model
$beta$	Beta (systematic risk of the equity)
BM	Business mix
bu	Subscript denoting business unit
β_n	Slope coefficient for model variables
$\beta_{e,n}$	Sensitivity of the equity risk to factor n
c	Unobserved effect
c_e	Cost of equity
CO	Cost efficiency
d	Decay rate
DD	Discounted dividend (model)
DIV	Dividends
E	Equity
d	Subscript denoting earnings before taxes
EE	Economic equity
$E(r_m)$	Expected rate of return on the market portfolio m
f	Subscript for explicit forecast interval (Phase 1)
FCF_e	Free cash flow to equity
BS	Branch structure
g	(Expected) growth rate
i	Subscript denoting individual banks
IR	Industry / bank type subsample (dummy variable)
IND	Interest rate (control variable)

IV	Intrinsic value
γ_n	Risk premium of the factor n
m	Subscript denoting the market
MV	Market value
n	Subscript denoting the country
$NOPAIT_{Adj}$	Adjusted net operating profit after interest and taxes
R_{bm}	Rate of return on the benchmark index
r_f	Risk-free rate of return
RC	Risk capabilities
REG	Regional subsample (dummy variable)
RI	Residual income
$RIOE$	Residual income on equity
ROE	Return on equity
$ROIC$	Return on invested capital
S	Sample type (control variable)
s	Subscript denoting the sector
t	Subscript denoting time (year)
T	Length of the explicit forecast period
TV	Terminal value
u	Regression residual (disturbance)
v	Random effects residual (disturbance)
$WACC$	Weighted average cost of capital
$YEAR$	Year (dummy variable)

I. Introduction

During the last few decades, the shareholder value approach has been the management concept that has most significantly shaped today's economies and the way companies do business. In fact, shareholder value has become the pre-eminent performance indicator for companies worldwide, and maximizing shareholder value represents the ultimate directive for managerial decisions in all industries and, in particular, in banking.[1]

The shareholder value approach has significantly affected the way banks carry out their business, and creating sustainable shareholder value has been the prime objective of European banks in recent years. The strategy chosen by Deutsche Bank, the leading German bank, illustrates this fact: The core of its strategy is to create shareholder value, and in line with this strategic goal, Deutsche Bank is making every effort to strengthen its share price. This is also reflected by the short and medium-term targets set by its chief executive, Josef Ackermann, who declared an ROE target of 25 percent to be the central target figure of the bank, before committing himself to reaching this target by the end of 2005.[2]

The Deutsche Bank example not only indicates the importance of a shareholder value orientation for banks, but also reveals the resistance that exists to this management concept within Germany, and in particular within the banking sector. Deutsche Bank's ambitious ROE target has and will require rigid cost reduction measures to be implemented by its management, and the resulting lay-offs have sparked a controversial debate on the shareholder value orientation of Deutsche Bank.[3] In the business press,

---

[1] See Coenenberg and Salfeld (2003), p. 3; Henzler (2003).

[2] See Steevens (2005); Hiller and Fehr (2005).

[3] See Wittkowski (2005).

Deutsche Bank has come to symbolize Germany's capitalistic, inhuman companies and this current controversy involving banks and shareholder value in itself suggests that objective examination of the subject is required.

This dissertation comprises three studies that relate to *Banks and Shareholder Value* and aims to clarify the subject both from a theoretical and empirical perspective. Starting with a review of the literature, the dissertation proceeds from general guidance on the derivation of shareholder value of banks to empirical analyses on the relevance of shareholder value and on value drivers for banks.

When applying the shareholder value approach to banks, the measurement of shareholder value, i.e. the valuation of a bank, is the prerequisite and the starting point for all research. For this reason, **Part II** addresses the fundamental question: *How to measure the shareholder value of banks?*

More than 15 years after the first appearance of Copeland et al. (1990) groundbreaking and standard-setting work on valuation and the countless articles and books on company valuation that followed in its wake, the question could well be asked: Why write another article on valuation?

The question is a legitimate one. However, having surveyed the wide-ranging literature available on valuation and on bank valuation in particular, one author concludes: "Literatur zur Unternehmensbewertung allgemein gibt es eher schon zuviel, aber zu den Besonderheiten bei Kreditinstituten eher zu wenig; die in unserem Lande berufsständisch (ich könnte mich auch versprechen: berufsständig) dazu berufenen Wirtschaftsprüfer sind – so jedenfalls meine Erfahrung – in diesen Besonderheiten nur unzureichend praxiserfahren."[4] Another author adds: "Selbst Bankiers als geborene Anlageberater passen, wenn sie ihre eigene Branche bewerten sollen, so als falle die

---

[4]   Müller (1994), p. 85.

Beurteilung von Kreditinstituten unter das Bankgeheimnis."[5] Ten years later, there is still a lack of comprehensive coverage of this subject. Moreover, the valuation literature that does focus on banks has rarely been practicable and theoretically satisfactory at the same time.[6]

The objective of Part II is therefore to give an overview of the current thinking on bank valuation and to serve as a comprehensive and at the same time practical guide to measuring shareholder value of banks. When valuing a bank, two questions immediately arise. First of all: Which valuation methods apply to banks and which do not? And secondly: In which cases do the standard valuation methods have to be adjusted and how?

To answer the first question, Part II studies the prevalent valuation methods such as multiples, and net asset values, as well as income-oriented and cash flow-oriented models, in order to examine the general applicability of these methods to banks. The conclusion is that the basic principles of valuation apply just as much to banks as they do to other industries, the required use of the equity approach being the essential dissimilarity between banks and other industries. In view of the special role of financing in banking, the equity approach is more appropriate for banks, and highly recommended for valuations based on multiples, discounted cash flow (DCF), and residual income.

Assessing valuation methods for their compliance with shareholder value does not differ from what is generally valid for other industries. As in the case of non-banks, the fundamental valuation models are superior ways of measuring the shareholder value of banks. The DCF and residual income model are preferable to alternative valuation

---

[5] Schmidt and Wilhelm (1988), p. 137.

[6] Section II.2 gives an overview of the existing literature on bank valuation and discusses these shortcomings in detail.

approaches, such as multiples and net asset values, which only play an auxiliary function in bank valuation.

With respect to the second question, we study the potential adjustments that are required to customize the standard DCF and residual income models for banks, and identify six key adjustments in this context.[7] We advise practitioners to follow these adjustments to obtain a reliable estimate of a bank's shareholder value. Furthermore, we prefer the residual income approach to DCF for its ease of use in the case of banks.

The analysis of bank valuation literature in Part II reviews current thinking on bank valuation and highlights the gaps in the empirical research on bank shareholder value. Empirical studies on shareholder value of banks are scarce. However, empirical evidence is required to overcome the doubts that still exist concerning the relevance of shareholder value for banks. Skepticism in this regard has subsisted amongst academics and bank managers because of the special role of banks in national economies and the complexity of bank valuation. **Part III** aims to overcome this skepticism by studying the *empirical relevance of shareholder value for banks*.

The initial hypothesis and precondition of the shareholder value approach is that the market value of a company approximates its intrinsic value. Our study examines the validity of this characteristic of market value and intrinsic value for banks. For a sample of 290 worldwide banks, we estimate an ex-post intrinsic value based on the operating performance of the sample banks and compare this value estimate to the market values observed between 1989 and 1998. With 2,900 bank-year observations, this is, to our knowledge, the first study to provide large-scale evidence on banks.

---

[7]   Section II.5.6 summarizes the key adjustments to the standard DCF and residual income model for banks.

The above-described model was designed based on two joint hypotheses: the fit of the applied valuation model for banks and the existence of market efficiency. In the course of our paper, we successively test the validity of these two hypotheses.

With respect to the fit of the valuation model, we first look at the existing research in this area. Accounting-oriented capital market research has extensively studied the reliability of value estimates in the past. In line with Feltham and Ohlson (1995), who rediscovered the residual income model for their academic research, most articles support the superiority of value estimates from the residual income model when measuring shareholder value.[8] Unfortunately, the empirical evidence found is based on data that explicitly excludes financial institutions.[9] Therefore, empirical evidence on the validity of the superiority of residual income for banks has yet to become available.

We estimate intrinsic value based on the residual income model and conduct several tests on the reliability of the value estimates produced by the residual income model for our sample banks. We first study the accuracy and explanatory value of the value estimates from the residual income model compared to the estimates from the discounted dividend model for our sample banks. Empirical evidence suggests that the residual income model is superior to the discounted dividend model when it comes to measuring bank shareholder value. We reconcile the results for our sample banks with the empirical evidence found for other industries. The results of the comparison suggest that value estimates from the residual income model are even more reliable for banks than for other industries. On this basis, we conclude that residual income is an appropriate value estimate for the shareholder value of banks.

---

[8] See Section III.2. Table III-1 gives a brief overview of existing studies and results.

[9] Typically studies exclude financial services providers and utilities, given the fundamental differences in the business economics of these industries.

To test the second hypothesis on market efficiency, we study the predictive power of market values concerning the fundamental performance of banks. We therefore analyze the observed prediction errors of market value and potential determinants, such as regional scope, bank type, bank size, profitability, and time effects.

Similar to other industries, the study findings for our banking sample suggest that the profitability of banks is one determinant of the prediction error of market values. Furthermore, the size of the prediction error significantly differs across regions and over time. These variations can be attributed to asset bubbles overlying the market development in the corresponding region. We find no evidence of bank type and bank size influencing the prediction errors.

In summary, we do not find determinants of prediction errors that are specific to banks, or any other factors that indicate that, unlike for non-banks, the predictive power of market values does not exist for banks. Based on the evidence found, we infer that the shareholder value approach is a valid measure of bank performance and a relevant strategic concept for banks.

The empirical evidence on the relevance of the shareholder value approach for banks provided in Part III immediately raises a further question: What drives the shareholder value of banks? **Part IV** therefore addresses this question and looks at the DNA of shareholder value creation in the case of banks. The research objective in this concluding part is the measurement of the *value drivers of retail banks*. The empirical study aims to understand the metrics behind bank value and to provide valuable insights into the management of banks.

We identify the business mix, the branch structure, the cost efficiency, and the risk capabilities in relation to banks as potential drivers of shareholder value. Applying a panel data analysis, we study the impact of the four value drivers on value creation and the underlying income, cost, and risk structure of our sample banks.

We look at a sample of 139 retail banks over the observation period from 1998 to 2003. The data set is unique for two reasons: Data for the retail units of worldwide universal banks combined with data for German savings banks allows us to concentrate on pure retail players and to perform an isolated analysis of the value drivers in retail banking. To our knowledge, this is the first study in this area. Besides accounting information, the data set includes unique information on the branch structure of our sample banks. Standard company databases typically do not provide such information, and the study thus promises to yield new insights.

Study findings suggest that the cost efficiency and risk capabilities of our sample banks are important drivers of their shareholder value. Concerning the business mix and the branch structure, the empirical evidence from our study is ambiguous. Regression results for the business mix, measured by the diversification of income, are controversial. We therefore cannot draw a conclusion on the value creation potential of the business mix of a bank based on our sample.

The empirical results provide only weak evidence of the branch structure being a value driver of banks. We study the ratio of customers per branch as well as several alternative parameters of a bank's branch structure. The evidence of a relationship between branch structure and value creation remains vague, however. We therefore conclude that the branch structure of a bank has no direct impact on value and that potential value implications are driven instead by the interdependence of the branch structure and other value drivers.

The study results represent a first step towards a better understanding of the empirical drivers of shareholder value in banking. However, a complete decoding of the DNA of shareholder value creation with respect to (retail) banks will require further research in the future.

This dissertation comprises four main sections including the above introduction. Each of the following three core sections addresses one of the above-described issues in the context of banks and shareholder value. To avoid redundancies, we dispense with a full description of the structure of the individual sections at this point and refer to the introduction of the relevant sections. For the same reasons, we do not repeated summaries of the core results and implications at the very end of the document.

II. How to measure the shareholder value of banks?

II.1 Motivation and key research questions

The shareholder value approach and its aim of shareholder value maximization is currently the most important comprehensive management tool in use. For banks, the shareholder value approach is not only an important strategic management tool; its overarching objective of shareholder value maximization is vital for banks to exist. Unlike non-banks, banks are required to secure their business with equity capital. Consequently, the provision of equity capital is conditional for the growth of banks' business volume and therefore is a highly critical function for banks. As higher shareholder value eases access to equity capital, a shareholder value orientation is especially important for banks. In addition, the equity returns of European banks and German banks in particular, are low relative to international banks, and this, coupled with the increasing competition and globalization in banking, makes it even more important to take action and to become more strongly oriented towards shareholders' interests. Despite its relevance to banks, the shareholder value approach has only recently gained importance in the banking industry.

The starting basis of the shareholder value approach is the measurement of shareholder value, i.e. the fundamental valuation of companies. Valuation is an important tool in many business situations, such as part of internal strategic planning processes or decisions concerning mergers and acquisitions. The multitude of literature on valuation theory reflects this importance. As the shareholder value approach was originally developed for industrial companies, most of the standard literature on valuation focuses on industrial companies and does not take into account the institutional specifics of banks. Copeland et al. (2000), authors of the standard work on valuation, devote only one chapter to the specifics of valuing financial institutions, and articles and doctoral thesis only sporadically cover issues relating to bank valuation.

Looking at the literature on the valuation of banks, some articles call for a proprietary valuation methodology for banks.[10] Others claim that while institutional specifics significantly affect the valuation of banks, they do not justify a proprietary valuation approach.[11] Irrespective of the answer to this question, the valuation of banks requires specific expertise in two special subjects: an in-depth knowledge of valuation techniques, and a deep understanding of the banking industry and the bank-specific characteristics of valuation.

This being the case, two key questions relating to the measurement of the shareholder value of banks immediately arise:

• Which valuation methods apply to banks and which do not?

• In which cases do the standard valuation methods have to be adjusted and how?

The study addresses these questions by summarizing the bank-specific literature on valuation and value-based management. We examine the applicability of valuation methods to banks and of adjustments to standard valuation models in order that they reflect the specific characteristics of banks.

In our paper, we summarize the small body of bank valuation literature published so far along with the bank-specific characteristics of valuation. The aim of the study is to serve as a comprehensive guide to the measurement of the shareholder value in the case of banks. The paper covers current thinking on bank valuation and discusses the relevant bank-specific characteristics, and we aim it at readers with a basic knowledge of valuation, without providing a general introduction to the principles of valuation.

Section II.2 gives an overview of the existing literature on bank valuation. Section II.3 derives the institutional specifics of banks in the context of valuation based on banking

---

[10] See Adolf et al. (1989), p. 485; Strutz (1993), p. 102; Höhmann (1998), p. 21.

[11] See Zessin (1982), p. 61; Koch (2002), p. 55.

definitions and the structure of the financial statements of banks. Section II.4 gives an overview of the prevalent valuation methods and assesses their applicability to the banking industry based on the institutional specifics of banks discussed in Section II.3. Section II.5 discusses the specific adjustments that are required to customize the DCF and residual income approach for banks. Section II.6 summarizes the results and provides an overview of the further research that will be required in the future.

II.2   Overview of bank valuation literature

The literature published in the area of shareholder value and value-based management
is manifold in nature. As the shareholder value approach was originally developed for
industrial companies, the majority of contributions focuses on the valuation of industrial companies and do not account for bank-specific issues. Copeland et al. (2000),
authors of the standard work on valuation, devote just a single chapter to bank valuation, while Stewart (1990) and Young and O'Byrne (2000), who set the standard in
value-based management, do not discuss the specifics of value-based management for
banks at all. Overall, coverage of bank-related valuation issues is sporadic.

Though the number of articles and doctoral thesis in the area of bank valuation and
bank management has increased recently, only a few contributions give a detailed and
comprehensive overview of the adjustments to valuation necessary in a banking context and go on to deliver practical, hands-on advice for valuing banks.

Early German contributions from the 1980s, such as Zessin (1982), Schell (1988), and
Adolf et al. (1989), focus on the subject from the purely accounting viewpoint long
promoted by German auditors, and do not share the cash orientation of Copeland et al.
(2000) and standard valuation literature. North American contributions in the 1990s,
such as Mercer (1992), Johnson (1996), and Rezaee (2001), give a comprehensive
overview of the banking industry, introduce the general principles of valuation, and
cover some of the bank-specific issues.[12]

Few recent authors cover existing bank valuation literature comprehensively. Most
articles are typically limited to a general discussion of valuation principles and their
application to banks instead of further developing existing insights on bank-specific
valuation issues. Seidel (2000) limits his work to a description of the valuation stan-

---

[12] Wariboko (1994) only loosely covers the general principles of valuation and bank specific issues.

dards set by Copeland et al. (2000), and does not cover the fundamental specifics when valuing a bank. Kirsten (2000), Geltinger (2003) and Kümmel (1995) also follow the work of Copeland et al. (2000), but illustrate the relevant specifics of banks in detail. Their work, however, remains very theoretical, and hands-on advice for practitioners is rare. A further indication of the loose and unsystematic coverage of bank valuation issues is the fact that typical German and Swiss contributions mostly ignore the North American literature on bank valuation published in the 1990s.

When comparing the DCF and residual income model, many bank specifics support the use of a residual income approach for bank valuation, as we will see in Section II.4.5 and II.5.6. As in the case of non-banks, however, the DCF approach is the standard valuation model that is generally focused on in bank valuation literature, with only a few contributions such as Uyemura et al. (1996), Bodmer (2001), and MSDW (2001) including the residual income approach in their discussion.

Some authors exhibit a good understanding of the banking industry and give practical insights into bank valuation. Höhmann (1998) and Merkle (2001) both discuss the data availability for bank valuation within the framework of HGB accounting standards. Hörter (2000) and Koch (2002) illustrate their insights using many practical examples, while Damodaran (1994) and MSDW (2001) give hands-on advice for the practical external valuation of banks. Other contributions, however, like those of Becker (1997) and Bodmer (2001), remain very much on a technical level and do not provide assistance with the practical issues involved in bank valuation.

Table II-1 gives an overview of the existing literature on bank valuation. The grey shadings indicate contributions that cover the main issues related to bank valuation.

Some interesting contributions focus explicitly on one process step of the valuation process: Behm (1994), Arnsfeld (1998), and Faust (2002) discuss in detail the estimation of the cost of equity for banks, and Schell (1988) and Wildgruber (1998) explicitly deal with the forecast of bank performance and potential problems. Both articles, however, remain very technical in their approach.

Table II-1: Overview of bank-specific valuation literature

Author and Year	Valuation Models						Measuring Shareholder Value					Managing Shareholder Value					
	Institutional specifics of banks	Market oriented approaches	Net asset value	Discounted income	DCF	Residual income	Definition of performance measure	Forecast of future prospects	Cost of equity	Terminal value	Valuation of business units	Value drivers	Strategic planning	Controlling systems	Incentive compensation	Mergers & acquisitions	Case studies / Examples
Adolf et al. (1989a)		(x)	(x)	x			x	x	x	x	x						
Arnsfeld (1998)									x								
Arnsfeld and Gehrke (2001)	x				x		(x)		x								
Becker, D. (1999)	(x)		x	x	x		x	x	x	x	x						
Becker, G. (1996)			x		x					x			x				
Becker, G. (1997)													x				
Behm (1994)					x		x	(x)	x	x	x	x					x
Bodmer (2001)		x	(x)		x	x	x		x	x	x	x			x	x	
Böhme (1997)				(x)	(x)												(x)
Börner and Lowis (1997)	x				x		x	x	x	x	x	x					
Bremke and Busmann (2000)									(x)				x				
Brüning and Hoffjan (1997)													x				
Brunner (1996)					(x)								x	x		x	
Cates (1991)						(x)						x	x				
Copeland et al. (2000)	x				x	(x)	x	x	x	(x)	x						
Damodaran (2004)	x	x	x		x	x	x										
Dombret and Bender (2001)			x	x	x		(x)	(x)	(x)	(x)	(x)						
Faust (2001)	x				x		x	x	x	x	x				x		
Fiordolesi (2002)							x	x									x
Fiordolesi and Molyneux (2004)							x	x									x
Geltinger (2003)		x	x	x	x		x	x	x	x	x				x		(x)
Höhmann (1998)	x	(x)	x		x	x	x	x	x	x		x					(x)
Hörter (1996)													x				
Hörter (1998)		(x)			x	x	(x)	x	x	x	x		x				(x)
Johnson (1996)			x									x					
Kirsten (1995)													x	(x)			
Kirsten (2000)	x	x			x	x	x		x	x	x						
Koch (2002)	x	x	x		x		x		x		x		(x)		x		
Kümmel (1995)	x				x		x	x	x	x			(x)				
Kunowski (2002)	x	x	x	x	x		x	x	x		x						
Leemputte (1989)												x	(x)			(x)	
Lehar (1998)										x			x				
Liebich (1995)			x	x	x	x											
Lottner (1997)													x	x	x		
Matten (2000)					x	x	x	x	x	x	x			x			x
Mercer (2002)	x			x		x	x	x						x	x		
Merkle (2001)	x	x	x	(x)	x	x	(x)	x	x		x			x	x		(x)
MSDW (2001)	x					x			x	x	x			x	x	(x)	
Rezaee (2001)	x	x			x	(x)	x	x	x	x						x	
Schell (1988)				x			x										
Schierenbeck (1997)													x	x			
Schierenbeck (1998)														x			
Schmittmann et al. (1996)									(x)					x			
Schroeck (2002)													x	x			
Seidel (2000)				x			(x)		(x)					x	(x)		
Sonntag (2001)				x								x					
Strutz (1993)			x		x		x	(x)	x	x	x	x				(x)	
Süchting (1996)													x				
Uyemura et al. (1997)						x	x				x		x			x	x
Vettiger (1996)		x			x	x	x	x	x		x		x	x		x	x
Wariboko (1994)	(x)	x	x		x						x						
Wilde (1982)									x								
Wildgruber (1998)				x	(x)				x	x							
Zessin (1982)	x		x	x			(x)	x	(x)								
Zimmer and McCauley (1991)									x								x
Zimmermann and Jöhnk (1998)													(x)				
Zimmermann and Örtmann (1996)									x								
Zimmermann (1995)									x								

Source: Own table

Further contributions highlight recent trends or specifics of the banking industry. Spurred on by the recent consolidation trend within the banking industry, Becker (1999) and Koch (2002) focus on the valuation of bank mergers and acquisitions, while Merkle (2001) illustrates the problems involved in valuing the individual business units of universal banks.

Other articles discuss the influence of interest rate risk and banks' asset-liability structures on bank value. Kümmel (1995) emphasizes the influence of interest rate risk on bank valuation, while Sonntag (2001) relates valuation and the value-based management of banks to the concept of funds transfer pricing. Further insights into the implications of asset-liability mismatch on a bank's value and cost of capital are found in the contributions on bank asset-liability management, such as that of Zimmermann (1995).

The situation with respect to bank-specific literature on value-based management is similar. Most contributions, like those of Brunner (1996) and Lottner (1997), illustrate the general issues involved in integrating a value orientation into the planning, controlling, and incentive systems of a company. Only a small number of authors deepen the general discussion on value-based management and illustrate bank-specific issues when measuring and managing value. These include Lehar (1998), Matten (2000), and Schroeck (2002), who have all published risk management-oriented contributions that discuss potential problems when integrating value management into the existing risk management systems of banks.[13] Further research in the area of value-based management for banks is required. The present work, however, focuses on bank valuation. We thus do not discuss bank-specific aspects of value-based management in this article.

Although a variety of authors exemplify their insights with case studies, as indicated in Table II-1, empirical work is rare. The empirical studies listed in Table II-2 are mostly

---

[13] Brüning and Hoffjan (1997) state that the potential integration of risk-adjusted return on capital (RAROC) into a broader shareholder value analysis is one of its strengths.

driven by consulting companies. Except for Fiordelisi (2002), purely academic studies
providing empirical evidence on banks and shareholder value do not exist.

Table II-2: Overview of empirical studies on bank shareholder value

Author and year	Affiliated institution	Regional scope	Sample (N=)	Time period	Performance measure
Barfield (1998b)	PWC	Banks world-wide (Top 25)	25	1992-1997	Total return to shareholders (TRS)
Barfield (1998a))	PWC	Banks world-wide (Top 50)	50	1993-1998	TRS
Fiordelisi (2002)	None	Italian banks	33	1995-1999	EVA
Kennedy (1999)	Roland Berger	European banks	60	1993-1998	Outperformance of index
Sinn et al. (2003)	BCG	Worldwide banks	700	1998-2002	(Risk-adjusted) TRS
Sinn et al. (2004)	BCG	Worldwide banks	750	1999-2003	(Risk-adjusted) TRS
OECD (2004)	OECD	Worldwide banking index	N/a	2000-2003	Return index for sector
Uyemura et al. (1996)	Stern Stewart	Banks world-wide (Top 100)	100	1986-1995	EVA
MSDW (2001)	MSDW	US financial institutions	39	2001	Residual income
MOW (2003)	MOW	Financial institutions worldwide	400	Annually since 1997*	(Risk-adjusted) TRS

* 5 year moving window of performance data

Source: Own table

In addition to the empirical literature cited in Table II-2, analyst reports on banks nicely illustrate the application of valuation techniques to banks. These reports, however,
are typically limited to a single bank or a small sample of banks. With respect to the
drivers of value, the theoretical derivation of the drivers of bank shareholder value is

rare and empirical evidence on the potential drivers in a banking context does not exist to date.[14] A multitude of articles focus on the relevance of shareholder value in a banking context and in particular on its applicability to public savings banks and cooperatives given their specific ownership structures.[15] The majority of these contributions conclude that shareholder value is just as relevant for private and public banks as it is for non-banks. The discussions, above all, are focused on the general debate on the shareholder vs. the stakeholder view and do not produce bank-specific results any different to those found for non-banking industries. We have therefore excluded these articles from the scope of this study.

---

[14] Leemputte (1989) studies the impact of strategic restructuring on bank value creation. Yet, the approaches identified for the maximization of shareholder value are universally valid and not specific to banks.

[15] See Amely (1997); Zimmermann and Jöhnk (1998); Hörter (2000); Schuster (2000); Shaw (2000).

II.3   Bank specifics in the context of valuation

Standard literature on valuation is directed towards industrial companies. However, banks differ significantly from industrial companies due to their role as a service provider and financial intermediary. The specifics of banks imply adjustments to the valuation of banks, and based on the definition of banks and the comparison of the structures of their balance sheets and income statements with those of industrial companies, we identify a number of value-relevant bank specifics. In particular, specifics in the area of financing and risk-taking, laws and regulations, as well as the operating business of banks, are relevant for the valuation of banks.

II.3.1   Definition and business structure of banks

II.3.1.1   Definition of banks

The essential function of a bank is to provide services related to the storing of value and the extending of credit. A bank is a financial institution that provides banking and other financial services, and the term *bank* is generally understood to refer to an institution that holds a banking license.[16] The banking licenses granted by financial supervision authorities allow banks to provide basic banking services such as accepting deposits and making loans. Typically, a bank generates profits from the interest spread on the resources it holds in trust for its clients while paying them interest on the assets, and from transaction fees on financial services.

Banking services include the deposit, transport, exchange and provision of liquid funds. Production and selling are thereby intertwined and cannot be isolated.[17] Further-

---

[16] The terms *bank* and *credit institution* are used synonymously in the following.

[17] See Faust (2002), p. 40.

more, the use of various banking products is interwoven for cross-selling purposes.[18] For example, it is almost impossible for customers to use a bank's credit services or most of its capital investment services without making use of its payment transaction services.

The main difference between the banking industry and industrial companies is that banking services are not concrete physical goods. Indeed, customers often do not perceive the intangible products offered as discrete, fee-worthy services.[19] Furthermore, banking services are not storable. Due to the missing shelf life of banking services, banks must hold out sufficient capacity.[20]

Due to the phenomena of universal banking and consolidation within the financial services industry, a large and increasing number of banks have become diversified financial institutions, operating in more than one area of business,[21] including insurance, investment banking and asset management. Conversely, institutions offering the latter types of financial services have also diversified and now too offer traditional banking services. These characteristics result in the value-relevant specifics described in Section II.3.2.

II.3.1.2 Analysis of the balance sheet and income statement

Analyzing the structure of the balance sheets and income statements of banks and industrial companies allows us to derive several banking specifics relevant to valuation.

---

[18] See Börner and Lowis (1997), p. 95; Kirsten (2000), p. 133.

[19] See Faust (2002), p. 40; Kunowski (2002), p. 20.

[20] See Kümmel (1995), p. 15; Börner and Lowis (1997), p. 95; Büschgen (1998), p. 312; Koch (2002), p. 41.

[21] See Damodaran (2004), p. 2.

As illustrated in Table II-3, the balance sheet structure of banks differs significantly from the balance sheet structure of industrial companies.[22]

Table II-3: Structure of the balance sheet of banks vs. non-banks

Germany, 2001, percent

Assets	Non-banks	Banks	Liabilities & shareholders' equity	Non-banks	Banks
Property, plant and equipment	25%	1%	Equity capital and reserves	18%	4%
Investments	13%	2%	Provisions	20%	1%
Inventories	23%	n/a	Liabilities	62%	91%
Receivables	33%	74%	Trade payables	12%	n/a
from customers	15%	49%	Liabilities to financial institutions	20%	29%
from credit institutions	n/a	25%	Liabilities to non-banks	n/a	38%
Other receivables	18%	~0%	Securitised loans	n/a	23%
Investment securities	3%	19%	Other liabilities	31%	5%
Cash and cash equivalents	4%	1%			
Other assets	~0%	2%			
Total assets	100%	100%	Total assets	100%	100%

Source: Buba (2003b); Buba (2002a)

The major positions on the asset side of the balance sheet of industrial companies are property, plant and equipment (25 percent of total assets), inventories (23 percent of total assets) and receivables (33 percent of total assets). The asset side of a bank balance sheet, however, is dominated by receivables from customers and from credit institutions, accounting for three quarters of total assets. Tangible assets are of minor importance (1 percent of total assets) for banks whose major input factors are personnel expenses and investment in knowledge.[23] Inventories and changes therein do not exist, as banks provide services that are not storable.[24] Consequently, bank earnings are usually collected in the period in which they accrue. The net income of banks before any risk adjustments therefore has the character of a cash equivalent.[25]

---

[22] A comparison of the balance sheet structure of banks vs. non-banks and a detailed discussion of the differences is also found in Mercer (1992), pp. 97-120.

[23] See also Süchting (1996), p. 412.

[24] See Börner and Lowis (1997), p. 95; Koch (2002), p. 41.

[25] The cash adequacy of net income in banking is illustrated in Section II.4.3.

If we look at the liabilities' side of the balance sheet, we see that industrial companies are financed to the tune of approx. 50 percent by debt and to the tune of approx. 50 percent by equity and provisions, whereas bank financing is dominated by debt capital (91 percent of total liabilities).

A significant part of this debt, however, relates to the deposit business, i.e. it has no financing function, but instead is part of the operating business of a bank.[26] In contrast to most industrial companies, banks create value on the asset as well as on the liabilities side of their balance sheets.[27] From an outside-in perspective, however, the function of debt is hard to determine.[28] Equity capital and provisions only account for a minor part of the liabilities side, with equity capital being on average 4 percent of total liabilities compared to 18 percent for non-banks. Equity in banks instead functions as a liability and compensation for losses incurred rather than as a source of funding for the lending business.[29]

Table II-4 compares the structure of the income statements of banks to non-banks.[30] Supplies expenses (61 percent of total expenses) and staff expenses (17 percent of total expenses) dominate the operating expenses of industrial companies. For banks, however, interest expenses (71 percent of total expenses) and staff expenses (10 percent of total expenses) account for the majority of operating expenses. Depreciation on fixed assets and intangibles accounts for 3 percent of the expenses of industrial companies,

---

[26] See Zessin (1982), p. 55; Merkle (2001), p. 37.

[27] See Copeland et al. (2000), p. 429. The potential value creation on the liabilities side of banks is also shown by the concept of transfer pricing. See Geltinger (2003), p. 115. For an overview of the concept of transfer pricing, see Schierenbeck (1991), pp. 78-136.

[28] See Section II.3.2.1.

[29] See Höhmann (1998), p. 14.

[30] See also Mercer (1992), pp. 122-140, who studies the income statement of a sample bank and its composition in detail.

whereas for banks depreciation on fixed assets is very low. Provisions on receivables and securities, on the other hand account for 5 percent.

Table II-4: Structure of the income statement of banks vs. non-banks

Germany, 2001, percent

Revenues	Non-banks	Banks		Expenses	Non-banks	Banks
Sales	93%	n/a		Supplies expense	61%	N/a
Change in inventories	1%	n/a		Staff expense	17%	10%
Interest income	1%	83%		Other administrative expenses	n/a	7%
Income from provisions	n/a	7%		Depreciation	4%	7%
Income from securities & investments	n/a	4%		- on fixed assets & intangibles	4%	1%
Net income from financing business	n/a	1%		Provisions on receivables & securities	n/a	5%
Other income	5%	5%		Interest expense	2%	71%
				Tax charges	3%	1%
				Other expenses	14%	4%
Total income	100%	100%		Total expenses	100%	100%

Source: Buba (2003b); Buba (2003a)

Banking revenues are dominated by interest income (83 percent of total revenues) and only a small portion of income comes from provisions (7 percent of total revenues). The revenue of industrial companies is mainly sales proceeds resulting from the exchange of goods (93 percent of total revenues). In contrast to banks, interest income and expenses are not part of the operating activities of industrial companies, but belong to financing activities. Again, the predominance of interest income and interest expenses for banks shows the specific role of the financing function in banking.

II.3.2   Value-relevant specifics of banks

II.3.2.1   Specific role of financing and risk-taking

The analysis of the structure of balance sheets and income statements of banks compared to non-banks in the previous section shows the importance of the financing function for banks. In contrast to industrial companies, the financing function is part of the operating business of banks.

Financing represents a major part of a bank's value chain. Debt is a raw material to a bank, and represents "what steel is to General Motors, something to be molded into other financial products which can then be sold at a higher price and yield a profit".[31] The financing function not only serves to refinance the funds granted to customers as credits, but also represents an original source of revenue for banks.[32] As a result, banks create value both on the asset as well as on the liabilities side of their balance sheets. This specific characteristic of banks affects the valuation method of banks significantly, as banks can be only valued correctly if all financing activities are included in the valuation model.

A further specific of banks in the area of financing is the role of liquidity. For industrial companies liquid funds are only a residual of the production process. However, the liquidity kept on a bank's books plays a central role as a basic input factor into its banking business.[33] As a result, cash flows are significantly more volatile in banking and therefore more difficult to plan and forecast than in other industries.

The financial market risks taken on by banks on both sides of their balance sheets play a significant role in their business. Whereas other industries incur risks as a side effect of their original business activities, the original business activity of banks is to incur, structure, assess, and manage financial market risks.[34] As shown above, receivables represent the major portion of a bank's total assets. Interest income accounts for 83 percent of total revenues, and interest expense accounts for 71 percent of total expenses. Consequently, banks are highly dependant on interest rate risk.[35] They consciously incur interest rate risks and earn part of their revenue through refinancing at

---

[31] Damodaran (2004), p. 4.

[32] See Zessin (1982), p. 55; Höhmann (1998), p. 13; Kirsten (2000), p. 135; Merkle (2001), p. 37; MSDW (2001), p. 11.

[33] See Zessin (1982), p. 16; Höhmann (1998), p. 13; Merkle (2001), p. 39; Kunowski (2002), p. 20.

[34] See Behm (1994), p. 77; Höhmann (1998), p. 13; Kirsten (2000), p. 134.

[35] See Johnson (1996), pp. 217-249.

mismatched maturities. Given the relatively low share of equity financing,[36] banks have a significantly higher leverage risk than other industries and are highly vulnerable to even small changes in interest rates.[37] Furthermore, banks run additional risks because of proprietary trading activities. Banks' income from trading on their own account has increased continuously over recent years, thereby increasing their vulnerability to capital market risks.[38] Furthermore, in addition to the risks inherent in balance sheet items, banks take on significant risks by entering off-balance sheet positions such as swaps, forward deals and options on foreign currencies or securities.[39] In summary, the risks taken on by banks and the dependency on external factors associated with these risks increase the volatility of a bank's equity value and significantly complicate the forecasting of the future performance of banks relative to that of industrial companies.[40]

The business activities of banks in the financial markets as described above result in a general dependency on exogenous factors such as the economic cycle or trends in money, capital or real estate markets.[41] This direct dependency on changes in the macroeconomic environment shows up in particular in changes in a bank's credit losses. Macroeconomic trends have an immediate impact on the value of a bank, and this direct dependency complicates bank valuation and requires a thorough analysis of the macroeconomic parameters and the forecasting of future trends.[42] The impact of

---

[36] See Table II-3, p. 20.

[37] See Behm (1994), p. 44.

[38] See Faust (2002), p. 43.

[39] See Höhmann (1998), p. 14; Merkle (2001), p. 39.

[40] See Vettiger (1996), p. 121.

[41] See Börner and Lowis (1997), p. 95; Höhmann (1998), p. 11; Becker (1999), p. 27; Kirsten (2000), p. 133; Merkle (2001), p. 39; Koch (2002), p. 42.

[42] See Adolf et al. (1989), p. 485; Kümmel (1995), p. 16; Kunowski (2002), p. 21.

inflation risk, however, is relatively low, as banks trade with monetary contracts and, unlike industrial companies, do not produce real products.[43]

II.3.2.2   Bank-specific laws and regulations

Due to the risks taken on by banks, their specific role in the economic system, and their dependency on economic cycles, banks are subject to various bank-specific rules and regulations,[44] and the effects of regulatory requirements on value have to be considered. In this context, the bank-specific accounting standards and the capital adequacy requirements of banks are of particular relevance.

Due to banks' specific dependency on macroeconomic factors, legislators give them specific rights to build up reserves. In their role as financial intermediaries, banks absorb imbalances in the savings and investment behavior of their customers, leading to high volatility in the profit contributions of different bank products before and after risks.[45] To compensate for this industry feature, bank-specific valuation rules grant banks special rights to steer accounting results by building up and reducing reserves.[46] From an external perspective, banks' rights to build up hidden reserves significantly complicate the outside-in analysis of bank performance.[47] Banks use hidden reserves to steer accounting results and the resulting tax charge, and as a result, external analysts

---

[43]   See Kirsten (2000), p. 134.

[44]   See Adolf et al. (1989), p. 485; Höhmann (1998), p. 12; Merkle (2001), p. 39; Koch (2002), p. 43.

[45]   See Koch (2002), p. 41.

[46]   See Höhmann (1998), p. 12; Merkle (2001), p. 40; Kunowski (2002), p. 21. Krag (1988) gives an overview of these rights for German banks. With regard to international accounting standards, IAS regulation no. 39 and 40 regulate accounting for financial instruments and hedges. Yet banks' freedom to build up hidden reserves is more limited in IAS compared to HGB. See Krumnow (2001), pp. 191-193. For an overview of HGB, IAS, and US-GAAP as well as existing differences in accounting standards for banks, see Buba (2002b).

[47]   See Adolf et al. (1989), p. 485; Börner and Lowis (1997), p. 96; Koch (2002), p. 42.

find it almost impossible to evaluate the quality of a bank's credit portfolio, as direct conclusions from the provisions made are not possible.[48] Valuation rights complicate the consistent valuation of banks, and require input parameters in valuation models to be corrected for existing hidden reserves.[49]

Apart from specific rules concerning the accounting of various balance sheet items, banks are subject to specific capital adequacy rules given their role as macroeconomic institutions, including the capital standards put forward by the Basle Committee on Banking Regulations and Supervisory Practices.[50] In addition, rules on the maintenance of minimum reserves and systems for the protection of deposits regulate capital management within banks.[51] These capital rules restrict the payout of distributable profits to investors and therefore determine largely the equity value of a bank.[52] Consequently, bank capital represents a bottleneck for bank managers and has to be considered when formulating bank growth targets.[53]

Further specifics may result from the legal form of banks, as well as their affiliation to a specific bank type. As for any other industry, differences in the taxation of public and private companies and the consequences for bank shareholders are also factors to be considered when valuing banks.[54] For savings banks and co-operatives, institute-specific regulations exist in addition to the general bank regulations. Based on their

---

[48] See Vettiger (1996), p. 120; Copeland et al. (2000), p. 434.

[49] See Höhmann (1998), p. 12.

[50] According to the Basle capital rules, the business volume of a bank has to be translated into risk assets with a capital backing of 8 percent, of which 4 percent is to be Tier-One capital. For a detailed overview of the new Basle standards, see Buba (2002b). For an overview of the regulatory capital components of banks, see Rezaee (2001), pp. 249-252.

[51] See Höhmann (1998), p. 13; Kunowski (2002), p. 21. For a detailed overview, see Behm (1994), pp. 45-49.

[52] See Börner and Lowis (1997), p. 95; Merkle (2001), p. 40.

[53] See Dombret and Bender (2001), p. 329; Merkle (2001), p. 85; Koch (2002), p. 43.

[54] See Kunowski (2002), p. 22.

legal form, equity financing through external markets is complicated and, as a result, funding out of retained profits represents the dominant source of financing for both groups.[55]

Savings banks are characterized by the public mandate and the state guarantees granted to them in the past.[56] Nonetheless, profit orientation has become the dominant objective of savings banks in recent years, so that systematic differences in the valuation process for savings banks do not exist.[57] Cooperatives are characterized by the mandate to support their members. As this support is mainly provided in the form of dividend payments, they too are driven by the need to make a profit. Again, no systematic adjustments to the valuation process are necessary.

II.3.2.3   Specifics of the operating business

Apart from the specific role of financing and risk in banking and bank-specific regulations, the specific nature of banking services and the relationship between banks and their customers also interfere with the valuation of banks.

Due to the intangible character of banking services, product differentiation within banking is low and no banking products are patented.[58] Consequently, forecasting the future performance of banking products and banks is complicated.[59] Conversely, the long-term contracts and customer relations of banks simplify the forecasting of future performance, as the long contract durations and the high percentage of existing lending

---

[55] See Koch (2002), p. 44.

[56] For an overview of the German public banking sector and the structural changes after June 2005, see Goldman Sachs (2001); Berndt (2002).

[57] See Kunowski (2002), p. 22.

[58] See Koch (2002), p. 42.

[59] See Hörter (1998), p. 148.

relative to new lending allow more precise planning of cash flows in early years.[60] For short-term contract durations, the knowledge of customer behavior gained during often long-lasting customer relationships provides insights that allow a more detailed estimate of new lending.

In contrast to the product-oriented organization of the majority of industrial companies, the organization of banks is customer-oriented. As mentioned in Section II.3.1.1, cross-selling exists between individual banking products, and this often results in the hybrid costing of banking products, with individual services that generate low or even negative value contributions being subsidized by the value contributions of other services.[61] A product-oriented valuation of banks based on the performance of individual products is therefore not possible.[62] Banks have to be valued based on customer structures that incorporate the cross-selling effects of banking products.

Furthermore, the individual steps contained in the value chain of banks are inseparable, as the production process of banking services is typically a "uno-actu" production process.[63] Internal transfer pricing and capital allocation between banking units mean that valuation at the business unit level is very complicated.[64] Another structural characteristic of banks is the relative high share of fixed costs, due to the necessary storage of capacity in the form of staff and information technology.[65] Both factors, as well as their resulting consequences for bank unit valuation, are illustrated in Section II.5.5.

---

[60] For industrial and trading companies, a higher uncertainty in the forecasting of future performance exists due to the shorter-term customer relationships. See Börner and Lowis (1997), p. 96; Faust (2002), p. 41.

[61] See Faust (2002), p. 43.

[62] See Börner and Lowis (1997), p. 95.

[63] See Merkle (2001), p. 41; Koch (2002), p. 43.

[64] See Vettiger (1996), p. 121; Merkle (2001), p. 41; Koch (2002), pp. 42-43.

[65] See Börner and Lowis (1997), p. 96; Merkle (2001), p. 41.

II.4   Valuation methods and their applicability to banks

The following sections discuss different approaches to bank valuation. When valuing a bank, we measure its value on a stand-alone basis and assume the going concern of the bank. The applicability of standard valuation models to banks is measured using a two-step approach. First, the emphasis is placed on the specific applicability of the approach to banking given the value-relevant specifics of banks discussed in Section II.3.2. Secondly, we assess the effectiveness of the valuation methods with regard to the purposeful measurement and successful management of shareholder value. We therefore use the general assessment criteria of valuation models discussed in literature, these being market orientation, a forward-looking perspective, risk-return consideration, and operational manageability and practicality.[66] Section II.4.5 concludes with a discussion of the advantages and disadvantages of the valuation methods.

II.4.1   Market-oriented approaches

Capital market-oriented approaches use the information efficiency of stock exchanges and form comparative multiples that compare the value of an asset with the values assessed by the market for similar or comparable assets.[67] The identification of an appropriate benchmark company as well as choice of reference value are essential, and require careful analysis of the company to be valued.[68]

---

[66] See Vettiger (1996), p. 123; Höhmann (1998), pp. 14-17; Hörter (1998), p. 129.

[67] See Liebich (1995), p. 22; Dombret and Bender (2001), p. 326; Merkle (2001), p. 73. Another widely used approach to measure the value of a company is the comparison of realizable transaction prices. This approach provides useful backup in the case of an M&A decision, but is not appropriate for shareholder value measurement and management since these multiples are typically biased by acquisition premiums. See Dombret and Bender (2001), p. 328; Koch (2002), p. 40.

[68] See Vettiger (1996), p. 158; Koch (2002), p. 40.

Equity multiples are much better suited for valuing banks than value multiples.[69] Firm value multiples such as EV/EBIT or EV/EBITDA are not applicable to bank valuation, as the operating and financing activities of banks cannot be clearly separated.[70] With respect to equity multiples, we examine two widely used concepts and their applicability to bank valuation: price-to-earnings (P/E) multiples and the market-to-book ratio (M/B).[71]

One of the most widely used multiples is the P/E ratio, defined as the ratio of the market price to the earnings per share (EPS) of a company.[72] The actual P/E multiple typically uses historical earnings as an approximate value for earnings, and therefore lacks a forward-looking perspective.[73] The use of predicted P/E ratios and an estimate of future earnings can solve this problem. Nevertheless, valuation using P/E ratios is still limited to a return view and does not consider risk.[74] For banks in particular, risk plays an important role when assessing future performance.[75] High earnings growth in the short-term may lead to the destruction of shareholder value for banks in the longer-term if earnings growth is realized by a decrease in the quality of the credit portfolio.[76] Consequently, the P/E approach tends to overvalue growing banks with a high share of interest income.

Furthermore, the explanatory power of P/E ratios depends on the quality of the underlying accounting variables. In the case of banks, the application of P/E ratios is espe-

---

[69] The advantages of the equity approach in bank valuation are discussed in detail in Section II.4.3.

[70] See Damodaran (2004), p. 32.

[71] Another widely used multiple is the price-to-sales (P/S) multiple. For banks, P/S multiples cannot be used, as sales or revenues are not measurable for banks. See Damodaran (2004), p. 32.

[72] See Brealey and Myers (2000), p. 76.

[73] See Bodmer (2001), p. 42.

[74] See Vettiger (1996), p. 157; Damodaran (2004), p. 34.

[75] Section II.3.2.1 describes the special role of risk-taking in banking.

[76] See Kirsten (2000), p. 189.

cially questionable, as banks can significantly manipulate the basis of these multiples by means of their risk policy measurements, e.g., the build up of provisions.[77] This potential bias in banks' P/E ratios is hard to measure from an outside-in perspective. For diversified banks, the application of P/E ratios at the bank level is not reasonable, and meaningful results can only be achieved at the business unit level.[78]

For non-banks, advanced P/E multiples such as EV/EBIT and EV/EBITDA[79] help overcome the shortcomings of standard P/E multiples by excluding distorting and extraordinary factors such as taxes and depreciation. Since banks' operating and financing activities cannot be clearly separated, however, these advances in the standard P/E approach are not applicable to them.[80]

In addition to the theoretical weaknesses of the P/E approach, empirical studies find only a very low correlation between EPS growth and P/E multiples.[81] Given the low empirical evidence, P/E multiples and their applicability to banks also have to be questioned from a practical viewpoint.

---

[77] The problem of the reliability of accounting numbers also exists for industrial companies. However, given the specific valuation options that exist in bank accounting (as described in Section II.3.2.2), the potential manipulations in banking have a much wider scope. See Vettiger (1996), p. 158; Kirsten (2000), p. 188; Damodaran (2004), p. 33.

[78] Multiples for the retail and wholesale banking business, for example, differ significantly. See Damodaran (2004), p. 33.

[79] The EV/EBIT multiple is defined as the ratio of enterprise value to earnings before interest and taxes. By excluding financing activities and tax payments, the EV/EBIT multiple gives a better picture of the operating performance of a company than the standard P/E multiple. The EV/EBITDA multiple, defined as the ratio of enterprise value to earnings before interest and taxes, depreciation and amortization, additionally corrects for depreciation and amortization. See Fernández (2002), p. 149.

[80] See Kirsten (2000), p. 188; Bodmer (2001), p. 50; Damodaran (2004), p. 32.

[81] Kirsten (2000), p. 190, finds only a low correlation between EPS-growth and P/E multiples for European banks for the years between 1997 and 1999 with an R^2 of 0.16. See also Uyemura et al. (1996), p. 99.

Another widely used multiple is the M/B ratio, which compares market value to book equity.[82] The M/B multiple is forward-looking and relates the market's expectations concerning future performance to invested capital. Due to the balance of risk ability and profitability, M/B multiples have a higher explanatory power than P/E multiples when it comes to banking.[83] The relationship between M/B ratios and returns on equity should be relatively strong for banks, as the book value of equity is much more likely to be close to the market value of equity invested in existing assets.[84] The strength of the relationship in theory is validated by empirical evidence, with a high correlation between M/B multiples and ROE.[85]

Another ratio that is widely used for the analysis of industrial companies is the M/A multiple, which compares the market value of a company to its book assets. Conclusions on the value of banks based on M/A ratios are misleading, as they do not include the off-balance business of banks that often accounts for a significant part of their business.[86]

In summary, multiples represent good rules of thumb for valuing banks, and practitioners make substantial use of multiples in day-to-day business situations as rough approximations.[87] The multiples approach is simple and the required bank information easily accessible. However, the availability of comparable assets is limited, and firm-specific factors that might affect a company's multiple can only be accounted for to a

---

[82] See Brealey and Myers (2000), p. 830.

[83] See Kirsten (2000), p. 192.

[84] See Damodaran (2004), p. 36.

[85] See Vettiger (1996), p. 157. Hörter (1998), p. 110, finds an R^2 of 0.79 for the correlation of ROE and M/B ratios for a sample of 22 large US and European banks between 1992 and 1996. Kirsten (2000), p. 192, finds an R^2 of 0.70 for a European bank sample in 1999. Damodaran (2004), p. 37, finds an R^2 of 0.70 for commercial banks in the US.

[86] See Vettiger (1996), p. 158.

[87] See Bodmer (2001), p. 47.

certain degree.[88] Consequently, the use of multiples is problematic in an academic context.[89] Furthermore, some of the shortcomings of multiples are even increased in a banking context, as illustrated above.

One general problem is that management cannot directly influence multiples.[90] Market-oriented approaches lack transparency when it comes to the underlying value drivers and are therefore not suitable for stand-alone use. Their use for the measurement and management of bank shareholder value is therefore limited. Nevertheless, multiples have an important auxiliary function and support the fundamental valuation methods as an early indicator, control methodology and negotiation tool. Market-oriented approaches serve as indicators if the business environment is changing quickly or the retrieval of data required for the fundamental approaches is complicated.[91] Practitioners often use them as a control methodology to assess whether the intrinsic value is in line with the market view of the comparables or to render financial forecasts more accurate.[92] In negotiations, multiples limit the number of variables and thus facilitate communication.

---

[88] See Liebich (1995), p. 22. An overview of firm-specific factors for which adjustments might be required due to a lack of comparability is given by Mercer (1992), pp. 254-255, and Rezaee (2001), pp. 181-182.

[89] See Merkle (2001), p. 74; Kunowski (2002), p. 44.

[90] See Vettiger (1996), p. 158; Bodmer (2001), pp. 43-44.

[91] See Kunowski (2002), p. 45.

[92] See Rezaee (2001), p. 340; Hamoir et al. (2002), p. 7. In addition, Koch (2002), p. 40, states that the calculation of continuing value with multiples in a DCF context, as frequently seen for invest-ment banks, is not reasonable on a stand-alone basis and should only be used as a control check.

II.4.2   Asset-oriented approaches

Net asset value methods take an individual approach when it comes to valuation and measure the value of asset and liabilities separately. Net asset value methods are based either on liquidation values or on the replacement values of the assets.

The net asset value of a bank based on replacement values is calculated as the difference between the replacement costs of on-balance-sheet assets and liabilities.[93] This value generally does not or only inadequately incorporates unrecorded goodwill and other unrecorded intangible assets as well as all off-balance sheet items.[94] These items, however, may account for a major part of the value of a bank.[95] In addition, banks' book assets and liabilities have to be corrected for hidden reserves in the investment portfolio, in real estate assets and in the risk provision.[96] These adjustments are necessary to determine the true value of a bank, but are almost impossible to estimate from an outside perspective. Not only does the net asset approach measure only part of a bank's value, it generally does not assign any value to future growth and resulting excess returns.[97] The net asset value is not meaningful from an economic perspective, as "the relevant value estimate is based on the future income-generating capabilities of the bank as a whole operating unit, not on the specific assets it happens to own".[98] For instance, the net asset value approach does not account for the synergies and effects of

---

[93] See Merkle (2001), p. 68; Kunowski (2002), p. 23.

[94] See Strutz (1993), p. 97; Becker (1996), p. 22; Merkle (2001), p. 69; Koch (2002), p. 22. The full reproduction method includes goodwill in the valuation. However, the calculation of goodwill as part of the net asset value is complex. See Bodmer (2001), p. 130.

[95] See Höhmann (1998), p. 15.

[96] See Dombret and Bender (2001), p. 325.

[97] See Merkle (2001), p. 68; Damodaran (2004), p. 31.

[98] Rezaee (2001), p. 333. See also Höhmann (1998), p. 15; Becker (1999), p. 29; Merkle (2001), p. 69.

mergers, nor, to take another example, does it consider value creation or destruction based on high or low quality management.[99]

The liquidation value is forward-looking and measures the value of a bank by subtracting the value of individual liabilities from the value of individual assets based on liquidation values. However, once again it is not subject to an economic profit consideration. The liquidation value as the so-called "raider" approach assumes the liquidation of the bank and therefore violates the principle of going-concern.[100] It represents a minimum value and serves as a lower limit for the objective value of a company.[101] The estimation of the liquidation value as a floor is essential in valuation. This is especially the case in buy and sell decisions and for the valuation of non-operating assets such as industrial holdings.[102]

In contrast to the above discussion, that rejects the use of net asset values as a measure of bank shareholder value, this approach is actually in widespread use in the banking industry. The reasons might be the relatively high liquidity of bank assets as well as the proximity of banking to the capital markets.[103] Nevertheless, the net asset value is only meaningful for the valuation of individual financial investments and not for the valuation of banks as a whole. On a stand-alone basis, the liquidation value does not have a proprietary function in the valuation of shareholder value and only complements existing methods.[104]

---

[99] See Becker (1999), p. 30.

[100] See Adolf et al. (1989), p. 487; Strutz (1993), p. 97; Becker (1996), p. 22; Höhmann (1998), p. 14; Merkle (2001), p. 71.

[101] See Zessin (1982), p. 33; Höhmann (1998), p. 14; Becker (1999), pp. 31-32; Dombret and Bender (2001), p. 332.

[102] See Koch (2002), p. 23.

[103] See Merkle (2001), p. 71.

[104] See Becker (1999), pp. 30 and 32; Kunowski (2002), p. 24. For the auxiliary function of the net asset value, see Zessin (1982), pp. 33 and 37; Strutz (1993), p. 98.

II.4.3   Cash flow-oriented approaches

Cash flow oriented approaches are based on the principle of future benefits, which states that the value of any business equals the net present value of all future economic benefits attained as a result of the ownership of the business.[105] Looked at from this perspective, the value of a bank is driven by its ability to create cash flows in the future. DCF approaches measure value by estimating future cash flows and taking into consideration the time value of money.

Three basic concepts essentially underlie the cash flow-oriented valuation approaches.[106] The entity approach uses the weighted average cost of capital (WACC) of shareholders and debt holders as a hurdle rate or discount factor and estimates the enterprise value of a company.[107] The equity approach uses the cost of equity as a discount factor, thereby directly deriving the value of equity.[108] The adjusted present value (APV) method measures shareholder value in two steps: First of all the value of the company were it to be entirely financed by equity is calculated. Secondly, the value of the tax benefit arising from debt financing is added.[109]

Whereas the entity approach is the most widely used approach for valuing industrial companies, it falls short when measuring the shareholder value of banks.[110] With respect to banks, there is general agreement in literature that the equity approach is the

---

[105] See Rezaee (2001), p. 175.

[106] See Copeland et al. (2000), p. 131. In the past, academic valuation literature in Germany was strongly influenced by income models that focused on accounting income rather than cash flows as performance measures. However, the cash flow orientation is widely accepted today and differences between these approaches are only of terminological character. For details see Drukarczyk (1995); Merkle (2001), pp. 49-53.

[107] See Copeland et al. (2000), pp. 132-137; Merkle (2001), pp. 54-55; Faust (2002), p. 61.

[108] See Copeland et al. (2000), pp. 150-152; Faust (2002), p. 62.

[109] See Copeland and Weston (1992), pp. 439-451; Brealey and Myers (2000), pp. 555-559; Copeland et al. (2000), pp. 146-150; Merkle (2001), pp. 56-57.

[110] See Copeland et al. (2000), p. 428.

more appropriate model to use and there are several reasons for this.[111] As described in Section II.3.2.1, operating and financing activities in banks are intertwined. A bank creates value on the liabilities' side of its balance sheet not only by using financing instruments more efficiently than other market participants, but also by collecting cheap financing through its deposit franchise.[112] From the outside, it is almost impossible to determine whether the role of debt is to be permanent capital or just an instrument of spread management.[113] For this reason, it is difficult to assign the proper cost of capital to deposits and refinancing instruments.[114]

Another reason is that debt capital is composed of a variety of debt tranches varying in amount and the interest rate paid. As a result, the estimation of the overall cost of bank debt is complicated.[115] Given the high leverage of banks and consequently the small share of equity on the liability side of bank balance sheets, the cost of equity has only a small impact on the weighted average cost of capital. In addition, the margin between equity cost and interest income is very small. Small errors in the calculation of capital cost may therefore lead to significant variations in the value of equity.[116] The capital structure and the structure of the debt capital of banks are continuously changing. For

---

[111] See Sonntag (2001), p. 5. Also see Zessin (1982), p. 54; Strutz (1993), p. 86; Behm (1994), p. 59; Kümmel (1995), p. 32; Vettiger (1996), p. 125; Börner and Lowis (1997), p. 104; Höhmann (1998), p. 32; Hörter (1998), pp. 57 and 146; Becker (1999), p. 59; Kirsten (2000), p. 138; Bodmer (2001), p. 35; Merkle (2001), p. 59; MSDW (2001), p. 11; Faust (2002), p. 63; Koch (2002), p. 44; Kunowski (2002), p. 38; Geltinger (2003), p. 115; Damodaran (2004), p. 7.

[112] See Zessin (1982), p. 55; Behm (1994), p. 59; Faust (2002), p. 63.

[113] See Copeland et al. (2000), p. 429; Kunowski (2002), p. 32; Geltinger (2003), p. 116.

[114] This is especially the case for non-interest bearing funds such as checking accounts or float. See MSDW (2001), p. 11.

[115] See Höhmann (1998), p. 50; Faust (2002), p. 64. For a detailed overview of the problems involved in estimating the market value of bank debt, see Koch (2002), p. 45.

[116] See Kümmel (1995), p. 32; Höhmann (1998), p. 193; Copeland et al. (2000), p. 489; Faust (2002), p. 64; Koch (2002), p. 45; Geltinger (2003), p. 116.

this reason, the cost of equity varies significantly with changes in interest rates, and assuming a constant debt ratio and cost of debt may lead to misinterpretations.[117]

Similar to the entity approach, the APV approach falls short as a valuation method for banks, as the separation of operating and (re)financing activities is problematic for banks, as mentioned above. The calculation of the tax benefits from debt financing for the different tranches of debt capital of banks is not realizable due to the complexity of such a task, and would result in pseudo-accuracy.[118]

The equity approach is therefore the most qualified for measuring the shareholder value of banks. In particular, it is more appropriate for the measurement of shareholder value on a business unit level and for the management of shareholder value.[119] The choice of the equity model for valuing financial companies means that all debt is regarded as part of operations rather than financing. Debt is not considered capital and interest paid on debt is an operating expense.[120]

The equity value of a company is calculated as described by Equation II-1.

$$Equity\ value = \sum_{t=1}^{t=T} \frac{FCF_e}{(1+c_e)^t} + \frac{\overline{FCF_e}}{c_e} \frac{1}{(1+c_e)^T} \qquad\qquad \text{II-1}$$

with FCF_e = Free cash flow to equity
       c_e = Cost of equity

The derivation of the input factors of the model, free cash flow to equity and the cost of equity, as well as potential adjustments in a banking context, are described in Section II.5.

---

[117] See Höhmann (1998), p. 150; Faust (2002), p. 64.

[118] See Arnsfeld and Gehrke (2001), p. 494; Merkle (2001), p. 59; Kunowski (2002), p. 41.

[119] See Höhmann (1998), p. 150.

[120] See MSDW (2001), p. 11.

As for non-banking industries, the DCF method is the most widely used approach for measuring the shareholder value of banks. The reason for this might be the high empirical correlation between intrinsic DCF values and market values.[121] Other reasons could include the fact that the DCF method is forward looking, as it derives the value from expected future performance. It is also capital market-oriented, as it uses a discount factor that is based on the market opportunity cost. Compared to the use of multiples or net asset values, the DCF approach is complex, with forecasting future performance representing the most difficult part of the valuation.[122]

While the DCF approach is a good tool for measuring shareholder value, its application as a periodical management tool is limited. Free cash flow to equity in one period does not explain the value created over the period in question.[123] In consequence, periodical performance can only be measured directly by means of the market value added (MVA), i.e. the difference between the value in t and t-1.

II.4.4   Residual income-oriented approaches

Residual income represents the value created by a company over a certain period. Residual income methods measure economic profit by considering not only the reported accounting expenses but also the opportunity cost of the capital employed. More precisely, residual income equals the spread between the return on invested capital and the cost of capital times the amount of invested capital, as illustrated by Equation II-2.[124]

Residual income = Invested capital $\times$ $(ROIC - WACC)$ II-2

---

[121] See Brunner (1996), p. 86.

[122] See Kunowski (2002), p. 46.

[123] See Brunner (1996), p. 86; Vettiger (1996), p. 152; Copeland et al. (2000), p. 143.

[124] See Stewart (1990), p. 137; Copeland et al. (2000), p. 143; MSDW (2001), p. 14.

with $ROIC$ = Return on invested capital
            $WACC$ = Weighted average cost of capital

Alternatively, residual income can be defined as operating earnings less a capital charge for the economic capital used by the company, as depicted in Equation II-3.

Residual income = Operating earnings - ($WACC \times$ Invested capital)   II-3

with $WACC$ = Weighted average cost of capital

The concept of economic profit is old, dating back to at least 1890.[125] The classical concept underwent a renaissance in the 1990s, when consulting companies developed and strongly promoted modern residual income models.[126] Among the multitude of performance measures, the most well known are economic value added (EVA) and economic profit (EP).[127] Both these modern residual income concepts differ from traditional residual income approaches in two ways. In contrast to classical models, EVA and EP focus on operating residual incomes,[128] and operating and non-operating activities are separated, as the underlying business risks differ. EVA and EP, like the classical residual income concepts, rely on accounting numbers, and in contrast to classical models, both adjust accounting numbers to correct for accounting distortions.[129] EVA and EP differ in their definition of operating earnings, invested capital and cost of

---

[125] See Copeland et al. (2000), p. 143; Matten (2000), p. 267.

[126] Academic literature on accounting-based valuation typically uses the term *abnormal earnings* for residual income type valuation models. From an academic perspective, the model was rediscovered by Feltham and Ohlson (1995) and is often referred to as the Feltham/Ohlson model in preceding articles. Rezaee (2001), pp. 359-360, briefly discusses the model and its application to banks.

[127] EVA is a trademark of Stern Stewart & Co. For details on EVA, see Stewart (1990) and Young and O'Byrne (2000). McKinsey & Co., Inc. have developed the EP approach. For details, see Copeland et al. (2000), pp. 143-146.

[128] See Bodmer (2001), p. 77.

[129] See Uyemura et al. (1996), p. 97.

equity.[130] Nevertheless, these differences are very much of a minor nature and the concepts are often identical in practice.[131]

As cash flow-oriented models, residual income models can be categorized into entity and equity approaches. As stated in Section II.4.3, the equity approach is more appropriate for valuing banks.[132] When calculating the residual income of banks, operating income includes the income and expenses from debt financing. Invested capital is defined as economic equity, and cost of capital equals cost of equity. Consequently, residual income for banks is calculated as illustrated by Equation II-4.

$$RI = NOPAIT_{Adj} - EE_{t/t-1} \times c_e$$

$$RI = \left(\frac{NOPAIT_{Adj}}{EE_{t/t-1}} - c_e \right) \times EE_{t/t-1}$$

II-4

with $NOPAIT_{Adj}$ = Adjusted net operating profit after interest and taxes

$EE_{t/t-1}$ = Average economic equity in year t and t - 1

c_e = Cost of equity

Some authors consider residual income models as having limited relevance, as they lack a forward-looking perspective.[133] This is the case for the residual income in a single period, but not for the valuation of a company based on expected residual incomes in the future. In terms of residual income, the value of a company can be expressed as the amount of capital invested plus a premium equal to the present value of the value created each year, as illustrated in Equation II-5.[134]

---

[130] See Fernández (2002), pp. 265-269.

[131] See Bodmer (2001), p. 78.

[132] See Vettiger (1996), p. 153; MSDW (2001), p. 11; Bodmer (2001), p. 79; Damodaran (2004), p. 26.

[133] See Merkle (2001), p. 62.

[134] See Vettiger (1996), p. 154; Höhmann (1998), p. 21; Hörter (1998), p. 109; Copeland et al. (2000), p. 144; MSDW (2001), p. 14.

Value = Invested capital + Present value of expected residual incomes   II-5

Consequently, the equity value can be calculated as illustrated by Equation II-6.

$$Equity\ value_t = EE_t + \sum_{t=1}^{t=T} \frac{RI_t}{(1+c_e)^f} + \frac{RI_t}{c_e} \frac{1}{(1+c_e)^T}$$ II-6

with EE_t = Economic equity in year t

$\quad\quad c_e$ = Cost of equity

$\quad\quad RI_t$ = Residual income in year t

$\sum_{t=1}^{t=T} \frac{RI_t}{(1+c_e)^f}$ = Present value of RI during explicit forecast period

$\frac{RI_t}{c_e} \frac{1}{(1+c_e)^T}$ = Present value of RI after explicit forecast period

NOPAIT is derived from operating income adjusted for transactions that are not cash-effective and accounting manipulations. Economic equity is estimated as the sum of equity and equity equivalents. The explicit derivation of the input parameters and accounting adjustments are described in Section II.5.

Comparing residual income and DCF approaches we see that residual income is a useful measure for understanding a company's operating performance in any single year, and that free cash flow is not.[135] Residual income can be used to measure the value of a bank's equity, as well as the periodic performance of a bank. Consequently, residual income is a useful concept for value-based management, as it serves as a tool for multi-year financial planning and periodic performance controlling and can be easily communicated.[136]

---

[135] See Copeland et al. (2000), p. 143; MSDW (2001), p. 14.

[136] See Cates (1991), p. 52; Vettiger (1996), p. 153; Merkle (2001), p. 57. Schierenbeck (1997) illustrates how residual income can be linked to operating performance and the ROE hierarchy of banks. See also Schierenbeck (1998).

From a theoretical perspective, the residual income and DCF approaches lead to identical results given the same assumptions.[137] In consequence, residual income can be understood as an extension of the DCF approach that improves the measurement and management of shareholder value creation.[138] However, this theoretical identity in practice essentially does not exist. The focus on accounting income is usually considered the most significant shortcoming of the residual income approach.[139] However, due to the cash adequacy of net income in banking, this problem is less critical in the case of bank valuation. In addition, book equity should be more reliable for banks than for industrial companies as depreciation is typically marginal in the case of banks.[140] Nevertheless, hidden reserves distort the value of equity, and the correction of these distortions is complex and problematic from an outside-in perspective.[141] Similarly, hidden reserves are often only partly or not all included due to limited data availability. In consequence, residual income is overestimated, as the required return on hidden reserves, i.e. equity equivalents, is not accounted for.

Although the application of residual income models to banks is a recent development, residual income models are now routinely used by a variety of banks in the US and Europe.[142] When it comes to the empirical evidence for residual income models and in particular the EVA approach, several authors have tested the statistical correlation

---

[137] See Hörter (1998), p. 103; Bodmer (2001), p. 133; Merkle (2001), p. 58. Whereas this identity exists when looking at the total value or value creation over all periods, value creation in a single period can differ, as the residual income approach smoothes out the impact of investments over time. See Vettiger (1996), p. 156.

[138] See Matten (2000), p. 254.

[139] See Höhmann (1998), p. 21; Hörter (1998), p. 105.

[140] See Damodaran (2004), p. 27.

[141] See Höhmann (1998), p. 21; Bodmer (2001), p. 79.

[142] Bodmer (2001), p. 78, names Centura Banks, Commercial Bank, Lloyds TSB, Merrill Lynch, HSBC, Deutsche Bank, J.P. Morgan, and NatWest as examples of banks that have implemented a residual income oriented approach in the 1990s.

between residual income and market value. Uyemura et al. (1996) relate MVA to various performance measures and find the highest correlation for EVA with an R² of 0.40.[143] MSDW (2001) examine the relationship between MVA and three performance metrics: residual income, net income and free cash flow, and find the highest correlation for residual income, with an R² of 0.39.[144] Matten (2000) regresses M/B ratios with accounting profit, EPS and residual income, and finds the highest correlation for residual income, with a R² of 0.76.[145] Fiordelisi (2002) finds evidence for the superiority of an adjusted EVA measure that accounts for banking specifics.[146]

II.4.5   Discussion

In general, all the valuation approaches discussed in the previous sections are applicable to banks. The institutional specifics of banks illustrated in Section II.3 affect bank valuation significantly, but do not justify a proprietary valuation approach for banks as argued by some authors.[147] The basic principles apply just as much to banks as they do to other firms.[148]

The specifics of the banking business, however, mean that adjustments are required to the valuation methodologies in specific areas. The most important adjustment results from the difficulties associated with defining and measuring bank debt. In consequence, estimating the value of a firm or the cost of capital is complicated, whereas the

---

[143] The basis of their analysis is a sample of the largest 100 US bank holding companies over the ten-year period from 1986 to 1995. See Uyemura et al. (1996), pp. 99-101.

[144] MSDW (2001) use a sample of 113 worldwide financial companies as the basis for their analysis and time intervals of five, 10, 15 and 19 years. See MSDW (2001), pp. 44-47.

[145] See Matten (2000), p. 257.

[146] The empirical investigation focuses on a sample of 71 European banks between 1996 and 2002. For details on the methodology and results, see Fiordelisi (2002), pp. 18-27.

[147] See Adolf et al. (1989), p. 485; Höhmann (1998), p. 21.

[148] See Zessin (1982), p. 17; Kümmel (1995), p. 16; Koch (2002), p. 55; Damodaran (2004), p. 43.

direct valuation of equity is much easier. The equity approach is the more appropriate method for valuing a bank for multiples, DCF and residual income approaches.

When it comes to asset-oriented approaches, net asset values based on replacement or liquidation costs can be applied to banks. Given the fact that intangible assets are excluded from these approaches, they do not reflect the true value of a bank, which is mainly comprised of intangible assets.

Although all models can in general be applied to banks, not all models comply with the general criteria of valuation from a shareholder value perspective. Figure II-1 gives an overview of the compliance of the discussed models with the shareholder value perspective and notes their practicability.[149]

As far as *market-oriented models* are concerned, equity multiples are in general applicable to banks. Some of their weaknesses, however, are aggravated in a banking context. While P/E multiples are widely applied to banks, they have to be interpreted very carefully, as banks' leeway for manipulation is relatively high and risks are not considered. The use of multiples represents an easy and practical method of getting an initial idea of the value of a bank. When measuring shareholder value, however, they are of limited use and have only an auxiliary function.

Asset-oriented models can easily be applied to banks and do not need bank-specific adjustments. Net asset values based on replacement costs, however, violate several principles of valuation and thus should be disregarded in relation to shareholder value questions. Liquidation values complement fundamental valuation models and function as minimum valuations. As market-oriented approaches, liquidation values cannot be used on a stand-alone basis, however, and merely have an auxiliary function.

---

[149] See also Vettiger (1996), p. 123; Hörter (1998), p. 129.

Figure II-1: Assessment of valuation models for banks

✓ Criteria fulfilled
(✓) Criteria partly fulfilled

Criteria	Market-oriented models: Price/ earnings ratio	Market-oriented models: Market / book ratio	Asset-oriented models: Replace-ment value	Asset-oriented models: Liqui-dation value	Discounted cash flows	Residual income
• Capital market orientation	✓	✓	–	–	✓	✓
• Accounting orientation	✓	✓	–	–	(✓)	✓
• Forward-looking perspective	(✓)	–	–	(✓)	✓	✓
• Risk-return consideration	–	(✓)	–	–	✓	✓
• Link to invested capital	–	(✓)	–	–	✓	✓
• Link to internal performance	–	–	–	–	✓	✓
• Use as management tool	–	–	–	–	(✓)	✓
• Ease of use/practicability	High	High	Low	Low	Medium	High

Source: Own graphic

The *DCF model* can be applied to banks using an equity approach. It is the most widely used method for measuring the shareholder value of banks as it is for non-banks. The advantages of the DCF method are that it represents an intrinsic value that is both market-oriented and related to internal bank performance. Moreover, it provides a bank-level as well as a business unit-level valuation. It does not provide, however, a direct measure of periodical performance as does the residual income approach.

The application of the *residual income model* to banks requires the use of an equity method similar to DCF models and multiples. The residual income approach is, above all else, a good tool for value-based management. By providing an estimate of value-creation on a year-by-year basis, value creation is directly tied to operating performance and competitive advantage. Like the DCF approach, it can be applied to banks at the firm or business unit level, and compared to the DCF approach, its advantages are ease of use in daily decision processes, coeval application as a performance measure, and ease of perception.

In the long-term, the DCF and residual income model lead to similar results if the assumptions underlying the two models are identical. The terminal value assumption in residual income approaches, however, is more reasonable. In addition, residual income is often easier to calculate than cash flow in the case of banks, as we will see in the following section. At the end of the day, the question of whether the DCF or residual income approach is to be preferred depends above all on the purpose of the shareholder value estimate and the data set. In the case of pure valuations, DCF and residual income are both appropriate measurement methods, and the choice of one over the other in many cases merely depends on the data availability. Whereas DCF and residual income are both viable options in the case of individual bank valuations, the residual income approach is more preferable for large-scale samples. If the purpose of the valuation is to establish metrics for value-based performance management, residual income is without a doubt the superior method. In summary, residual income is preferred over DCF in the majority of cases when valuing banks.

In the following, we take a simultaneous look at the valuation process and bank-specific characteristics of both methods, i.e. DCF and residual income, and illustrate the bank-specific problems and adjustments that are required during the valuation process. The final choice concerning which of the two methods to use is always an individual decision based on the purpose of the valuation, the internal or external perspective of the valuator, and the availability of data.

II.5   Measuring the shareholder value of banks

II.5.1   Definition of a performance measure

II.5.1.1   Cash flow to equity

II.5.1.1.1   Use of the indirect approach

As discussed in Section II.4.3, the equity method is the most appropriate cash flow-oriented valuation approach as far as banks are concerned. To value the equity of a company, we normally use free cash flow to equity as a performance measure.

Practitioners often approximate free cash flow to equity by using net income as reported in banks' accounts.[150] Among the practical reasons for the use of net income are ease of use and the availability of data. In practice, the cash adequacy of the net income of banks, problems with the estimation of the reinvestment rate for banks, and bank-specific capital requirements account for the preferred use of income or dividends instead of cash flows. Nevertheless, focusing on income and expenses alone is not sufficient for deriving a performance measure. The implications of volatile investment flows on effective capital commitment have to be taken into account by adopting a cash flow perspective.[151]

In general, cash flows can be determined using a direct approach or an indirect approach.[152] The direct approach subtracts cash-in and cash-out flows to derive free cash flow, and is the theoretically correct approach to use. The indirect approach adjusts net income to derive a cash flow measure, and defines free cash flow to equity (FCF_e) in the way illustrated in Equation II-7.[153]

---

[150] See Becker (1997), p. 106; Arnsfeld and Gehrke (2001), p. 494; Geltinger (2003), p. 116.

[151] See Zessin (1982), p. 59; Koch (2002), p. 55.

[152] See Höhmann (1998), pp. 39-41.

[153] See Damodaran (2004), p. 7.

$$FCF_e = \text{Net income} + \text{Cash-ineffective transactions} - \Delta\text{Non-cash working capital} \atop - \text{Net capital expenditures} - (\text{Debt repaid} - \text{New debt issued})$$ II-7

For banks, applying the direct approach is not feasible in the majority of cases and therefore the indirect approach is widely used in practice.[154] Both from an internal and external perspective, the availability of the data required for the direct approach is limited and the quality of the data, if available, low. Internal bank planning is typically not cash flow-oriented.[155] Only a few banks base their multiple-year-planning on cash flows, and banks usually forecast their future performance using both a bank-specific economic performance measure and their income statement.[156] Typically, internal bank planning covers only the risk assets on their balance sheets, so that comprehensive forecasts of balance sheet positions do not exist. Consequently, it is very difficult to derive a cash flow calculation for banks.

From an external perspective, cash flow calculation is even more difficult. Figure II-2 gives an overview of the components of consolidated financial statements required by US GAAP, IAS, and HGB.[157] IAS and US GAAP both require a statement of cash flows, whereas a cash flow statement report is not mandatory under HGB standards. Both IAS and US GAAP recommend using the direct approach to derive cash flows. Banks, however, typically base their cash flow statement on the indirect approach.

---

[154] See Höhmann (1998), p. 44; Kunowski (2002), p. 51.

[155] See Kunowski (2002), p. 52. Faust (2002), p. 58, states that cash flow calculation is widely used in banking, e.g., for the valuation of transactions in the trading and investment book. In addition, he sees an increase in the significance of a cash flow orientation in the area of risk controlling. As this might only be the case for certain banking areas, banks overall do not forecast performance in terms of cash flows.

[156] See Geltinger (2003), p. 117.

[157] See Prangenberg (2000), p. 119.

Consequently, the information content of the data is limited, as differentiating between the cash flows that result from interest, provisions and trading is impossible.[158]

Figure II-2: Components of consolidated financial statements

		✓ Required	
Component	**US GAAP**	**IAS**	**HGB**
Group income statement	✓	✓	✓
Group balance sheet	✓	✓	✓
Notes	✓	✓	✓
Group management report	For exchange–listed corporations	Recommended	For corporations
Cash flow statement	✓ (actual and past two years)	✓	For capital market oriented firms
• Direct method	Recommended	Recommended	n/a
• Required classification	Operating/financing/ investment activities	Operating/financing/ investment activities	n/a
Segmental reporting	For exchange–listed corporations	✓	For capital market oriented firms
Changes in equity	✓	✓	For capital market oriented firms

Source: HGB, IAS, US GAAP

IAS and US GAAP both require the classification of cash flows resulting from operating, investment, and financing activities. Since the allocation of cash flows to operating, investment, and financing activities is not clearly defined and the separation of the operating and financing function is impossible in banking, however, bank cash flow statements are difficult to interpret, often ambiguous and cannot be compared.[159] Furthermore, the cash flow statement gives no information on credit losses, so that the

---

[158] See Koch (2002), pp. 47-49.

[159] See Vettiger (1996), p. 120; Koch (2002), pp. 49-51.

income statement remains as before the main source for the assessment of the quality of a credit portfolio.[160]

The information on cash flows for banks is limited, both from an internal and external perspective. The conjecturable problems when deriving cash flow indirectly are small, however, as differences between the income and cash flow perspectives for banks are marginal, as will be seen in the following section.

II.5.1.1.2 Derivation of free cash flow to equity

Figure II-3 shows the indirect derivation of cash flow to equity based on the income statement and balance sheet.[161] First, we derive Cash Flow I by adjusting net income for cash-ineffective income and expenses and the effects of extraordinary events. While for non-banks Cash Flow I represents cash flow from operations, in the case of banks further cash in- and outflows relate to their operating business.[162] The usual classification of cash flows into cash flows from operations, investments and financing is difficult to carry out in the case of banks, as it is almost impossible to separate their investment and financing functions from their operating business.[163]

To arrive at the free cash flow to equity figure we subtract net investments as a cash outflow and add the net increase in debt as a cash inflow. Copeland et al. (2000) use

---

[160] See Copeland et al. (2000), p. 434; Koch (2002), p. 55.

[161] Vettiger (1996), p. 129, and Kunowski (2002), p. 56, use the statement of cash flows required by IAS regulations as their basis. As illustrated above, this approach does not improve the quality of data since the majority of banks use an indirect approach to calculate reported cash flows.

[162] See Faust (2002), p. 70. Although many authors treat Cash Flow I as cash flow from operations, this is not appropriate in the case of banks. See Vettiger (1996), p. 129; Copeland et al. (2000), p. 430.

[163] Vettiger (1996), p. 129, categorizes cash flow into cash flow from changes in fixed and current assets and cash flow from banking business. Separating operating and non-operating cash flows, however, is almost impossible in the case of banks.

the terms uses and sources.[164] Important above all else is that consideration is given to both sides of the balance sheet.[165]

Figure II-3: Derivation of Free Cash Flow to Equity for banks

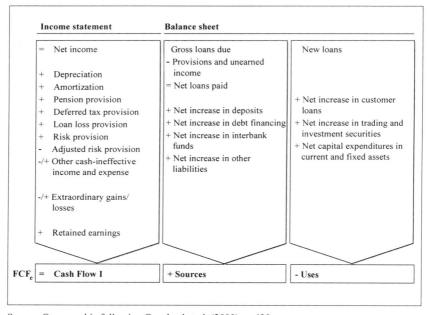

Source: Own graphic following Copeland et al. (2000), p. 430

While the adjustments for cash-ineffective transactions can be extensive for non-banks, the periodical differences between income and expense versus cash-in and cash-out in banking are marginal. One reason for this is that stock value does not exist in banking, and income is a receipt, as it accrues in the majority of cases.[166] Another reason is that investment in plant, equipment and other fixed assets in the case of banks is very low

---

[164] See Copeland et al. (2000), p. 430. See also Wariboko (1994), p. 144.

[165] See Kirsten (2000), p. 140.

[166] See also Section II.3.1.2.

and stable, unlike for industrial companies.[167] Consequently, a bank's statement of cash flows to its shareholders contains little or no capital expenditure and depreciation is correspondingly low.[168]

As in the case of non-banks, net income has to be adjusted both for the depreciation of fixed assets as well as for the amortization of goodwill and other intangible assets.[169] Provisions are made for pensions, deferred taxes and risk. Cash-ineffective entries for pension provisions and deferred taxes present no problems and are added back to net income in the same way as happens in the case of non-banks.[170] In summary, the main positions on a bank's income statement before risk considerations are strongly cash flow-oriented.[171]

Risk provisioning is problematic as provisions typically do not reflect economic reality. Instead, they are mainly driven by accounting considerations and the wish to smooth out earnings over time.[172] The provision for risk is often derived as a residual value to meet income targets, and has no explanatory power when it comes to the actual risks that are likely to be incurred.[173] Both the loan loss provision and the general risk provision have to be corrected if a risk-adjusted performance measure is to be derived that approximates cash and is sufficiently free of manipulation.[174] One way of

---

[167] Exceptions exist, e.g., extraordinary IT investments or significant strategic investments such as the expansion of the branch network. See Süchting (1996), p. 412; Koch (2002), p. 55.

[168] See Zessin (1982), p. 41; Kümmel (1995), p. 27.

[169] Depreciation and provisions relating to the trading book are not reported separately but are included instead in the net income from financing activities. Therefore, it is almost impossible to account for non-cash effects from an external perspective. See Höhmann (1998), p. 47.

[170] See Höhmann (1998), pp. 48-49; Faust (2002), p. 33.

[171] See Zessin (1982), p. 60; Geltinger (2003), p. 117.

[172] See Liebich (1995), p. 23; Uyemura et al. (1996), p. 102; MSDW (2001), p. 11; Damodaran (2004), p. 39.

[173] See Geltinger (2003), p. 159.

[174] See Geltinger (2003), p. 118; Damodaran (2004), p. 39.

correcting the opportunistic provisioning of risk is to consider net charge-offs as the current period estimate of losses due to credit risk instead of reported provisions for loan losses.[175] Another option is to use the benchmarks of comparable bank loss rates as reality checks, and to correct reported provisions on loan losses if necessary.[176] These adjustments are reasonable from an internal perspective.

For external valuators, the amount of accounting information on cash flows resulting from the non-payment of loans is usually limited. Thus, from an external perspective it is often easier to treat loan-loss provisions as though they were an actual cash flow.[177] In addition, cumulative risk provisions over time should equal the cumulated bad debts over the same period.[178] In consequence, adjustments to risk provisions could well prove immaterial if the analytical timeframe is long enough. If a bank maintains an excessive loss reserve over the economic cycle, however, it is inevitable that reported provisions will need to be adjusted.[179] In future, stricter criteria on the use of general provisions under IAS 39 may potentially lead to a reduction in the safety cushion of provisions.[180] As a result, provision figures will provide a better reflection of economic reality, and the adjustments to cash flow referred to above will become obsolete.

We also adjust for extraordinary losses and gains. We exclude extraordinary events from the valuation because we focus only on the value of the core business and, by definition, we cannot forecast extraordinary events in future periods.[181] We also take

---

[175] See Uyemura et al. (1996), p. 102; Damodaran (2004), p. 39.

[176] For a detailed overview of the necessary adjustments to reported risk provisioning, see Geltinger (2003), pp. 159-162.

[177] See Copeland et al. (2000), p. 429; MSDW (2001), p. 11.

[178] See Damodaran (2004), p. 39.

[179] See MSDW (2001), p. 11; Damodaran (2004), p. 40.

[180] See Merrill Lynch (2005), p. 31.

[181] See Börner and Lowis (1997), p. 107; Höhmann (1998), p. 46; Kirsten (2000), p. 144.

into consideration the retention of income due to capital adequacy requirements, as illustrated in Section II.5.1.1.3.

In addition to Cash Flow I, the operating activities of banks result in various other sources and uses of cash. Net investments include changes in asset items resulting from business activity, in particular in customer loans, the trading book and financial investments.[182] Further non-operating investments that reduce cash flow are net capital expenditures of current and fixed assets such as IT investments or strategic participations.[183] These investments, however, are only considered if they relate to ordinary business and are not extraordinary events. Also, net investments incorporate all losses from the liquidation of assets such as credit and trade losses and direct charge-offs from asset sales.[184]

On the liabilities side of the balance sheet, free cash flow only incorporates changes in debt capital. Net increases in debt capital include all the changes in deposits as operative financing, as well as changes in debt financing such as bonds and debentures.[185] Also, all net increases in interbank funds are considered. Free cash flow to equity does not take into consideration equity transactions such as capital increases, buybacks, and dividend payments, as these transactions in the context of equity approach represent a use of shareholder value.[186]

---

[182] Börner and Lowis (1997), p. 106, include new loans in cash flow from operations, but exclude repayments of loans. We, however, recommend a consistent handling of changes in loans.

[183] See Kirsten (2000), p. 148.

[184] See Faust (2002), p. 70.

[185] See Kirsten (2000), p. 151.

[186] See Vettiger (1996), p. 128; Kirsten (2000), p. 150. In contrast, Kunowski (2002), p. 62, explicitly includes increases and decreases in equity capital when determining free cash flow to equity.

The cash flow derivation approach described above is overall a reasonable approach to use. Nevertheless, bank-specific aspects could well require individualized deviations from the cash flow calculations.[187]

II.5.1.1.3 Estimation of reinvestments

One important difference between a cash flow- and an income-oriented view is the inclusion of reinvestments. Measuring the amount of reinvestment in the case of banks is problematic, however. Whereas reported reinvestment in tangible assets is marginal, banks invest heavily in intangible assets and regulatory capital. Investments in intangible assets, such as a brand name or human capital, are often categorized as operating expenses in accounting statements.[188] In analogy to research and development (R&D) expenses for technology companies, we could capitalize the expenses associated with developing human capital if human capital is a large factor in determining the success or failure of a bank. These expenses, however, are more difficult to capitalize than R&D expenses for two reasons:[189] First, employee development costs are typically not reported as a separate item and could be spread over several different expense items. The second reason is that the patents and licenses that result from research work belong to companies, whereas a bank's employees are mobile and may move to competitors. For these reasons, capitalizing for investment in human capital is theoretically correct, but in practice usually not feasible.

Banks' reinvestment rate in regulatory capital is regulated by capital adequacy requirements.[190] These capital ratios require equity capital in support of risk assets and

---

[187] See Faust (2002), p. 71.

[188] See Damodaran (2004), p. 6.

[189] See Damodaran (2004), p. 25.

[190] For a detailed overview of the capital adequacy regulations, see Merkle (2001), p. 87.

thus limit the amount of net income available to be distributed to shareholders. Due to these capital requirements, the classic hypothesis on the full distribution of profits does not hold in banking.[191] Whereas some authors adhere to the classic hypothesis,[192] consideration of retention in the definition of bank cash flow is widely accepted in literature.[193] Several arguments support consideration of the retention required by regulators. First, equity capital is necessary for the expansion of investments and directly limits the business volume of banks.[194] Retention therefore represents a reinvestment in a bank to be considered in the same way as other investments in current and fixed assets.[195] Nevertheless, the argument that retention represents a reinvestment in a bank only holds if the bank utilizes its larger capital base to grow.[196] Whether a retention rate is used or not, a focus on free cash flow after required retention is necessary in order to avoid the double-counting of the retained cash flows.[197] Above all else, bank valuation must incorporate the risks incurred by a bank's operations. By taking into consideration the equity required by capital ratios, the valuation process explicitly models the degree of risk pertaining to assets.

---

[191] See Kümmel (1995), p. 29; Geltinger (2003), p. 178.

[192] See Behm (1994), p. 61.

[193] See Adolf et al. (1989), pp. 489 and 546-548; Strutz (1993), p. 89; Kümmel (1995), p. 112; Vettiger (1996), p. 147; Börner and Lowis (1997), p. 111; Hörter (1998), p. 56; Becker (1999), p. 60; Matten (2000), p. 276; Dombret and Bender (2001), p. 329; Merkle (2001), p. 96; Koch (2002), p. 45; Kunowski (2002), p. 62; Geltinger (2003), p. 187; Damodaran (2004), p. 25. Kirsten (2000) agrees on the value relevance of capital requirements, but rejects subtracting the required retention from free cash flow to equity. Instead, he proposes reducing total assets to reflect bank capital requirements. See Kirsten (2000), p. 141.

[194] See Börner and Lowis (1997), p. 111; Merkle (2001), p. 85.

[195] See Damodaran (2004), p. 26. If the self-financing potential of a bank's operations is not high enough, external capital must be raised. Banks therefore regularly depend on external sources of equity to fund their growth. For an overview of the historical internal and external equity funding of German banks, see Koch (2002), p. 52.

[196] See Damodaran (2004), p. 26.

[197] See Adolf et al. (1989), p. 485.

In addition, it is possible to argue that retention above the required rates is necessary, as banks need self-financing potential to maintain the flexibility needed to react to investment opportunities.[198] Consequently, maintaining this flexibility is a worthwhile act in itself. However, we do not account for the potential value of flexibility, as estimating this value would be too complex. In particular, it is almost impossible to conclude with any degree of certainty whether a retention rate is economically rational or is merely a way for management to withhold cash flows.[199]

We adjust for the retention rate in two steps. The balance sheet for the base year is checked for compliance with the regulatory capital requirements, and, where necessary, part of the income retained.[200] Furthermore, we incorporate the required retention for future periods by multiplying the long-term growth rate for risk assets with the required Tier-One capital ratio.[201] Another reasonable calculation to make is to calculate the required retention according to economic capital requirements and to give consideration to the economic risk capital in years in which economic risk capital is higher than regulatory risk capital.[202]

II.5.1.2   Residual income

As discussed in Section II.4.4, residual income for banks is calculated using the equity approach. In the following, we once again include Equation II-4, which defines resid-

---

[198] See Vettiger (1996), p. 148. Merkle (2001), p. 86, finds a markup for flexibility of 2 percent for the capital ratios of Deutsche Bank between 1990 and 1998.

[199] See Vettiger (1996), p. 148.

[200] For a detailed overview of the calculation of capital requirements, see Höhmann (1998), pp. 70-73; Merkle (2001), pp. 88-95.

[201] See Adolf et al. (1989), pp. 489 and 548; Geltinger (2003), p. 187.

[202] See Strutz (1993), p. 89.

ual income as adjusted NOPAIT less the economic equity multiplied with the cost of equity.

$$RI_t = NOPAIT_{Adj} - EE_{t/t-1} \times c_e$$

with $NOPAIT_{Adj}$ = Adjusted net operating profit after interest and taxes

$EE_{t/t-1}$ = Average economic equity in year t and t - 1

c_e = Cost of equity

Although residual income is based on accounting statements, the reported NOPAIT and equity are both adjusted in order that they reflect the economic performance of the bank better. Financial reporting practices under generally accepted accounting principles often distort the quality of accounting variables as economic performance measures.[203] To correct for the deficiencies of standard financial reporting practice, a multitude of potential adjustments for improving the quality of conventional accounting income and equity are discussed in literature.[204] The aim being to have them is to reflect the current economics of the business better.

Figure II-4 shows potential accounting adjustments to bank residual income. These adjustments are also briefly discussed in the following. For banks, common adjustments include adjustments to the loan loss reserve, taxes, extraordinary gains and losses, goodwill, and securities accounting.[205] While all the adjustments are material to

---

[203] For an overview of the potential sources of distortions to accounting numbers, see Young and O'Byrne (2000), pp. 107-111. Generally, accounting standards under IAS and US GAAP are closer to being economic performance measures than European accounting standards and thus require fewer adjustments to net income. See Bodmer (2001), p. 80.

[204] Stern Stewart & Co. proposes about 150 potential adjustments to accounting numbers when calculating EVA. For an overview of potential adjustments, see Stewart (1990), pp. 112-117; Young and O'Byrne (2000), pp. 206-255. Weaver (2001), p. 54, reports that from a potential 150 adjustments, the average EVA user carries out 19. See also Fiordelisi (2002), p. 8.

[205] See Uyemura et al. (1996), pp. 101-103; Matten (2000), pp. 271-272; MSDW (2001), p. 11; Fiordelisi (2002), pp. 8-10.

performance measurement in banking, the data for them is not always available. Especially when performing an outside-in valuation, data availability is limited or the
increase in accuracy achieved through the adjustment does not justify the effort
involved in carrying it out.

Figure II-4: Accounting adjustments to bank residual income

	Adjusted NOPAIT =	Economic equity =
	Net operating profit after interest and taxes (NOPAIT)	Common equity
Risk provision	+ Loan loss provisions – Net charge-offs + General risk provision	+ Net loan loss revenue + General risk reserve
Deferred taxes	+ Increase in deferred tax reserve	+ Deferred tax reserve
Goodwill	+ Goodwill amortization + Unrecorded goodwill	+ Cumulative goodwill amortization
Restructuring costs	+ Restructuring charge*	+ Cumulative restructuring charges*
Securities accounting	+/– Loss (gains) from securities +/– IAS 39 adjustments	+/– Cumulative loss (gains) from securities +/– Cumulative IAS 39 adjustments

* Possibly other unusual gains and losses

Source: Own graphic

A specific adjustment in the case of banks relates to the *loan loss reserve*, as already
discussed for the derivation of cash flow to equity in Section II.5.1.1. The provisions
for loan losses primarily serve to smooth out earnings for financial statement purposes,
but it is not a cash cost.[206] Though some authors disregard any adjustment to the loan

---

[206] See Uyemura et al. (1996), p. 102; MSDW (2001), p. 11; Fiordelisi (2002), p. 8.

loss reserve,[207] using net charge-offs as the current period estimate of losses due to credit risk is, in general, a reasonable adjustment to make.[208] As discussed in Section II.5.1.1, the decision concerning whether to adjust risk provisions is an individual choice and depends on the analytical period, the availability of data, and the accounting policy of the bank. As in the case of the loan loss reserve, any other general risk reserve that is not required to support an existing or expected deterioration in the value of assets should not be included in residual income.[209] In addition, as mentioned previously, the provision requirements under IAS 39 lead to provision figures that reflect economic reality better. Reported earnings will therefore become more meaningful and adjustments to provisions may potentially no longer be needed.

With regard to *taxes*, the two standard adjustments used to customize them are also relevant to banks. First, tax provision amounts in general do not equal the amount of taxes paid due to differences between IAS and tax accounting.[210] Since these differences are quasi-permanent, the deferred tax reserve resembles an equity equivalent that should be added back to equity. Analogously, the increase in deferred taxes is not a cash-out. Thus, it should be added back to income.[211] Secondly, the income taxes paid are often substituted by effective average taxes to correct for accounting distortions in the individual tax rates applicable to companies.[212] Adjustments for effective taxes are

---

[207] See Copeland et al. (2000), p. 429; MSDW (2001), p. 11. Matten (2000), p. 271, criticizes the disregard of the loan loss provision as an inherent cost factor of banking, but also warns of general provisions that are not supported by the underlying loss levels.

[208] See Uyemura et al. (1996), pp. 101-102; Bodmer (2001), p. 88. For a detailed discussion of the adjustments, see Section II.5.1.1. See also Geltinger (2003), pp. 159-162.

[209] See Matten (2000), p. 271; Fiordelisi (2002), p. 9.

[210] See Stewart (1990), p. 113; Young and O'Byrne (2000), pp. 218-222.

[211] See Uyemura et al. (1996), p. 102; Matten (2000), p. 272; Bodmer (2001), p. 90; MSDW (2001), p. 11.

[212] See Kirsten (2000), p. 145.

reasonable if reliable data on effective taxes exists and the bias in actual taxes paid is significant.

In general, adjusted NOPAIT should focus on operating income and expenses, and should not consider *extraordinary gains and losses*.[213] One relevant adjustment is to the restructuring charge, which is a common non-recurring cost in the case of both banks and non-banks. If the restructuring effort presents a disinvestment, the charge must not reduce operating income but must be deducted from capital instead.[214] The adjustment of the restructuring charge and other non-recurring events has to be considered on a case-by-case basis given the character of the charge.[215] Since assessing the character of the restructuring charge, i.e. the extent of real disinvestment, is almost impossible from an outside perspective, this adjustment is usually only relevant for internal valuations.[216]

The amortization of *goodwill* is a non-cash expense and thus should be added back to operating income.[217] Goodwill is not amortized from an economic perspective, as goodwill does not wear out like other fixed assets.[218] Consequently, equity should be corrected for cumulative goodwill amortization. To date the availability of data on the amortization of goodwill has been limited for most countries. With the adoption of IAS, however, this adjustment to residual income is no longer necessary, as IFRS 3

---

[213] See Matten (2000), p. 272.

[214] See Uyemura et al. (1996), p. 102; Fiordelisi (2002), p. 14.

[215] See Uyemura et al. (1996), p. 102; Matten (2000), p. 272.

[216] See Fiordelisi (2002), p. 9.

[217] See Stewart (1990), p. 114; Matten (2000), p. 271; Young and O'Byrne (2000), pp. 236-244; MSDW (2001), p. 11.

[218] See Copeland et al. (2000), p. 177.

disallows the practice of amortizing goodwill and requires goodwill to be capitalized on the balance sheet.[219]

For North American banks, another measurement problem exists when accounting for acquisitions using the pooling-of-interest method.[220] In these transactions, goodwill, i.e. the difference between the book value and market value of acquired securities, is not recognized at all. This unrecorded goodwill resembles an equity equivalent and should be added back to equity.[221] As international accounting standards no longer permit merger accounting, this adjustment will become irrelevant in future.[222]

A further important adjustment with respect to banks concerns *securities accounting*.[223] Securities accounting is often used as a tool for earnings management and consequently does not reflect business economics. If this is the case, securities transactions should neither be rewarded nor penalized. The effect of gains and losses should be excluded from income when incurred, but amortized over the remaining lives of the securities sold.[224] This adjustment is particularly relevant in value-based management as it prevents managers from increasing residual income and shareholder value creation through securities transactions. Since the data for making both of these adjust-

---

[219] See Merrill Lynch (2005), p. 33.

[220] The pooling-of-interest method is the accounting treatment required by US GAAP to account for the mergers of equals. In pooling-of-interest transactions, two companies merge by adding together the book value of their assets and equities. These book values are carried forward to the consolidated financial statements without writing-up assets to their fair value. For a detailed discussion of pooling vs. purchase accounting, see Stickney and Weil (1997), pp. 714-718; Rezaee (2001), pp. 217-222.

[221] See Stewart (1990), pp. 114-115; Young and O'Byrne (2000), pp. 245-247.

[222] See MSDW (2001), p. 11.

[223] Gebhardt et al. (2002) illustrate the changes in accounting regulations for financial instruments after the implementation of IAS 39, and study the implications for banks under different interest rate scenarios.

[224] See Uyemura et al. (1996), p. 102.

ments is almost impossible to obtain in the case of an outside-in analysis, correcting for securities accounting usually only makes sense for internal valuations.[225]

A standard adjustment to residual income is to capitalize tangible and intangible investments and amortize these assets over their useful life. IAS 38 in this case allows some development expenses to be capitalized such as for internally developed computer software.[226] As stated in Section II.5.1.1.3, banks mainly reinvest in intangible assets such as brand names and human capital. Training expenses, therefore, are another item for which capitalization on the balance sheet might result in a more accurate reflection of economic reality.[227] However, due to the limited availability of data on training expenses and similar investments, coupled with the mobility of human capital, we do not adjust for investments in intangible assets.[228]

Finally, residual income should be corrected for required equity retention, as in the case of the DCF approach.[229]

Figure II-4 summarizes the adjustments to net income and equity that might be considered reasonable for the derivation of an adjusted income and economic equity figure. To arrive at the economic equity figure we use common equity, which is composed of equity and equity reserves, and potentially add back a number of equity equivalents. To calculate adjusted income we use NOPAIT, and as when calculating economic equity, we add back the corresponding average increase in equity equivalents. Also, we recalculate taxes using the effective average tax rate for each country. As mentioned above, the data required to make the proposed adjustments is often limited, especially

---

[225] See Fiordelisi (2002), p. 9.

[226] See Merrill Lynch (2005), p. 33.

[227] See Fiordelisi (2002), p. 9.

[228] See Section II.5.1.1.3. See also Damodaran (2004), p. 25.

[229] See Adolf et al. (1989), p. 489; Dombret and Bender (2001), p. 329. For details, see Section II.5.1.1.3.

when valuing a bank from an outside-in perspective. As a result, the trade-off between a pragmatic approach with only a few adjustments and a detailed valuation approach with higher accuracy is an individual choice that needs to be decided on a case-by-case basis.

II.5.2   Forecasting of future prospects

II.5.2.1   Specifics in bank planning

The forecasting of expected cash flows and therefore future bank performance represents a major difficulty in valuation.[230] The quality of the forecast significantly affects the validity of the estimated equity value and depends above all on the accuracy and certainty of the forecasts.[231] The complexity lies in the fact that forecasts are based on knowledge about the development of chances and risks in the future, all of which are retrieved using historical and actual data. In the following, we pay no attention to the general difficulties of forecasting, and focus instead on potential bank-specific problems.[232]

The institutional specifics of banks as illustrated in Section II.3.2 significantly affect the forecasting of bank performance, and several factors complicate the forecasting of future bank performance. First, bank performance significantly depends on macroeconomic factors and financial market trends.[233] As a result, macroeconomic and financial parameters such as insolvency rates or interest rates need to be forecast and included in bank planning. In addition, the specific dependence of banking on macroeconomic

---

[230] See Börner and Lowis (1997), p. 103; Becker (1999), p. 60.

[231] See Kunowski (2002), p. 66.

[232] For a detailed discussion of the general difficulties of forecasting, see Wildgruber (1998), pp. 99-114; Brealey and Myers (2000), p. 283; Kunowski (2002), pp. 66-67.

[233] See Hörter (1996), p. 148; Becker (1999), p. 62; Faust (2002), p. 76.

factors leads to particularly high forecasting uncertainty when it comes to bank planning. Banks as service providers are directly affected by fluctuations in demand, as they cannot store the products that they produce.[234] Fluctuations in demand are largely determined by external effects and therefore depend on quick changes in market data. Planning difficulties are aggravated by the double dependency of banks on the capital market, as banks offer both lending and deposit services and thus have to combine two converse markets.[235] Due to the high transparency of banking markets and the non-existence of patents, product innovations in banking are rapidly imitated, and a competitive advantage similar to the one that exists for industrial brands does not exist.[236] Furthermore, the difficulties inherent in the measurement of the reinvestment rate, as described in Section II.5.1.1.3, complicate the estimation of expected future growth.[237]

The restriction of bank autonomy by laws and regulations is often seen as a further aggravating factor for bank planning. Nevertheless, the legal restrictions on bank balance sheets do not lead to a narrowing of the principal planning options, but instead reduce autonomic planning through the specification of norms. This eases bank planning, as these norms predefine the structure of bank balance sheets.[238]

In addition, several other factors aid the planning of bank performance. The accounting systems of banks are highly developed,[239] and the high degree of transparency in banking markets allows relatively reliable forecasting of the expected behavior of competitors – an important input factor in bank planning.[240] Due to the long contract

---

[234] See Zessin (1982), p. 65; Kunowski (2002), p. 69. See also Section II.3.1.1.

[235] See Kümmel (1995), p. 55; Vettiger (1996), p. 131.

[236] See Zessin (1982), p. 66; MSDW (2001), p. 27.

[237] See Damodaran (2004), p. 6.

[238] See Zessin (1982), p. 67; Becker (1999), p. 61.

[239] See Kümmel (1995), p. 55; Kunowski (2002), p. 69.

[240] See Zessin (1982), p. 67.

durations and long-term customer relationships in banking, the forecasting of future banking performance is more certain and therefore easier than in the case of many other industries.[241]

In summary, planning bank performance is possible. The planning process for banks, however, is more complicated than for industrial companies, as macroeconomic factors and financial indicators also have to be considered. Two additional difficulties are the difficulty in retrieving available information and the increasing uncertainty of this information the longer the forecast interval. These problems, however, are not specific to banks, but instead are confronted by planners in all industries.[242]

II.5.2.2   Forecast horizon

Basic valuation models usually incorporate two phases, the first phase representing an explicit forecasting period and the second phase describing the remaining life of the company, which corresponds to its terminal value.[243] The length of the first phase is determined by an individual trade-off between the accuracy provided by detailed forecasts, and the increasing uncertainty and lower quality of forecasts the longer the forecasting period.[244] A longer duration for the explicit forecasting period is preferable, as it leads to a better balance between the terminal value and the total value of a bank.[245] For industrial companies the length of the detailed forecasting period is usually between 5 and 10 years.[246]

---

[241] See Becker (1999), p. 61; Faust (2002), p. 76; Kunowski (2002), p. 69.

[242] See Faust (2002), p. 76.

[243] See Copeland et al. (2000), p. 136.

[244] See Zessin (1982), p. 62; Adolf et al. (1989), p. 488; Kümmel (1995), p. 54; Börner and Lowis (1997), p. 99; Kirsten (2000), p. 175; Faust (2002), p. 75.

[245] See Copeland et al. (2000), p. 234; Faust (2002), p. 75.

[246] See Rappaport (1986), p. 40; Copeland et al. (2000), p. 236.

The main difference when forecasting the future performance of banks compared to that of industrial companies is that the detailed forecasting period is shorter.[247] The main reason for shortening the forecasting period for banks compared to non-banks is the strong dependency of bank performance on macroeconomic factors, as already mentioned. The choice of the forecasting period, however, has to take into consideration the volatile banking environment as well as accommodate a long-term strategic perspective. Choosing a very short-term forecasting perspective can lead to significant distortions, as exceptionally negative or positive periods might be extrapolated.[248]

The length of the forecasting period generally complies with the predictability of free cash flows and the strategic horizon of the planning and controlling departments of banks.[249] Furthermore, the forecasting interval has to be long enough to cover the duration of an economic cycle, to fully incorporate the implications of structural changes, and to ensure a stable economic situation in which competitive advantages are eroded.[250] Other than for non-banks, the product life cycle of banking products is not a good indicator for the forecast horizon.[251]

Appendix 1, p. 237, gives an overview of the bank forecast horizons proposed in the literature. As illustrated, the average planning horizon is approx. five years, although horizons of up to ten years are possible. During this period existing lending is paid

---

[247] See Zessin (1982), p. 70; Hörter (1996), p. 156; Becker (1997), p. 106; Börner and Lowis (1997), p. 99.

[248] See Kümmel (1995), p. 55; Kunowski (2002), p. 69.

[249] See Behm (1994), p. 60; Kümmel (1995), p. 60; Vettiger (1996), p. 124.

[250] See Hörter (1998), p. 156; Copeland et al. (2000), p. 234; Faust (2002), p. 75; Kunowski (2002), p. 68.

[251] See Rappaport (1986), p. 41. Wildgruber (1998), p. 200, and Kunowski (2002), p. 68, propose setting the length of the forecasting period according to bank product life cycles. While this is a legitimate approach for non-banking industries, the approach is not appropriate for the banking industry as product life cycles often last for decades and product innovations are rare. See Faust (2002), p. 76. For a detailed discussion of the value-oriented product life cycle management, see Schlund (2001), pp. 30 – 42.

back, newly established branches potentially break even, and the impact of acquisitions on the business structure is apparent.[252] Nevertheless, the length of the forecast interval still allows the implications of the economic cycle to be estimated.

Figure II-5 illustrates the forecast horizon for bank valuation using a DCF approach. Phase 1 is often split into two sub phases,[253] and forecasts cash flows explicitly based on detailed budgeted financial statements. In phase 2, trends alone are forecast, based on changes in key parameters that remain constant over individual years in phase 2. Appendix 2, p. 238, illustrates the forecast horizon using a residual income approach.

Figure II-5: Forecast horizon for banks using a DCF approach

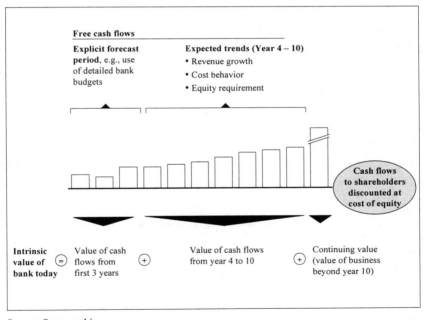

Source: Own graphic

---

[252] See Zessin (1982), p. 69; Kümmel (1995), p. 55.

[253] See Adolf et al. (1989), p. 488; Börner and Lowis (1997), p. 100; Copeland et al. (2000), p. 234.

II.5.2.3   Forecast method

Forecast methods are categorized into qualitative and quantitative forecast methods.[254] Appendix 3, p. 239, gives an overview of the different methods. As in the case of non-banking industries, we forecast bank performance primarily using quantitative methods.[255] Nevertheless, qualitative methods have an important auxiliary function. For instance, expert interviews help to forecast trends such as technological innovations, customer behavior and market developments.[256] Furthermore, they represent an essential control check for the planning data resulting from quantitative forecasts.[257]

As in the case of non-banks, time series analysis is a good starting point for forecasting bank performance. Höhmann (1998) tests various forecasting periods for forecasting quality and plausibility of results, and finds that five-year moving averages and budgeted financial statements yield the best results.[258] Damodaran (2004) finds correlations between past earnings growth and expected future growth to be much higher for banks than other industries.[259] Time series analysis is appropriate when past performance exhibits a reasonably steady growth pattern.[260]

If this is not the case, the use of value drivers helps to obtain a deeper understanding of banking performance and possible levers, and thus leads to more accurate performance

---

[254] For a detailed discussion of qualitative and quantitative methods, see Höhmann (1998), pp. 92-99; Becker (1999), pp. 63-80; Kunowski (2002), pp. 70-75.

[255] See Höhmann (1998), p. 93.

[256] See Kunowski (2002), p. 72.

[257] See Vettiger (1996), p. 133.

[258] See Höhmann (1998), pp. 136-141. Wilde (1982) develops a comprehensive econometric model based on quantitative risk analysis. While such an approach might be reasonable in relation to internal strategic planning, the amount of work involved outweighs the benefit as far as valuation is concerned.

[259] See Damodaran (2004), p. 12.

[260] See Rezaee (2001), p. 189.

forecasts. For banks, these value drivers are not only internal, but also external value drivers, given the high impact of external factors on bank valuation, as discussed in Section II.5.2.1.[261] These value drivers have to be identified for each banking income category, along with the corresponding value and quantity components. Analogously, the different components of a bank's expenses have to be forecast. For a detailed discussion of the analysis and forecasting of bank performance, we refer to Becker (1999), Geltinger (2003), and Kümmel (1995), who discuss the steps involved in detail.[262]

In general, future performance is forecast from the bottom up as well as separately for each business unit.[263] In the case of internal valuations, forecasting can usually be based on the planning data resulting from internal planning and budgeting systems.[264] This data is not available for external valuations, and therefore the forecast must rely on historical accounting performance and defined value drivers.

II.5.3   Determination of terminal value

II.5.3.1   Cash flow-oriented approaches

To accommodate for the growing uncertainty and increased planning effort in later years, a terminal value is used to estimate value creation after the detailed forecast horizon.[265] Given the relatively short forecast interval in bank valuation, the significance of a bank's terminal value is high.[266] The terminal value of a bank typically

---

[261] See Höhmann (1998), p. 96.

[262] See Kümmel (1995), pp. 57-69; Becker (1999), pp. 91-114; Geltinger (2003), pp. 123-165.

[263] See Kümmel (1995), pp. 56-57; Vettiger (1996), p. 131; Hörter (1998), p. 156; Faust (2002), p. 76.

[264] See Vettiger (1996), p. 132; Faust (2002), p. 76.

[265] See Faust (2002), p. 77.

[266] See Hörter (1998), p. 148.

accounts for 75 percent of a bank's total value.[267] A high-quality estimate for the terminal value is therefore essential in bank valuation.

Typically, the terminal value is calculated as a perpetuity that assumes the bank will be a going concern.[268] As illustrated by Equation II-8, the main input parameters for the calculation of the terminal value (TV) are the expected free cash flow to equity and the expected growth rate of cash flows after the explicit forecasting period.[269]

$$TV_T = \frac{FCF_{e,T+1}}{c_e - g}$$ II-8

with $FCF_{e,\ T+1}$ = Free cash flow to equity in $T + 1$ and thereafter
c_e = Cost of equity
g = Expected growth rate
T = Length of the explicit forecast period

A universally valid method for calculating the terminal value and input parameters in bank valuation does not exist. Given the high share of the terminal value in total bank value, however, the assumptions should be defined carefully. FCF_e in year T is often not the best estimate of the long-term performance of a bank and should be checked for sustainability.[270] For instance, approximating FCF_e in year T+1 with the average FCF_e during the explicit forecast period T might be more reasonable.[271]

---

[267] See Koch (2002), p. 29. For non-banking industries, Copeland et al. (2000), p. 267, find that the weight of the terminal value ranges between 56 and 125 percent.

[268] Alternatively, the terminal value can be calculated using a market-oriented approach. For a detailed overview, see Faust (2002), p. 80. In order to ensure consistency of the valuation model, the use of a market-oriented approach for determining the terminal value in a DCF or residual income model is not recommended. See Höhmann (1998), p. 142; Copeland et al. (2000), p. 268; Kirsten (2000), p. 178; Faust (2002), p. 82.

[269] See Copeland et al. (2000), p. 269.

[270] See Becker (1999), p. 119.

[271] For a detailed overview of possible estimates of free cash flow to equity in T+1 and thereafter, see Geltinger (2003), pp. 58-59.

The assumptions in relation to the growth rate generally depend on the industry structure and the competitive position of the company as well as on the company-specific strategy.[272] Appendix 4, p. 240, gives an overview of growth rate estimates for the banking industry assumed in literature.

The estimation of the growth rate is simplified by relating the perpetuity formula to the value drivers of cash flow, as depicted in Equation II-9 below.[273]

$$TV_T = \frac{NOPAIT_{T+1}(1 - g/ROIC)}{c_e - g}$$ II-9

with $NOPAIT_{T+1}$ = Net operating profit after interest and taxes in $T+1$
c_e = Cost of equity
$ROIC$ = Return on invested capital
g = Expected growth rate
T = Length of the explicit forecast period

Whereas some authors include the inflation rate in the growth rate,[274] the use of a nominal growth rate that includes inflation is questionable. In contrast to non-banking industries, banks do not deal in real goods, but in monetary contracts.[275] The inflation rate, therefore, does not represent an explicit valuation parameter in banking.[276] It still influences bank value indirectly, however, as it significantly affects value drivers such as the interest rate, for example.

In general, we warn against using a growing perpetuity, which is only a plausible assumption if competitive advantage remains constant. Only a few companies, how-

---

[272] See Behm (1994), p. 62; Kümmel (1995), p. 62; Faust (2002), p. 81; Damodaran (2004), pp. 14-15.

[273] See Hörter (1998), p. 157; Copeland et al. (2000), p. 269.

[274] See Adolf et al. (1989), p. 548; Kümmel (1995), p. 42.

[275] For the low relevance of inflation risk for banks, see Section II.3.2.1.

[276] See Kirsten (2000), p. 134; Geltinger (2003), p. 61.

ever, can be expected to grow faster than the economy over long periods, and in the long-run returns converge to the average growth rate of the industry.[277] In particular, banks do not maintain their competitive advantages indefinitely as product innovations are rare and rapidly imitated by competitors due to non-existent patent protection.[278] Therefore, it is valid to assume that bank earns on average the cost of capital on new investments after the explicit forecast interval. Using $c_e = ROIC$ the growth term disappears from the equation and leaves a constant perpetuity for estimating the terminal value of a bank, as illustrated by Equation II-10.[279]

$$TV_T = \frac{FCF_{T+1}}{c_e}$$ II-10

with $FCF_{e,T+1}$ = Free cash flow to equity in $T+1$ and thereafter
c_e = Cost of equity
T = Length of the explicit forecast period

II.5.3.2   Residual income approaches

In residual income approaches, the terminal value does not represent the value of the bank after the explicit forecast period, but instead represents the incremental value over the bank's invested capital at the end of the explicit forecast period.[280]

Using the value driver formula, the terminal value of the residual income approach is calculated as illustrated by Equation II-11.[281]

---

[277] See Rappaport (1986), p. 42; Becker (1999), p. 119; Faust (2002), p. 80; Geltinger (2003), pp. 61-62.

[278] See MSDW (2001), p. 27; Faust (2002), p. 80; Geltinger (2003), p. 196.

[279] See Copeland et al. (2000), p. 282. Another valid but more complicated option is to model the length of the growth period as an explicit value driver. See Behm (1994), p. 65; Börner and Lowis (1997), p. 122.

[280] See Copeland et al. (2000), p. 271.

$$TV_T = \frac{RI_{T+1}}{c_e} + \frac{NOPAIT_{T+1}(g/ROIC)(ROIC - c_e)}{c_e(c_e - g)} \qquad \text{II-11}$$

with $NOPAIT_{T+1}$ = Net operating profit after interest and taxes in T+1

$\qquad RI_{T+1}$ = Residual income in year $T+1$ and thereafter

$\qquad c_e$ = Cost of equity

$\qquad ROIC$ = Return on invested capital

$\qquad g$ = Expected growth rate

$\qquad T$ = Length of the explicit forecast period

As in the case of the DCF approach, the calculation of the terminal value in the residual income approach depends on the industry structure and competitive situation of the company. Assuming banks earn on average the capital cost on new investments after the explicit forecast period, the second part of the equation equals zero. Moreover, assuming that a bank does not maintain its competitive advantage indefinitely, the value created after the explicit forecast period, and thus residual income, erodes over time.

Therefore, the introduction of a decay rate that erodes residual income in the terminal value calculation and the concept of a declining perpetuity, as illustrated by Equation II-12, is a legitimate assumption for banks.[282]

$$TV_T = \frac{RI_{T+1}}{c_e - d} \qquad \text{II-12}$$

with RI_{T+1} = Residual income in $T+1$ and thereafter

$\qquad c_e$ = Cost of equity

$\qquad d$ = Decay rate

$\qquad T$ = Length of the explicit forecast period

---

[281] See Copeland et al. (2000), p. 272; MSDW (2001), p. 27.

[282] See MSDW (2001), p. 27.

Decay rate d is a function of a bank's brand or franchise strength. In practice, decay rates between 5 and 10 percent are used for banks, reflecting the relatively weak brands in the banking industry.[283]

II.5.4   Estimating the cost of equity

The capital cost used in the DCF and residual income models is not regulatory but instead is the economic capital cost and represents the minimum return shareholders require from a bank. The following section gives an overview of the most popular approaches used to estimate this minimum return. We confine ourselves here to examining the validity and practicability of these approaches for bank valuation, and do not discuss the underlying theories and assumptions in detail.

II.5.4.1   Capital Asset Pricing Model

The Capital Asset Pricing Model (CAPM) is the most widely used approach for estimating the cost of equity, both in the case of banks and industrial companies.[284] "The CAPM postulates that the opportunity cost of equity is equal to the return on risk-free securities plus the company's systematic risk (beta) multiplied by the market price of risk (market risk premium)."[285] Given these assumptions, the CAPM estimates the cost of equity as depicted in Equation II-13:

---

[283] See MSDW (2001), p. 28.

[284] See Damodaran (1994), pp. 20-26; Kümmel (1995), p. 40; Copeland et al. (2000), p. 435; Kirsten (2000), p. 155; MSDW (2001), p. 48.

[285] Copeland et al. (2000), p. 214.

$$c_e = r_f + \left[E(r_m) - r_f \right] \times (beta) \qquad\qquad \text{II-13}$$

with $r_f =$ Risk-free rate of return

        $E(r_m) =$ Expected rate of return on the market portfolio m

$\left[E(r_m) - r_f \right] =$ Market risk premium

        $beta =$ Systematic risk of the equity

The market risk premium is equal to the difference between the expected return on the equity market portfolio and the risk-free rate of return. Beta is defined as the covariance between the returns on the individual stock and the market portfolio.[286]

The CAPM itself is the subject of much debate and there is disagreement concerning the estimation of the CAPM's variables, i.e. the *risk-free rate*, the *market risk premium*, and *beta*. In the following, we give a brief overview of the possible ways in which these parameters can be estimated. It should be noted, however, that the discussion on the input parameters is not specific to banks but applies to all industries.

A good proxy for the *risk-free rate* in bank valuation is the yield on the benchmark indices of ten-year government bonds.[287] Recent research has shown that long-term bonds are not completely risk-less and that unlevering the risk-free rate and combining the systematic equity risk of stocks and bonds into one premium is overall a reasonable adjustment.[288] However, for the market as a whole or any stock with a beta close to 1.0 the net effect of this adjustment approximates to zero.

---

[286] For a detailed overview of the CAPM and the underlying assumptions, see Copeland and Weston (1992), pp. 193-202; Brealey and Myers (2000), pp. 187-203; Pettit (2001).

[287] See Behm (1994), p. 120. For an overview of alternative estimates of the risk-free rate, see Damodaran (1994), pp. 24-26; Copeland et al. (2000), p. 216.

[288] The beta of long-term bonds has varied from -0.1 to over 0.4 in the past, with the current beta estimated at 0.25. See Pettit (2001), pp. 5-6.

Given historic banking betas close to 1.0,[289] this adjustment does not yield an observable benefit for the analysis of banks. The use of a national risk-free rate is typically preferred over estimates of a global risk-free rate as a local estimate incorporates the inflation risk related to the investment in domestic stocks.[290] Using a yearly average of the risk-free rate is the theoretically correct way of calculating the capital charge in the residual income equation. When calculating a discount rate, however, it is also possible to argue for the use of the risk-free rate at the time of valuation or of a long-term average.

The *market risk premium* can in general be estimated using two broad approaches: The first approach is historical and is based on the past performance of stock prices.[291] The second approach is forward-looking and is based on the projections implied by current stock prices.[292] Using a historical approach, estimates of the market risk premium vary between 3 and almost 8 percent depending on the underlying assumptions.[293] Most practitioners, however, use a narrower range of 3.5 to 5.0 percent.[294]

---

[289] See Schmittmann et al. (1996), p. 648. For an overview of typical betas for different bank types, see Matten (2000), p. 287. Zimmer and McCauley (1991), p. 53, give an overview of bank betas for different countries. Zimmermann and Oertmann (1996) study the differences between global and local bank betas in detail. Appendix 5, p. 241, gives an overview of historical industry betas for banks for the period between 1989 and 2003.

[290] See Faust (2002), p. 116; Geltinger (2003), p. 68.

[291] See Goedhart et al. (2002), pp. 11-12. For a detailed discussion on the derivation of the market risk premium, see Damodaran (1994), pp. 21-24; Copeland et al. (2000), pp. 217-221; Pettit (2001), pp. 1-5.

[292] For a detailed discussion of the forward-looking approach, see Copeland et al. (2000), pp. 221-223. See also Gebhardt and Daske (2004).

[293] See Copeland et al. (2000), p. 216. The main assumptions causing this variance concern the measurement interval of returns and the use of arithmetic vs. geometric averages.

[294] See Damodaran (1994), p. 22; Copeland et al. (2000), p. 221; Pettit (2001), p. 1; Goedhart et al. (2002), p. 11.

Current research suggests using a published estimate of *beta* based on a multi-factor approach, such as the one provided by BARRA.[295] However, published company betas from different providers often vary significantly, as shown in Appendix 6, p. 242. Existing variances often cannot be explained, as the methodology and assumptions that underlie these beta estimates are usually not published. Therefore, an estimate of beta based on historical return volatility is often more reliable and easier to interpret. Another option is to construct an industry average assuming that the systematic risk of an industry applies to all the firms that operate within it.[296] As measurement errors tend to cancel each other out, industry betas are typically more stable and reliable than individual company betas.[297]

As illustrated in Appendix 5, p. 241, and Appendix 7, p. 243, banking betas vary significantly according to the type and regional scope of the bank. [298] Therefore, industry peer groups have to be carefully defined to reflect the equity risk of the bank in question.

Correcting for leverage, i.e. unleveraging the beta of benchmarks and releveraging it thereafter so that it reflects the specific leverage ratio of the valuation target, is a reasonable and generally accepted practice for non-banks. For banks, the effect of leveraging is usually ignored, which in turn might be the result of several factors. First of all, the fact that the operating and financing activities of a bank cannot be separated means that the business risk and financial risk of banks cannot be separated either. This being the case, unleveraging and releveraging the betas of banks has no purpose.

---

[295] See Copeland et al. (2000), p. 223; Matten (2000), p. 287; MSDW (2001), p. 52.

[296] As a rule of thumb, current research prefers industry averages to individual betas where published betas differ by more than 0.2. See Copeland et al. (2000), p. 224.

[297] See Brealey and Myers (2000), p. 224; Annema and Goedhart (2003), p. 10.

[298] See Hörter (1998), p. 73. For a detailed discussion of the differences in the bank cost of capital and potential causes, see Zimmer and McCauley (1991).

Secondly, bank leverage is regulated by capital adequacy requirements. Consequently, the differences in the leverage ratios between banks are low compared to other industries. Finally, the leverage ratio reported in a bank's balance sheet is potentially distorted by off-balance sheet positions.

For banks, the value both of assets and of liabilities fluctuates with interest rate changes. Consequently, the asset-liability mismatch is at least as important as the equity ratio when deriving equity betas from a given business risk.[299] Therefore, it is the effect of the asset-liability mismatch profile of banks rather than the leverage effect that needs to be considered in cost of equity. Whereas the asset-liability mismatch can be accurately quantified from the inside, the mismatch can only be roughly estimated from the outside.

The CAPM is based on several simplifying assumptions, all of which provide grounds on which to criticize its methodology.[300] In addition, there are limitations in its application.[301] For instance, one major flaw is that the CAPM is not directly applicable to non-listed banks. This problem can be solved by using benchmark betas of comparable exchange-traded banks.[302] Again, the peer group has to be composed of banks of the same bank type, exposed to the same business risks and with a similar asset-liability mismatch. As one might expect, the number of specialized public banks with comparable characteristics is limited.[303]

---

[299] See Section II.5.4.2. See Zimmermann (1995) for the influence of asset-liability mismatch on banks' equity risk.

[300] See Höhmann (1998), p. 162; Merkle (2001), p. 64. For an overview of the underlying assumptions, see Faust (2002), p. 91. For an overview of the criticism of CAPM, see Damodaran (1994), pp. 27-28; Arnsfeld (1998), pp. 126-128; Copeland et al. (2000), pp. 224-226.

[301] See Kümmel (1995), p. 34; Kirsten (2000), p. 155.

[302] See Arnsfeld and Gehrke (2001), p. 495. For alternative ways of estimating the equity risk for non-public banks, see Höhmann (1998), pp. 159-162.

[303] See Vettiger (1996), p. 144.

II.5.4.2   Arbitrage Pricing Theory

An additional problem with the CAPM is that it treats the sensitivity of equity returns as the only source of equity risk. The Arbitrage Pricing Theory (APT) solves this problem by using a multifactor model to measure equity risk.[304] Instead of one measure of risk, the APT includes many factors, as illustrated by Equation II-14.

$$c_e = r_f + \gamma_1\beta_1 + ... + \gamma_n\beta_n \qquad\qquad\qquad \text{II-14}$$

with r_f = Risk-free rate of return

$\quad\quad\;\; \gamma_n$ = Risk premium of the factor n

$\quad\quad\;\; \beta_n$ = Sensitivity of the equity risk to factor n

Each beta measures the sensitivity of a company's return to a separate underlying factor. The main macroeconomic factors generally included in the APT are the growth of industrial production, changes in the yield curve, changes in the short- and long-term inflation rates, and changes in the credit default risk.[305] Although the APT is the theoretically more correct approach when measuring equity risk, its application is complicated and the empirical evidence available for multi-factor models is low due to their high degree of complexity.[306]

The main advantage of the APT over the CAPM is the fact that it explains systematic risk using a multitude of factors. So far, however, the approach lacks theoretical and empirical proof, as the question as to which factors are relevant and to what extent they

---

[304] For a detailed overview of APT and the underlying assumptions, see Copeland and Weston (1992), pp. 219-228; Brealey and Myers (2000), pp. 205-211.

[305] See Behm (1994), p. 117; Börner and Lowis (1997), p. 119; Arnsfeld (1998), p. 96; Copeland et al. (2000), pp. 274-275; Kunowski (2002), p. 92.

[306] See Vettiger (1996), p. 142.

influence the cost of equity has not been answered satisfactorily, neither for companies nor more specifically for banks.[307]

As far as banking is concerned, the parameters should reflect bank-specific risk factors such as the interest rate, exchange rates or insolvency rates.[308] While the default risk is already incorporated into the cash flow calculation, the impact of interest rates, exchange rates and general economic development has to be explicitly included in the cost of equity.

Since a bank's exposure to interest rate risks is significant, the cost of equity should above all reflect the risks associated with future changes in interest rates.[309] Zimmermann (1995) studies the relation between asset-liability mismatch and the equity cost of banks. He describes the impact of the bank-specific risk profile from a theoretical standpoint and illustrates it by means of several calculations. Having proved the strong influence of asset-liability mismatch on the cost of equity, he goes on to state that this factor is only one of many and that further research on the factors that influence banks' cost of equity is required.[310] Given the need for further research on multi-factors models, another option proposed in literature is to extend the CAPM's risk premium so that it accounts for the interest rate risk of a bank.[311]

---

[307] See Behm (1994), p. 117; Kunowski (2002), p. 94.

[308] See Börner and Lowis (1997), p. 119. For an overview of bank specific risks, see Section II.3.2.1. For a detailed discussion of the internal and external determinants of the capital cost of banks, see Arnsfeld and Gehrke (2001), pp. 187-270.

[309] See Vettiger (1996), p. 143.

[310] Kirsten (2000), pp. 165-172, follows the approach of Zimmermann (1995) and finds anecdotal evidence for mortgage banks which are required by regulators to closely match their assets and liabilities and historically have low equity betas. Again, the question that needs to be asked is to what extent are the low equity betas the result of the ALM profile of mortgage banks or the result of the typically low general business risks of mortgage banks.

[311] See Flannery and James (1984).

The question of whether the APT produces better empirical results than the CAPM has been the subject of controversial debate not only in the banking arena.[312] In spite of this, however, differences between the CAPM and the APT with respect to the banking industry are low compared to other industries.[313]

II.5.4.3   Alternative approaches

A simple alternative to the approaches described above is to use an *opportunity rate*. Using this approach, the cost of equity represents the risk-free rate plus a risk premium that is estimated based on investor-specific alternatives.[314] This alternative approach overcomes some of the shortcomings of the market-oriented models as its underlying assumptions are not as simplified.[315] On the other hand, the use of an opportunity rate is very subjective and is therefore only valid as a supplement to the above approaches.[316]

Several other approaches base the estimation of the cost of capital on performance measures. The *dividend return model* uses the actual dividend return as a proxy for the cost of equity.[317] Another approach that is often used in practice approximates the cost of equity with the reciprocal of the P/E ratio.[318] The *Gordon Growth Model* extends this

---

[312] See Copeland and Weston (1992), pp. 228-230; Brealey and Myers (2000), pp. 199-203 and 206-207; Copeland et al. (2000), pp. 224-228.

[313] Copeland et al. (2000) estimate equity risk based on APT and the factors described above. The risk premiums of all factors are positive and range between 0.0 and 0.5 percent. In summary, the equity cost estimated with APT is 1.0 percent higher than the CAPM estimate. See Copeland et al. (2000), pp. 275-278.

[314] See Adolf et al. (1989), pp. 549-554.

[315] See Adolf et al. (1989), p. 551; Kirsten (2000), p. 156.

[316] See Vettiger (1996), p. 144.

[317] See Behm (1994), p. 105; Faust (2002), p. 117.

[318] See Behm (1994), pp. 109-111; Faust (2002), pp. 118-120.

basic model by including a constant growth rate for income and dividends.[319] In summary, all these approaches fail to consider bank-specific risks as well as macro-economic factors such as the market premium or the risk-free rate. As both bank-specific risks and the macroeconomic environment have a significant impact on banks, the use of these performance-oriented models as cost of equity for banks is not recommended.[320]

From an internal perspective, the cost of equity can be estimated on the basis of the *earnings volatility* or *cash flow volatility* of a bank. Several empirical studies show that the volatility of income is a good proxy for the systematic risk of banks.[321] Yet the implied assumption that different types of cash flows or income are correlated in the same way has to be questioned. When calculating the equity cost of non-traded banks, the income volatility approach might indeed represent a good alternative to the CAPM if no reliable benchmark betas are available. Furthermore, it is also helpful when estimating the business-specific cost of equity. Section II.5.5.3 illustrates how accounting betas estimated using earnings volatility can be used to approximate the cost of equity for individual banking units.

II.5.4.4   Discussion

The estimation of the cost of capital and the usefulness of market-oriented models such as the CAPM and the APT has been the subject of considerable debate. While there are advocates of alternative methods of estimating cost of equity, such as the use of an

---

[319] See Behm (1994), pp. 106-109; Kunowski (2002), pp. 82-84.

[320] See Kirsten (2000), p. 160; Kunowski (2002), p. 94.

[321] See Bremke and Bußmann (2000), p. 130; Matten (2000), p. 228; Arnsfeld and Gehrke (2001), p. 495.

opportunity return rate or the measurement of the volatility of free cash flows, the CAPM and the APT remain the preferred methods both for banks and for non-banks.

In the majority of papers, the CAPM is preferred over the APT for reasons of practicability and ease of use. The APT represents the better alternative from a theoretical standpoint, as it overcomes some of the shortcomings of the CAPM. In practice, however, its application is complicated and empirical evidence for the relevant factors to be included in the case of banks is hard to come by. Therefore, the APT and all other sophisticated methods should only be used to the extent that the expected benefits of the new information exceed the cost of providing it. For external valuation, in particular, the CAPM remains the method of choice.

Several studies have been published on the empirical cost of equity for banks. Zimmer and McCauley (1991) examine the historical cost of equity for a sample of international banks between 1984 and 1990. They compare the resulting cost of equity for different countries and analyze the potential reasons for these differences. Furthermore, they study the consequences of bank cost of equity on the spread required to cover the cost of equity for different products. Behm (1994) compares the cost of equity for banks in 1993 using the CAPM, the Gordon Growth model and alternative dividend return models.[322]

II.5.5   Valuation of business units

An analysis done at group level assesses the overall company value based on company-specific factors, but is likely to overlook important aspects when it comes to the value of each business unit. The valuation of business units is very important for banks. Especially for universal banks, missing transparency concerning the value of individual

---

[322] See Behm (1994), pp. 125-144. Böhme (1997), pp. 205-207, estimates bank cost of equity using CAPM for a German bank sample for the years between 1983 and 1995.

business units is seen as one potential reason for the low market value of universal banks.[323] Furthermore, valuation at the business unit level is the key to the implementation of value-based management and the optimal allocation of resources.[324]

II.5.5.1   Definition of business units

The definition of business units should be oriented at the strategic business units of a bank. A typical separation criterion is independence from other banking units, which in turn allows isolated steering of the business unit and the well-defined definition of cash flows.[325] For banks, the definition of business units is usually customer-oriented, as product-oriented segmentation is not free of overlap due to existing synergies and cross-selling between product groups.[326] Other than for non-banks, cross-selling effects also exist between a bank's strategic business units, complicating the separation of a bank's individual business units.[327] This separation problem results in various income and cost allocation problems that are widely discussed in banking literature.[328] However, in the following we do not discuss general separation problems between bank units but instead focus on value-relevant issues.

External valuation should be carried out on the basis of the existing segmentation of business units used in segmental reporting. For internal valuation purposes, existing internal business units can be assumed to reflect strategic business units.[329] To ensure

---

[323] See Merkle (2001), pp. 6-7.

[324] See Börner and Lowis (1997), p. 101; Kirsten (2000), p. 178.

[325] See Adolf et al. (1989), p. 488; Becker (1997), p. 107; Börner and Lowis (1997), p. 101; Kunowski (2002), p. 77.

[326] See Kümmel (1995), p. 57; Becker (1999), p. 58; Kunowski (2002), p. 78.

[327] See Börner and Lowis (1997), p. 102.

[328] For an overview of the general separation problem, see Büschgen (1998), pp. 715-716.

[329] See Kunowski (2002), p. 78.

incentive compatibility within value-based management, the segmentation of business units should be consistent with the existing organizational structure of banks. Typical banking business segments include retail customers, corporate and institutional customers, and corporate center. Other potential segments include real estate, investment banking, and asset management, depending on the strategic positioning of the bank.[330]

II.5.5.2   Definition of a business unit-specific performance measure

The definition of free cash flow to equity and residual income is carried out analogously to the definition of these performance measures at the bank level, as described in Section II.5.1.1 and II.5.1.2. From an external viewpoint, the main problem encountered when valuing business units is the limited data availability on the input parameters for the valuation model at the business unit level when looking in from the outside. For internal valuations, general bank-specific separation problems between the different business units aggravate the valuation of business units.[331] We discuss potential solutions to these valuation problems in the following. There is no "correct" solution, however, and the allocation method must be in keeping with the overall management philosophy of the bank.[332]

---

[330] See Kirsten (1995), p. 674.

[331] See Hörter (1998), p. 153. General allocation problems within banks, such as the allocation of income from cross-selling activities or the cost allocation of internal services such as transaction services or credit processing, are relevant for valuation at the business unit level. As said earlier, we avoid discussing these problems here and focus instead on issues specific to valuation.

[332] See Matten (2000), p. 279.

II.5.5.2.1 Allocation of interest income using funds transfer pricing

The allocation of income to the individual business units is unproblematic as far as fees, provisions, and income from business unit trading activities are concerned.[333] With regard to interest income, the concept of funds transfer pricing allows cash flow to be calculated in isolation for each business unit.[334]

As illustrated in Section 0II.3, banking business units create value both on the asset and liability sides of their balance sheets. The concept of fund transfer pricing involves using market rates as the opportunity costs of refinancing, thereby separating the value created by the customer and treasury units by calculating the corresponding spread on lending and deposit transactions. Interest income is separated in the spread on loans, the spread on deposits, and the mismatch profits, as illustrated in Figure II-6. The spread income on loans and deposits is allocated to the corresponding customer units, whereas any mismatch profits are allocated to the treasury unit.[335]

Internal valuation should adopt this transfer pricing system and calculate the value creation of customer units free of mismatch profits. The calculation and especially the forecasting of the value created by the treasury unit are problematic, as this value creation is illusory assuming market efficiency.[336] The bank treasury borrows from the deposit businesses of the bank and lends to its lending businesses of the bank. In addition, it handles the bank's proprietary trading business and is responsible for centralized risk management.[337]

---

[333] See Vettiger (1996), p. 133; Börner and Lowis (1997), 105.

[334] See Börner and Lowis (1997), p. 103; Hörter (1998), p. 153. For a detailed illustration of the concept of funds transfer pricing, see Schierenbeck (1991), pp. 78-136.

[335] For a detailed discussion on the use of funds transfer pricing for the allocation of interest income to individual banking units, see Strutz (1993), pp. 49-53; Behm (1994), pp. 86-89; Kirsten (2000), pp. 179-181.

[336] See Copeland et al. (2000), p. 445; Merkle (2001), p. 83.

[337] See Kunowski (2002), p. 177.

Figure II-6: Allocation of interest income using funds transfer pricing

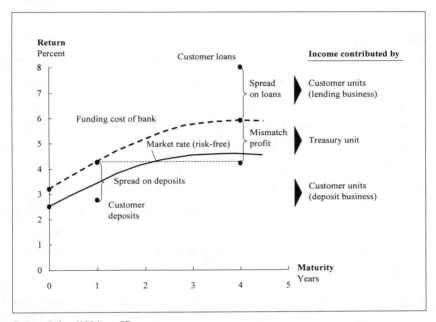

Source: Behm (1994), p. 87

In arbitrage-free markets, however, profits from mismatched securities and proprietary trading converge to zero in the long run. Thus, the value creation by the treasury unit cannot be justified assuming efficient markets. In consequence, mismatch profits in the base year have to be identified when valuing banks and individual banking units. When calculating residual income created at the business unit level, the mismatch profits must be allocated to the treasury unit.[338] When forecasting expected future cash flows or residual incomes, the valuation has either to fully disregard mismatch profits or to

---

[338] See Uyemura et al. (1996), p. 105.

include a conservative estimate of mismatch profits in the forecast income of the treasury unit.[339]

From an outside-in perspective, the question that raises itself is whether the reported net interest income of the business segments is calculated based on actual income or based on a matched opportunity rate, i.e. measured against the true wholesale price that corresponds to the maturity and risks of the loan or deposit for the bank. In line with internal valuations, mismatch profits should be identified for the base year and disregarded in the forecast of future performance. For segmental reporting based on a matched opportunity rate, potential mismatch profits are already included in the treasury income. If segmental income is reported based on actual income, potential mismatch profits can be identified by means of a rough estimate, as illustrated in Appendix 8, p. 244. Again, the forecasting of future mismatch profits is in general possible, but is usually not reasonable from an economic perspective, as mismatch profits are not systematic under efficient markets.

Another issue concerns the accounting for profit on equity allocated to banking units. The funding benefit attributed to shareholders' equity that is allocated to the business unit can be either allocated to the banking unit or included in the income of the corporate center or treasury unit. Since the cost associated with the equity is allocated to the banking units, the "equity profit" should also be allocated to the banking units to guarantee consistency. In the case of external valuations, financial reports usually indicate where the non-interest bearing contribution is included. If the equity profits are included in the income of the corresponding banking unit, no adjustment to reported

---

[339] Kunowski (2002), pp. 177-187, combines the concepts of funds transfer pricing and elasticity balance to forecast the future interest rate risks of a bank. Future mismatch profits can be estimated using a similar methodology. Also, future interest income through mismatch can be estimated using duration analysis, as illustrated by Johnson (1996), pp. 241-249. Both methodologies, however, are complicated and usually only applied in internal valuations when based on existing analysis performed by the treasury or risk controlling department.

income is required. If not, required equity has to be estimated, multiplied with the funding rate, and the benefit added back to the banking unit result.

II.5.5.2.2 Allocation of overhead costs

The problem of overhead cost allocation is particularly severe for banks as the indirect costs of banks are extraordinarily high, accounting for up to 80 percent of total costs.[340] Most banks try to use cost accounting systems to push all overhead costs down to the business unit level, yet it is better to allocate only those costs that the business units would incur if they were standing alone.[341]

From an external perspective, unallocated overhead costs should be kept as a head-quarters cost center, as the availability of the data necessary to allocate overhead costs is limited. In the case of internal valuations, costs are allocated partly in order to obtain a realistic picture of the value created at the business unit level.[342] One way of doing this is to allocate only budgeted overhead expenses, thereby preventing cost overruns in overhead units from affecting value creation at the business unit level.[343] Another overhead cost allocation option is activity-based costing.[344] Traditionally internal valuation involves adopting existing internal cost allocation systems.

---

[340] This is mainly accounted for by the high share of staff and IT expenses. See Strutz (1993), p. 53; Börner and Lowis (1997), p. 108. See also Section II.3.2.3.

[341] The main argument against fully allocated overhead costs is the accountability principle, which argues that only those costs over which business units have management control and are account-able for should be allocated. See Adolf et al. (1989), p. 489; Uyemura et al. (1996), p. 106; Vettiger (1996), p. 135.

[342] See Adolf et al. (1989), p. 489.

[343] See Uyemura et al. (1996), p. 106.

[344] See Strutz (1993), p. 53; Börner and Lowis (1997), p. 108; Hörter (1998), p. 154.

II.5.5.3   Estimation of the business unit-specific cost of equity

Approximating the cost of equity at the business unit level across the board with the overall cost of equity of the bank at the group level yields misleading results. Costs of equity have to be differentiated based on the differing systematic risk of the individual business units to avoid misallocation.[345]

We warn against using complicated mathematical models to estimate the cost of equity at the business unit level. The results produced by such models are bogusly accurate, whereas in practice the application of rough estimates is sufficient.[346] Again, we use the CAPM as the methodological basis for estimating the business unit-specific cost of equity, as it is also the model that we recommend for estimating the overall cost of equity in Section II.5.4.4.

One possible solution is the so-called "*pure player approach*" which uses the betas of "pure players", i.e. specialized, exchange-traded banks, as benchmarks.[347] The systematic risk of business units can be approximated in this case by the systematic risk of individual specialized banks or by the industry average of the systematic risk of the banking sector. Potential benchmarks have to be corrected for differences in the risk profile, as well as for national trends in the capital markets that influence systematic risk. The number of specialized public banks with comparable characteristics is, however, limited.[348]

If benchmark betas are not available, the estimation of an *accounting beta* via the earnings volatility is a viable alternative. This approach measures the systematic risk of a business unit as the covariance of the earnings growth of the business unit and that of

---

[345] See Hörter (1998), p. 148; Matten (2000), p. 270.

[346] See Kirsten (1995), p. 675.

[347] See Hörter (1998), p. 149; Becker (1999), p. 123; Arnsfeld and Gehrke (2001), p. 495.

[348] See Behm (1994), p. 92; Hörter (1998), p. 149.

a diversified bank portfolio divided by the variance of the portfolio, as depicted in Equation II-15.[349]

$$\beta_a = \frac{\text{cov}(g_{ebt,bu}g_{ebt,m})}{\text{var}(g_{ebt,m})} \qquad \qquad \text{II-15}$$

with $g_{ebt,bu}$ = Growth rate of earnings before taxes of business unit bu

   $g_{ebt,m}$ = Growth rate of earnings before taxes of market portfolio m

Another option is to estimate the *volatilities of the free cash flow* of individual business units compared to the overall cash flow at the group level.[350] However, this method neglects the diversification effects between the systematic risks of the individual business units.[351]

Arnsfeld (1998) derives a marginal cost calculation for equity cost and studies its role as a tool for internal bank management that corresponds to capital market theory. His approach is not only applicable at the level of individual banking units, but also at the product level. However, given the data requirements and the extensive calculations involved, it is more suited as a tool for internal bank control rather than for valuation.

II.5.6   Discussion

In the previous sections, we identified several adjustments to the DCF and residual income models that are necessary in order that these standard models reflect the institutional specifics of banks. Figure II-7 summarizes the key adjustments and the underlying rationale.

---

[349] See Behm (1994), pp. 92-93; Hörter (1998), pp. 149-152; Kirsten (2000), pp. 164-165; Matten (2000), pp. 288-290.

[350] See Kirsten (1995), p. 675.

[351] See Hörter (1998), p. 152; Matten (2000), pp. 236-241.

Figure II-7: Key adjustments to DCF and residual income models for banks

Adjustment specific to banks	Rationale
(1) Consider retention rate in CF calculation	• Required retention presents a reinvestment
(2) Adjust provisions for loan losses and general risks*	• Provisions typically serve as safety cushion and do not reflect economic reality
(3) Shorten explicit forecast horizon	• High dependence on exogenous factors complicates long-term forecasts
(4) Apply conservative estimate of growth rate in terminal value	• Banks' brand/franchise strength is relatively low; sustainable competitive advantage over long periods is rare
(5) Estimate cost of equity using CAPM; possibly adjust beta for bank individual risk profile	• CAPM yields relatively accurate results; the greater amount of work involved with the sophisticated models is typically not worthwile in practice
(6) Adjust business unit performance** —Identify mismatch profits and disregard them in performance forecast —Include equity profit in business unit income if data is available —Use existing overhead cost allocation rationale	• Several unit separation problems exist – Mismatch profits are not systematic (i.e. converge to zero assuming efficient markets) – Business units also pay cost of equity – Pushing overhead costs down might lead to misallocation as the available data is limited

* Also, adjust for hidden reserves in deferred taxes and pension provisions as for non-banks
** Follow existing segmentation of business units when valuing non-banks

Source: Own graphic

During our examination of the application of different valuation models to banks in Section II.4, we identified the use of the equity method as the main specific of bank valuation. When it comes to the definition of a measure of performance, the calculation of free cash flow to banks is in some ways difficult. The direct calculation of cash flows is problematic due to limited data availability, both from an external and internal perspective, and as a result, cash flows are typically calculated indirectly by adjusting net income.

Regardless of whether a direct or indirect cash flow approach is used, the estimation of the reinvestment rate for banks is difficult, as banks mainly invest in human capital and regulatory equity capital. While the estimation of the reinvestment in human capital is usually too complex a calculation, it is essential that consideration be given to the *required retention rate* when forecasting future cash flows, as the retention of capital required by capital adequacy regulations represents a reinvestment for banks.

Given the cash adequacy of net income in banking, the calculation of residual income for banks involves fewer adjustments and is usually easier than the somewhat more complicated derivation of free cash flow to equity holders.

In the case of both methods, i.e. DCF and residual income, risks have to be explicitly modeled in the performance measure. This involves above all substantial *adjustments to the risk provisioning* reported in financial statements, which typically does not reflect economic reality and includes hidden reserves. Correcting for these equity reserves, however, is in general difficult and from an external perspective often not practicable given the limited availability of data.

The forecasting of bank performance is relatively complicated due to the high dependence of banking performance on exogenous macroeconomic factors. As a result, in the case of banks it is usually necessary to *shorten the forecast horizon* compared to non-banking industries. Furthermore, the performance forecast needs to include predictions of macroeconomic and financial market trends.

The formulation of the terminal value requires a *conservative estimate of the growth rate* to be made. Sustainable competitive advantage in the case of individual banks over longer periods is rare given the relatively low brand and franchise strength of banks. It is therefore reasonable to assume that individual bank performance will converge to the industry average after the explicit forecast horizon, and consequently we use a constant perpetuity to calculate terminal value in DCF models. In the case of residual income models, the terminal value formula includes a decay rate to account for the erosion of competitive advantage over time.

Like for non-banks the *CAPM* is the preferred model for estimating the cost of equity, given its ease of use. Although the APT might be the better option from a theoretical standpoint, there is still a lack of clarity concerning which input factors should be selected. Furthermore, differences in the empirical results for the CAPM and the APT are relatively low where banks are concerned. In contrast to non-banks, a bank's capital structure is typically ignored when estimating the beta, whereas its individual asset-liability mismatch plays an important role.

The valuation of *individual banking units* is complicated by the problems inherent in separating banking units. Important adjustments in this respect concern the allocation of interest income and overhead costs to the individual banking units. With regard to interest income, mismatch profits have to be identified and disregarded in the forecasts of future performance. In addition, the equity profit has to be allocated to the individual banking unit. When it comes to overhead cost allocation, the best approach is to follow the existing allocation methodology. From an internal standpoint, the valuation of banking units should in general be carried out on the basis of the bank's internal allocation methodologies, which are assumed incentive-compatible. Alternative allocation methods for pushing down unallocated overhead costs to the banking unit level do not exist for external valuations, given the limited availability of data. As for non-banks, the cost of equity for individual business units can be estimated using a pure-player approach or an accounting beta methodology.

Appendix 9, p. 245, gives an overview of the key articles in bank valuation and summarizes their position regarding the key adjustments to be made to DCF and residual income referred to above.

In summary, the majority of adjustments result from the specific risk-taking role adopted by banks. Bank valuation models have to explicitly model the risks incurred by banks, and the default risk is considered in the definition of cash flow and residual income by adjusting the risk provisioning of banks. Risks resulting from macroeconomic and financial market trends are explicitly included in the forecast of future performance, and the calculation of the cost of equity can include, if necessary, the ALM profile of the individual bank. The identification of these risks when valuing banks and quantifying their influence on value requires a thorough understanding of a bank's individual performance, the banking industry overall as well as the underlying forces.

II.6   Conclusions and outlook

After examining the applicability of standard valuation models to banks, we conclude that the models, i.e. multiples, net asset values, DCF, and residual income, are all applicable to banks if the corresponding equity approach is used. When it comes to measuring shareholder value, DCF and residual income are superior models, and multiples and net asset values play only a complementary or auxiliary role.

Besides the choice of equity method, additional adjustments to DCF and residual income models are required to customize these standard models for banks. In total, six key adjustments are identified. When valuing banks, practitioners are advised to consider the required retention (in the cash flow calculation), correct the risk provisioning for hidden reserves, shorten the explicit forecast horizon, and apply a conservative estimate of the growth rate implied in the terminal value. For the estimation of the cost of equity, we suggest the use of the CAPM (taking into consideration the bank-specific risk profile). At the banking unit level, the performance measure and in particular interest income and overhead costs have to be potentially adjusted.

In summary, residual income is preferred over DCF when valuing banks. From a theoretical standpoint, the terminal value assumption is more reasonable in the case of the residual income model. In addition, the latter model is easier to use than DCF in a banking context given the cash adequacy of bank income and the corrections for the retention rate required by DCF. There is, however, a need for further research, as little research into the application of the residual income model to banks has been carried out up until now. No empirical studies on its relevance for banks exist apart from one study by Fiordelisi (2002), who studies the superiority of residual income compared to traditional bank performance measures.

The fulfillment of the performance goals set by the capital market is becoming increasingly important to banks. To meet these performance goals, bank managers need to understand the fundamental drivers of value. This raises the question as to what drives shareholder value in the case of banks. Empirical evidence for value drivers specific to banks has yet to be published, and therefore there is a need for empirical studies in which the potential value drivers for different bank types are measured and ranked. The implications for bank management derived from such evidence could then serve as a basis for value creation within banks.

Zimmermann (1995) nicely illustrates the influence of a bank's asset-liability mismatch on its value and capital cost in particular. Further research, both from a theoretical and empirical standpoint, on the asset-liability mismatch and the influence of other relevant factors on banks' cost of capital is required to complete the picture.

In this article, we provide an overview of bank valuation literature and illustrate the adjustments that are required to customize valuation models so that they reflect the institutional specifics of banks. At the same time, more research on value-based management for banks is required. Section II.2 contains an initial overview of bank-specific literature on value-based management. As stated in relation to the valuation literature above, standard literature on value-based management focuses on traditional industrial companies, while literature on the specifics of managing bank value is rare. Analogously to our research on bank valuation, a detailed analysis on the applicability of value-based management and the specific issues encountered when introducing value-based management into banks is required. Anchoring value-orientation in the planning, controlling, and incentive systems of banks is critical to the success of shareholder value management and therefore the maximization of shareholder value. As for bank valuation, substantial adjustments to the standard framework of value-based management are to be expected, as bank management differs significantly from planning and controlling systems used by industrial companies. In particular, the challenges involved in integrating value-based management into the risk management systems of banks, and potential trade-offs between minimizing risk and maximizing shareholder value can be expected to increase the need for extensive research in the future.

III. Empirical relevance of shareholder value for banks

III.1 Motivation and key research questions

The concept of shareholder value has gained worldwide acceptance since the constitutional work of Rappaport (1986). Based on the idea that the management's primary responsibility is to increase value, shareholder value has become not only the standard for measuring business performance, but also an important tool in strategic management. The basis of the shareholder value approach is the assumption that the capital market prices a company's shares according to the market's expectations of its long-term productivity, i.e. its sustainable competitive advantage.[352] In consequence, a company creates shareholder value by creating sustainable competitive advantage. This basic assumption turns the shareholder value approach into a holistic management approach that links the operating performance of a company to an external market view.

For a long time the shareholder value approach was primarily used in relation to industrial companies, while academics and practitioners ignored or doubted its relevance for banks. In the banking industry there was intense debate on the legitimacy of the shareholder approach, due to the responsibility held by banks in national economies as financial intermediaries, and the importance of stakeholder oriented governance structures in banking, such as savings banks and cooperatives.[353] One pragmatic reason for the late adoption of the concept of shareholder value in banking is that applying the principles of valuation to banks is complicated in practice due to a number of bank specifics. Especially when looked at from the outside, valuing banks seems problematic, e.g., determining the quality of the loan portfolio or measuring the share of profits

---

[352] See Rappaport (1986), p. 69.

[353] See Amely (1997); Zimmermann and Jöhnk (1998); Schuster (2000).

attributable to interest rate mismatch.[354] In addition, banking is extremely reliant on financial market trends and general economic cycles, and is highly vulnerable to technological disruption.[355] These facts considerably exacerbate the forecasting of the future performance of individual banks and the banking industry overall. Yet, shareholder value and its management have gained importance in the banking industry during the last few years. Looking forward, this trend is expected to strengthen even further as a result of the changing ownership structures in banking, continuing industry consolidation, high competitive pressure due to globalization and the deregulation of financial markets, as well as competition by non-banks.[356]

While the importance of shareholder value for the management of banks is set to increase further, skepticism on the relevance of the shareholder value approach for banking still exists. The practical problems inherent in bank valuation justify the doubts held concerning the ability of stock prices to reflect the future competitive advantage of banks: How meaningful are stock prices given the relatively low transparency of current and, in particular, future bank performance? Does the market have any predictive power when it comes to the future performance of individual banks and the banking industry as a whole?

The objective of our study is to answer these questions concerning the empirical relevance of shareholder value as a measure of bank performance and the applicability of this strategic concept to the management of banks. We investigate the predictive power of the market in regard to bank performance for a sample of 290 banks from around the world between 1989 and 1998.

---

[354] See Copeland et al. (2000), pp. 431-439.

[355] See MSDW (2001), p. 27; Koch (2002), pp. 41-42.

[356] See Kirsten (1995), p. 1; Hörter (2000), pp. 13-15; Fiordelisi (2002), pp. 1-2.

Our analysis compares the market value, as the market's expectation of future competitive advantage, with an ex-post intrinsic value based on historical operating performance, as illustrated in Figure III-1. Thereby we use an individual security approach and expect the market value of a bank in year t to approximate the ex-post intrinsic value of this bank in year t. The key figure in our analysis is the ratio of market value to intrinsic value minus 1, which we hereafter call the prediction error. As basic hypothesis, we expect the resulting prediction errors for our sample banks to approximate zero.

Figure III-1: Model design

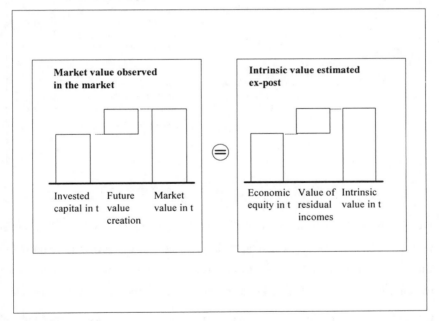

Source: Own graphic

The assumed identity of market value and intrinsic value is based on two underlying hypotheses. First, the valuation model used returns reliable estimates of intrinsic value of banks, and second, markets are efficient and value a bank at its intrinsic value. In the course of our paper, we test the validity of the two hypotheses for the banking industry, as illustrated in Figure III-2.

Figure III-2: Outline of analysis

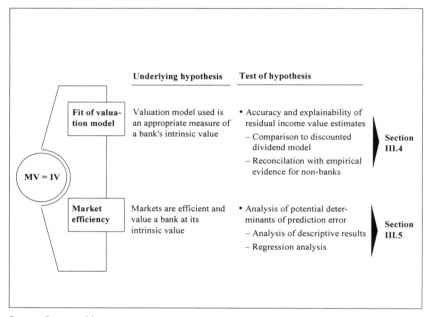

Source: Own graphic

We estimate intrinsic value based on the residual income model. We use the residual income model since prior research has found evidence for its superiority compared to alternative valuation models, such as the DCF or discounted dividend model, when valuing a firm in general. For banks, the residual income approach is more preferable

for banks from a methodological and practical perspective.[357] However, empirical evidence for the superiority of the residual income model for the banking industry does

---

[357] See Section II.4.5.

not exist so far. Therefore, Section III.4 examines the accuracy and explanatory value of value estimates from the residual income model for banks. Using data from our sample banks, we compare the value estimates from the residual income model to the value estimates from the discounted dividend model.[358] Thereafter, we reconcile the results for our banking sample with the empirical evidence found for other industries.

To test the second hypothesis on market efficiency, Section III.5 studies the prediction errors of the value estimates and potential determinants, such as regional scope, bank type, bank size, profitability, and time effects. If market efficiency exists for banking markets, existing prediction errors will follow patterns similar to non-banking industries and general principles of capital markets will provide explanations for the observed patterns.

Based on the empirical evidence on the two hypotheses for our banking sample, we draw conclusions on the relevance of shareholder value as a measure of bank performance and on the validity of the approach as a strategic concept for bank management.

The paper is organized as follows. Section III.2 puts our analysis into perspective of the existing research. Section III.3 describes the data set used and the methodology employed to construct the valuation models and estimate the model parameters. Section III.4 discusses the empirical results on the accuracy and explanatory value of the residual income model for banks. Section III.5 summarizes the descriptive statistics and regression results on potential determinants of the prediction errors. Section III.6 assesses the robustness of results based on several sensitivity analyses. Section III.7 presents the conclusions.

---

[358] The comparison with the discounted dividend model is consistent with the empirical studies on industrial companies in prior research. See Table III-1, p. 109. A comparison with results from the DCF model is preferable, but not feasible due to limited data availability in the case of our sample banks.

III.2   Overview of existing research

To put our analysis into perspective and delineate it from existing research, the following section gives a review on the various empirical studies that examine the relationship between market returns and economic performance in one way or another. Tests for return predictability, on asset pricing models, and on the empirical evidence of performance indicators are important areas of research that relate to our study and the underlying assumptions, as shown in Figure III-3.

The tests for *return predictability* are associated with one of the most important research fields in empirical economics, this being the research on market efficiency. Market efficiency claims that "security prices fully reflect all available information".[359] The efficient-market hypothesis has been intensively tested in empirical studies since its formulation by Kendall (1953) in the 1950s.[360] In addition to event studies and tests for private information, tests for return predictability represent an additional important category of work on market efficiency.[361] The key question is whether return predictability reflects rational variation through time in terms of expected returns or irrational deviations of price from fundamental value.[362] The tests therefore examine the forecasting power of past returns, but also of such variables as dividend yields and interest rates for the prediction of future market values and returns respectively.[363]

The majority of these studies finds evidence on the semi-efficient behavior of markets, therefore supporting the efficient market hypothesis. As described above, the existence

---

[359] Fama (1991), p. 1575.

[360] See Copeland and Weston (1992), pp. 361-392; Brealey and Myers (2000), pp. 358-368. For a detailed review of the literature on market efficiency, see Fama (1970) and Fama (1991).

[361] See Fama (1991), pp. 1576-1577.

[362] See Fama (1991), p. 1577.

[363] See Fama (1991), pp. 1577-1599.

of market efficiency is an important hypothesis in our model. We examine the fore-casting power of current market value of banks and banking returns for the prediction of future economic performance conditional on market efficiency and thus implicitly test market efficiency.

Figure III-3: Research on market value and economic performance

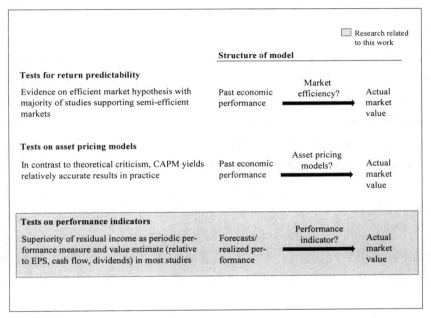

Source: Own graphic

Studies on *asset pricing models* provide further empirical research concerning the re-lationship between market returns and economic performance indicators. In this paper, market efficiency is not the subject of the tests, but is a maintained hypothesis. Asset pricing models are tested conditional on market efficiency, whereas in tests for the predictability of returns, market efficiency is assessed conditional on asset pricing models.[364] The problem is that such tests always provide combined evidence on market efficiency and asset pricing models, and the results are therefore ambiguous.[365]

In our analysis, however, we do not test the relevance of an asset-pricing model, but maintain the hypothesis that the CAPM is a good estimator of asset prices within our model. This assumption is in line with empirical findings that show that the CAPM, contrary to the theoretical criticism to which it has been subjected, in practice yields relatively accurate results.

A more practice-oriented area of research associated with our model is the research on the empirical evidence of innovative *performance indicators* based on fundamental valuation models. This area of research examines the relationship between market values and the fundamental value estimates of companies to test the relative superiority of the fundamental valuation model and its corresponding performance indicator. This work can in general be divided into two categories.

Whereas a large number of studies are completed by consultants searching for empirical evidence for the superiority of their proposed performance measures,[366] a small group of accounting-oriented researchers examines instead the empirical relationship between market values and fundamental value estimates based on accounting information from a neutral perspective.[367]

---

[364] See Fama (1991), p. 1589. For an overview of the literature on the empirical testing of the CAPM and the APT, see Copeland and Weston (1992), pp. 212-217 and 228-231 respectively.

[365] See Copeland and Weston (1992), pp. 350-351.

[366] Practitioner literature usually suggests that EVA is superior to traditional performance measures as it allegedly explains market values better. See O'Byrne (1996); Uyemura et al. (1996); MSDW (2001), pp. 44-47.

[367] Academic literature on accounting-based valuation also uses the term abnormal earnings for residual income type valuation models. This accounting-oriented research area found its seeds in the article of Feltham and Ohlson (1995) that rediscovered the residual income model for their academic research in the early 1990s. The model is therefore often referred to as the Feltham/Ohlson model in literature.

Table III-1 gives an overview of existing research in this area and describes the scope and results of the relevant studies.

Table III-1: Overview of empirical evidence on performance indicators

Article and Year	Scope of Analysis	Empirical Results
Studies on periodic performance measures		
Biddle et al. (1997)	Residual income, CF, and earnings	No superiority of residual income model
Frankel and Lee (1998)	Residual income vs. traditional performance measures	Superiority of residual income model
Lee (1999)	Residual income vs. traditional performance measures	Superiority of residual income model
Fiordelisi (2002)	Residual income vs. traditional performance measures	Superiority of residual income model
Studies on fundamental value estimates		
Bernard (1995)	Residual income model vs. discounted dividend model	Superiority of residual income model
Penman and Sougiannis (1998)	Residual income model, discounted dividend model vs. DCF model	Superiority of residual income model
Dechow et al. (1999)	Residual income model vs. DCF model	No superiority of residual income model
Courteau et al. (2000)	Residual income model, discounted dividend model vs. DCF model	No superiority of residual income model
Francis et al. (2000)	Residual income model, discounted dividend model vs. DCF model	Superiority of residual income model
Subrahmanyan and Venkatachalam (2004)	Residual income model vs. DCF model	Superiority of residual income model

Source: Own table

The existing contributions focus either on periodic performance indicators or on fundamental value estimates. The first group, the studies on periodic performance measures, examines the information content of market prices and the relevance of past or anticipated periodic performance indicators for current changes in market prices.

Indicators are innovative measures of performance such as residual income and cash flows, but also traditional measures such as income or EPS. The second group of research compares fundamental value estimates from the residual income, DCF, and discounted dividend model to stock prices observed in the market.

The empirical results suggest the superiority of the residual income model. In seven out of the ten listed studies, residual income dominates the alternative periodic performance indicators or fundamental value estimates. Unfortunately, the existing studies do not provide empirical evidence for this superiority for the banking industry. Except from Fiordelisi (2002), none of the listed contributions differentiates by industry and most of the studies explicitly exclude banks and other financial services providers. Fiordelisi (2002) focuses on the banking industry and provides evidence supporting the superiority of residual income compared to traditional performance measures. Evidence on the validity of fundament value estimates from the residual income model does not exist for banks.

The articles quoted in Table III-1 can be further discriminated along two dimensions. With respect to the point of view of the analysis, the majority of studies applies an *ex-ante view* and calculates the value estimates based on anticipated accounting variables. Few studies use an *ex-post analysis* based on historical operating performance reported in financial statements and thus realized attributes. Another differentiating factor is the level of granularity in the analysis. While the majority of studies with large sample evidence on the relative performance of valuation models uses *portfolio value estimates*, a few articles provide empirical evidence using *individual security value estimates*.

The methodology of our paper is closely related to the studies described in Table III-1. Since we aim to study the predictive power of market value with respect to the future competitive advantage of banks, we use an ex-post analysis and derive intrinsic value based on realized attributes. We choose an individual security approach since the use of a portfolio design averages out the expectations on the bank level. Unlike existing articles, which typically focus on industrial companies and exclude financial services providers from their analysis, our study focuses on banks only. To our knowledge, this is the first study to provide large-scale evidence on the relative performance of valuation models for the banking industry.

III.3   Data and methodology

III.3.1   Data

III.3.1.1   Data set used

We take our sample banks from the Datastream (DS) database[368] and choose those firms that conform to the DS industry definition of Banks, Investment Banks, Consumer Finance, and Mortgage Finance, covering the regions of North America, Europe, and Asia. We focus on financial services providers that conform to the bank definition in the narrow sense.[369] We exclude financial services providers such as Insurance Companies, Investment Companies, and Asset Managers, due to the differences in the business models. Also, we exclude specialist financial areas, e.g., Mining Finance.

Furthermore, we concentrate on North America, Europe, and Asia, and exclude countries which have had limited economic or political stability over the observation period such as South and Central America, Russia, Eastern Europe, the Middle East, India, and China.

When performing a shareholder value analysis, we concentrate by definition on banks that were exchange-listed during the observation period. An explicit sample restriction with respect to company size is not necessary as exchange-listing automatically implies a minimum bank size.

Although DS data dating back to 1985 is available, we restrict our focus to the years after 1988 in order to have a sample of significant size. The restricted data availability

---

[368] Datastream is a product of Thomson Financial, and contains both securities market data and the accounting data of companies worldwide.

[369] The DS industry definitions used mainly correspond to SIC codes 6021, 6022, 6029, 6035, 6141, 6162, and 6211; approx. 5 percent of the banks are covered by other SIC codes.

of the accounting variables used in the residual income calculations for the years between 1989 and 2002 limits the sample size to 290 banks.[370]

We use DS Worldscope[371] as our source for the accounting variables used in the residual income calculation. For the calculation of the cost of equity and market value of the sample banks, we draw on the market data available in DS. The information on pooling-of-interest transactions between 1989 and 2002 has been obtained from the Securities Data Company (SDC)[372].

III.3.1.2 Sample characteristics

The 290 sample banks accounted for a total market capitalization of USD 545 bn in 1989, growing to USD 1,646 bn in 2002. Table III-2 includes a number of statistics illustrating key characteristics of the sample banks.

Table III-2: Descriptive statistics of sample characteristics

(1989 – 2002, USD bn, N=2,900)

Statistic	Market Value	Book Equity	Total Assets	ROE
Mean	3.7	1.8	36.9	10.4
Median	0.9	0.6	10.0	12.3
Standard Deviation	8.9	3.9	83.9	31.2
Interquartile Range	2.5	1.5	29.5	12.7

Source: Own calculation

---

[370] For 350 of 1,600 banks with the defined industry and region, accounting data from 1989 until 2002 is available. Further correction for incomplete data records results in a sample of 290 banks.

[371] DS Worldscope is the former Worldscope company database, which has been acquired by DS and recently integrated into the DS platform.

[372] Securities Data Company (SDC) is a product of Thomson Financial, and provides detailed information on financial transactions such as new issues, mergers and acquisitions, syndicated loans, private equity, project finance, poison pills and much more.

The average market value of a bank is USD 3.7 bn, while average book equity is USD 1.8 bn. Average bank size, measured by the mean of total assets, is USD 36.9 bn.

Medians are significantly lower than standard means, indicating positive skewness for these variables. Profitability measured by ROE averages at a mean of 10.4 percent and is negatively skewed. The dispersion is relatively high for all characteristics, as shown in Table III-2.

Appendix 10, p. 246, shows the development of the above described sample character-ristics over the observation period from 1989 to 2002.

Figure III-4: Development of return – Total sample vs. DS World Banks

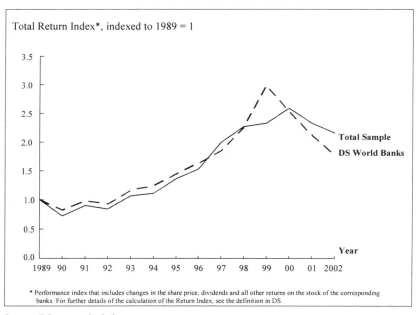

Source: DS, own calculation

Figure III-4 describes the development of the total return index of the sample weighted by the market value of the individual banks relative to the development of the DS World Banks index. The performance of the total sample and the DS World Banks is closely related except for the year 1999, in which the sample index significantly underperforms the market. In 2002, the total return index of the sample and the DS World Banks is 2.2 and 1.8 respectively.

We divide the sample into subsamples for different regions and bank types. The regional subsamples are North America, Europe, and Asia, as shown in **Error! Not a valid bookmark self-reference.**. In addition, Appendix 11, p. 247, gives a detailed overview of the sample banks by country.

Figure III-5: Characteristics of the sample by region

Market value by region
2002, percent (number of banks)

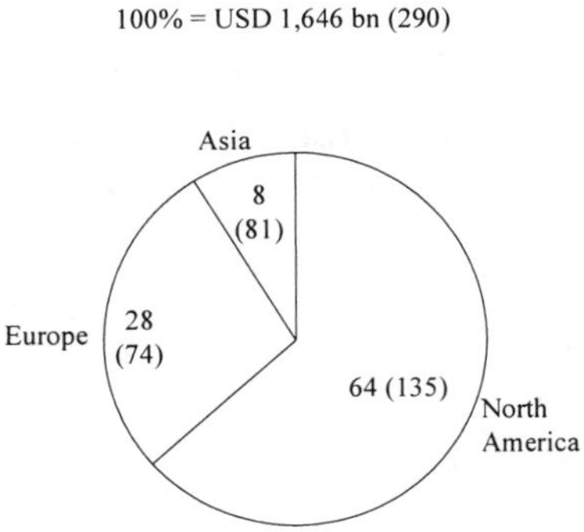

100% = USD 1,646 bn (290)

Asia 8 (81)

Europe 28 (74)

64 (135) North America

Characteristics by region
1989 – 2002, mean, USD bn

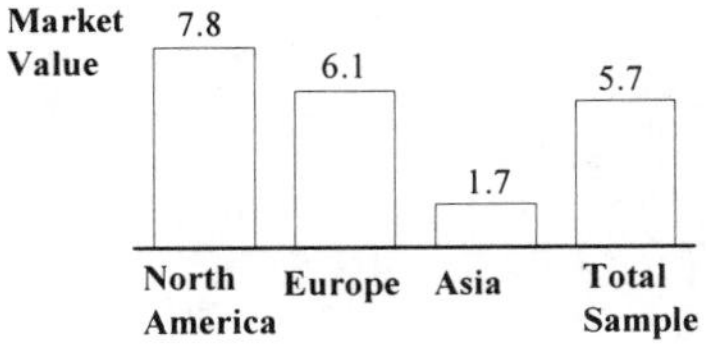

	North America	Europe	Asia	Total Sample
Market Value	7.8	6.1	1.7	5.7
Book Equity	3.8	4.2	1.6	3.3
Total Assets	61.5	104.0	30.1	63.5
ROE (percent)	17.0	9.9	-5.7	8.9
N	1,350	740	810	2,900

Source: Own calculation

North America is the largest subsample with 135 banks accounting for 64 percent of the total market value of the sample. With 74 European and 81 Asian banks, Europe and Asia are about the same size in terms of the number of banks. Asia, however, has a lower share of market value given the low average market value per bank (USD 1.7

bn) relative to North America (USD 7.8 bn) and Europe (USD 6.1 bn). Furthermore, the subsamples differ significantly with respect to profitability, with ROE ranging between 17.0 percent for North America, 9.9 percent for Europe and -5.6 percent for Asia.

Bank type subsamples are comprised of Banks, Investment Banks, Consumer Finance, and Mortgage Finance, as shown in Figure III-6 below.

Figure III-6: Characteristics of the sample by bank type

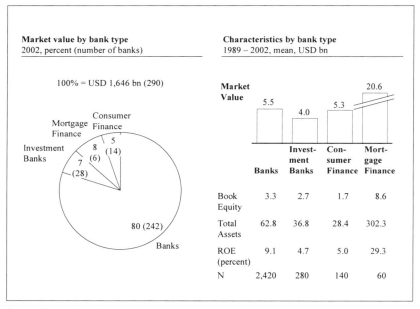

Source: Own calculation

Banks represent by far the largest subsample, with a market value of 81 percent of the total market value and accounting for 242 of the 290 banks. Profitability differences seem to be driven more by regional effects, with Banks being more profitable than Investment Banks and Consumer Finance. The Mortgage Finance sample is small and characterized by a few large, high-performing US players. Whereas a further differentiation of the sample banks in the Banks subsample would be preferable, more detailed bank type-related information for this subsample is not available neither via DS industry codes nor via SIC codes.

The distribution of bank types by regional subsample is relatively balanced, as illustrated in Appendix 12, p. 248. Within all the regional subsamples, Banks are the largest group, accounting for 77 percent to 89 percent of the banks. The share of Investment Banks and Consumer Finance is higher in the European and Asian subsamples. The Mortgage Finance banks are all located in North America except for one bank.

III.3.1.3   Sample coverage

We examine the coverage of the banking industry in our sample by using the sum of the market value of the DS World industry indices for Banks, Investment Banks, Consumer Finance, and Mortgage Finance as a proxy for the size of the banking industry. Using this proxy as a benchmark, we examine the market coverage as described in Figure III-7.

The total sample covers, on average, 44 percent of the worldwide banking industry during the years between 1989 and 2002. We also examine the coverage of the regional subsamples by comparing the sum of the market values of each subsample with the market value of the corresponding DS index. While North American and European subsamples cover, on average, 74 and 47 percent of the North American and European banking industry respectively, the coverage of the Asian banking market by the corresponding subsample is lower, with a mean value of 27 percent.

In addition, the Asian sample is biased, with 69 out of 81 banks coming from Japan, and a subcritical number of banks for the rest of the Asian countries, as shown in Appendix 11, p. 247. Given these facts, the Asian subsample is less representative and data quality considerably lower. For an overview of the development of sample coverage over time, see Appendix 13, p. 249.

Coverage of the DS banking indices in the sample is, on average, relatively high. Nonetheless, the representativeness of the sample is limited for several reasons. The sample excludes by definition banks that are not exchange-listed. This group, however, constitutes an important part of the banking industry, as it comprises such bank types as savings banks and cooperatives. Furthermore, there is a survivorship bias in the sample, since we look at a stable sample of banks, with no banks entering or exiting the sample over the observation period.

Figure III-7: Sample coverage of DS banking indices

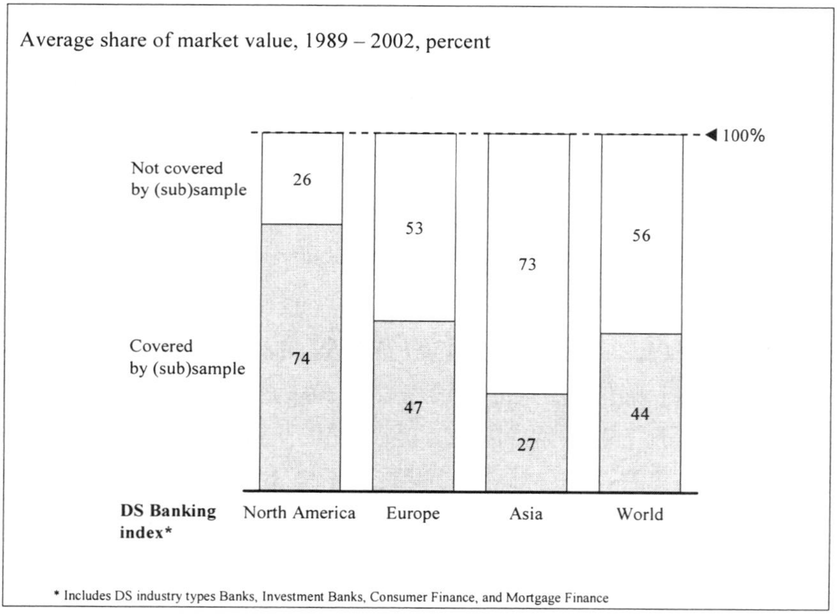

Average share of market value, 1989 – 2002, percent

Source: DS, own calculation

Consequently, inductive conclusions concerning the banking industry based on the sample results can only be drawn after careful consideration of the limited representativeness of the sample. In the following sections, we present and discuss the empirical results of our analysis. Based on the findings, we formulate conclusions for the banking industry as hypotheses and subsequently discuss their feasibility.

III.3.2   Residual income model

III.3.2.1   Structure of the model

In the following, we introduce the general concept of residual income to estimate the intrinsic value of a company and define the specific model structure used for the analysis on the banking industry in our case.[373] Residual income (RI) is generally defined as operating earnings less a capital charge for the economic equity used by the company, as described by Equation III-1:[374]

$$RI = \text{Operating Earnings-(Cost of Equity} \times \text{Economic Equity)} \qquad \text{III-1}$$

Furthermore, we use the equity approach rather than the entity model of valuation to calculate residual income. In literature, the use of an equity approach is recommended for banks, as debt has an operating and financing function in banking that is almost impossible to separate.[375] As it is difficult to define the debt capital used for financing, and to assign the proper cost of capital to this debt, the equity approach is more appropriate for valuing banks.[376] Therefore, we do not consider debt as capital and consider interest paid as an operating expense. Economic capital is simply defined as equity plus equity equivalents, and the cost of capital equals the cost of equity in the following.

Residual income measures shareholder value creation based on operating performance, but does not directly relate to market expectations.[377] Nonetheless, assuming market

---

[373] For the application of the residual income approach for measuring shareholder value in the banking industry, see Uyemura et al. (1996), pp. 99-100; MSDW (2001), pp. 44-47; Fiordelisi (2002), pp. 18-27.

[374] See Rappaport (1986), p. 121.

[375] See Copeland et al. (2000), pp. 428-429.

[376] For a detailed discussion of the specifics of banks and the reasons for the use of an equity approach when valuing banks, see Börner and Lowis (1997), pp. 94-104; Kirsten (2000), pp. 133-135; Koch (2002), pp. 44-45; Damodaran (2004), pp. 4-7.

[377] See Fernández (2002), p. 282.

efficiency, residual income can be linked to market value, as illustrated by Equation III-2:

Market value added = Market value - Economic equity
$\qquad\qquad$ = Present value (PV) of expected future RI $\qquad\qquad$ III-2
$\qquad$ Market value = Economic equity + PV of expected future RI

Assuming market efficiency, market value added incorporates the market expectations of future value creation, i.e. the present value of all future residual incomes of a company expected by the market.[378] We solve the equation for market value and obtain a comprehensive model of equity value incorporating changes in operating performance and market expectations.

Based on this conceptual framework, we calculate intrinsic value (IV) of bank i in year t, as illustrated by Equation III-3:

$$IV_{it}^{RI} = EE_{it} + \sum_{f=1}^{f=5} RI_{i,t+f} \times \left[1/(1+c_{e_{it}})^f \right] + \frac{\overline{RI}_{i,t+1/t+5}}{c_{e_{it}} + d} \times \frac{1}{(1+c_{e_{it}})^5} \qquad III-3$$

where EE_{it} = Economic equity of bank i in year t

$\qquad RI_{it}$ = RI of bank i in year t

$\overline{RI}_{i,t+1/t+5}$ = Average RI of bank i during the years $t+1$ and $t+5$

$\qquad t$ = Observation year

$\qquad f$ = Explicit forecast interval (Phase 1)

$\qquad d$ = Decay rate, constant over banks and time

$\qquad c_{e_{it}}$ = Cost of equity of bank i in year t

Figure III-8 illustrates the structure of the model used to estimate the value of equity. We construct our residual income model as a two-phase model, with Phase 1 representing an explicit forecast period similar to the one in traditional DCF-type

---

[378] See MSDW (2001), p. 18.

approaches, and Phase 2 describing the remaining life of bank i, corresponding to the
"terminal value".[379]

Figure III-8: Structure of the model

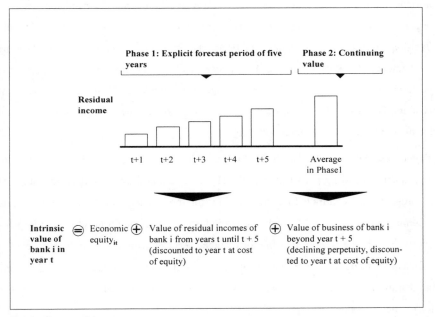

Source: Own graphic

In Phase 1 we measure historic residual income based on the operating performance of
bank i between the years $t+1$ and $t+5$. Afterwards, we calculate the present value of
the value created in Phase 1 by discounting residual income in the years $t+1$ and $t+5$
with the cost of equity of bank i in t.

---

[379] DCF-approaches typically use a two-phase model with an explicit forecast period in Phase 1 and
an estimate of the terminal value in Phase 2. See Copeland et al. (2000), pp. 233-234.
Alternatively, some models use three phases and subdivide the forecast period into two phases,
with a higher level of detail in the forecasts of Phase 1. See Adolf et al. (1989), p. 488; Börner and
Lowis (1997), p. 100.

We assume the explicit forecast period f to be five years, which corresponds to the length of forecast periods put forward in literature.[380] Other factors, too, serve as indicators for the selection of a forecast horizon, including the length of the strategic horizon and the term of an economic cycle.[381] A five-year forecast period appears to be a good proxy given the strategic horizon of approx. three to five years of internal decision makers within banks, such as the strategic planning and controlling departments. Also, external decision makers such as research analysts forecast the performance of financial stocks for no longer than five years.[382] Since the duration of economic cycles is about five years, a five-year period is long enough to fully account for the implications of structural changes.

To measure value creation in Phase 2 most models calculate the continuing value with a constant or growing perpetuity and thereby assume that the competitive advantage of a company will continue forever.[383] Unlike for most other industries, however, this assumption does not hold for the banking industry. The assumption of erosion in competitive advantage is more feasible for financial services firms due to industry specifics such as the strong bargaining power of customers, the high vulnerability to technological disruption, as well as the ease of imitation and the absence of patents and licenses for financial products.[384]

In Phase 2, we use the average of the residual incomes examined in Phase 1 as a starting basis for the estimation of potential value creation. Assuming that the competitive advantage that led to this average residual income in Phase 1 will gradually erode, we use a declining perpetuity with a decay rate d to estimate expected value creation in

---

[380] See Wilde (1982), p. 467; Rappaport (1986), p. 44; MSDW (2001), p. 24.

[381] See Faust (2002), p. 75.

[382] See MSDW (2001), p. 24.

[383] See Copeland et al. (2000), pp. 267-272.

[384] See MSDW (2001), p. 27; Faust (2002), p. 80; Geltinger (2003), p. 196.

Phase 2. The decay rate is an inverse function of the strength of the brand and franchise of bank i.[385] Given the relatively weak brands in the banking industry, decay rates between 5 and 10 percent are reasonable for banks.[386] While brand and franchise strength vary for different banks, bank types, and regions, we make the pragmatic assumption of a constant decay rate of d = 0.1 for all the banks in our sample. After estimating value creation in Phase 2 using the method described above, we calculate the present value of the expected value created in Phase 2 by discounting the declining perpetuity with the cost of equity in year t.

We use end-of-year market values as reported in DS. The market value of bank i in year t is defined as the market capitalization, i.e. the price per share of bank i at the end of year t multiplied with the common shares outstanding of bank i at the end of year t.

The estimation of the economic equity and residual income used to calculate intrinsic value involves potential adjustments to accounting variables that are discussed in Section III.3.2.2. Thereafter, the calculation of economic equity and residual income is described in the Section III.3.2.3 and III.3.2.4. The estimation of cost of equity as the third input parameter of the model is complex and involves several assumptions. Section III.3.4 describes these assumptions.

III.3.2.2   Potential adjustments to accounting variables

Financial reporting practices under generally accepted accounting principles often distort the quality of accounting variables as economic performance measures.[387] To correct for the deficiencies of standard financial reporting practice, a multitude of

---

[385] See MSDW (2001), p. 28.

[386] See MSDW (2001), p. 33.

[387] For an overview of potential sources of distortions to accounting numbers, see Young and O'Byrne (2000), pp. 107-111.

potential adjustments to improve the quality of conventional accounting income and equity to better reflect the current economics of the business are discussed in literature.[388]

For banks, common adjustments relate to *taxes, loan loss reserves, goodwill*, and *securities accounting*.[389] While all the adjustments are material to banking performance measures, data is not available for all of them in the case of our sample. In the following, we briefly discuss potential adjustments and data availability with respect to our sample.

A specific adjustment in the case of banks relates to the *loan loss reserve*. The provision for loan losses serves primarily to reduce taxes for financial statement purposes, but it is not a cash cost. Thus, using net credit losses plus a provision for known loan problems as the current period estimate of losses due to credit risk is in general a reasonable adjustment to make.[390] Still, we do not substitute net credit losses for the provision, as the corresponding data between 1989 and 2002 is only available for a few banks. In addition, estimating the provision for known loan problems is complicated and the quality of the estimate is quite low.

With regard to *taxes*, the two general adjustments used to customize taxes are also relevant for banks. First, the tax provision typically does not equal actual taxes paid, due to differences between IAS and tax accounting.[391] Thus, the deferred tax reserve resembles an equity equivalent and has to be added back to equity.[392] Analogously, the

---

[388] Stern Stewart & Co. propose about 150 potential adjustments to accounting numbers when calculating EVA. See Stewart (1990), pp. 112-117. For a detailed discussion of the required accounting adjustments to banks, see Section II.5.1.2.

[389] See Uyemura et al. (1996), pp. 101-103; Matten (2000), pp. 271-272; MSDW (2001), p. 11; Fiordelisi (2002), pp. 8-10.

[390] See Uyemura et al. (1996), p. 102; Fiordelisi (2002), p. 8.

[391] See Stewart (1990), p. 113; Young and O'Byrne (2000), pp. 218-222.

[392] See Bodmer (2001), p. 90; MSDW (2001), p. 11.

increase in deferred taxes is not a cash-out and has to be added back to income. Secondly, income taxes paid are often substituted by effective average taxes to correct for accounting distortions in the individual tax rate applied to a company.[393] We correct income and equity in our model for both these tax adjustments.

The amortization of *goodwill* is a non-cash expense and should be added back to operating income.[394] Consequently, equity should be corrected for the cumulative goodwill amortization. However, no data on the amortization of goodwill is available in DS prior to 2001. Another measurement problem exists when accounting for acquisitions using the pooling-of-interest method.[395] In these transactions, goodwill, i.e. the difference between the acquired book value and the market value of the securities offered, is not recognized at all. This unrecorded goodwill resembles an equity equivalent and has to be added back to equity.[396] Data for this adjustment is available in SDC and allows us to correct equity.[397]

A further important adjustment in the context of banks relates to *securities accounting*. Securities accounting is often used as a tool for earnings management and as a result, does not reflect the economic reality. The effect of gains and losses therefore should be excluded from income when incurred, but amortized over the remaining lives of the securities sold.[398] Since the data needed to make these theoretical adjustments can

---

[393] See Kirsten (2000), p. 145.

[394] See Stewart (1990), p. 114; Matten (2000), p. 272; MSDW (2001), p. 11.

[395] The pooling-of-interest method is the accounting treatment used in US GAAP to account for a merger of equals. In pooling-of-interest transactions, two companies merge by adding together the book value of their assets. These book values are carried forward to the consolidated financial statements without writing-up assets to their fair value. For a detailed discussion of the pooling-of-interest method, see Stickney and Weil (1997), pp. 714-718.

[396] See Stewart (1990), pp. 114-115; Young and O'Byrne (2000), pp. 245-247; MSDW (2001), p. 11.

[397] In our sample, this adjustment only refers to the North American subsample.

[398] See Uyemura et al. (1996), p. 102.

hardly be retrieved in an outside-in analysis, we do not correct for securities accounting in our study.

As discussed above, the data necessary to make the proposed adjustments is in many
case neither available for our sample nor for the observation interval, which dates back
to the year 1989. Consequently, we adopt a pragmatic approach and adjust accounting
income and equity for deferred taxes, average effective taxes, and unrecorded goodwill
as described below.

III.3.2.3   Calculation of economic equity

We calculate the economic equity of each individual bank for the years between 1989
and 2002 based on accounting numbers as reported in DS Worldscope and SDC. Given
the limited data availability for correcting for accounting distortions, we adopt a
pragmatic approach and adjust for deferred taxes and unrecorded goodwill. Equation
III-4 describes the calculation of economic equity of bank i in year t as follows:

$$
\begin{aligned}
\text{Economic equity}_{it}\,(EE_{it}) = \ & \text{Common equity}_{it} \\
& + \text{Deferred taxes}_{it} \\
& + \text{Unrecorded goodwill}_{it}
\end{aligned}
\qquad \text{III-4}
$$

We use common equity, which is composed of equity and equity reserves, as reported
in DS Worldscope as a base. To arrive at economic equity we add back deferred taxes
as reported in DS Worldscope. Furthermore, we derive unrecorded goodwill from the
pooling-of-interest transactions reported in SDC, and add it back to equity.

III.3.2.4   Calculation of residual income

We calculate the residual income of each individual bank for the years between 1989
and 2002. Again, we use a pragmatic approach with only a few adjustments. We cor-

rect income for effective average taxes and for deferred taxes. We calculate residual income of bank i in year t as described in Equation III-5:

$$\text{Residual income}_{it} \ (RI_{it}) = \text{Adjusted income}_{it} - EE_{i,t/t-1} \times c_{e_{nst}} \qquad \text{III-5}$$

where $EE_{i,t/t-1}$ = Average EE of bank i in the years t and t - 1

$c_{e_{nst}}$ = c_e of regional industry s for country n in year t

Equation III-6 defines the calculation of adjusted income of bank i in year t:

$$
\begin{aligned}
\text{Adjusted income}_{it} = \ &\text{Income available to common shareholders}_{it} \\
&+ \text{Income taxes}_{it} \\
&- \text{Effective average tax rate}_{ct} \times \text{Pre-tax income}_{it} \\
&+ \text{Increase in deferred taxes}_{i,t/t-1}
\end{aligned} \qquad \text{III-6}
$$

When calculating adjusted income, we use the income available to common share-holders as reported in DS Worldscope, as a base. Analogously to the calculation of economic equity, we add back the average increase in deferred taxes in year t and t - 1. Furthermore, we recalculate taxes using the effective average tax rate of the corresponding country. We add back income taxes as reported in DS Worldscope and deduct effective average taxes. To calculate effective average taxes, we multiply pre-tax income in year t as reported in DS Worldscope, with the effective average tax rate as estimated by Devereux et al. (2002).[399]

When calculating economic equity for bank i we adjust for deferred taxes and unre-corded goodwill as described above. To calculate residual income in year t, we use the average economic equity in year t and t-1 to account for the capital costs incurred

---

[399] Devereux et al. (2002) estimate an effective average tax rate for all countries in our sample except for a number of the Asian countries. As data is missing for only twelve banks in five Asian countries, we assume the effective average tax rate to equal the statutory tax rate in these countries. For a definition of the effective average tax rate used, see Devereux and Griffith (2003).

during year t. We calculate cost of equity of bank i in year t by constructing beta for twelve regional industries s and using a risk-free rate of country c as described in Section III.3.4.

III.3.3   Discounted dividend model

The discounted dividend (DD) model equates the value of a company's equity with the sum of the discounted expected dividend payments over the life of the company, with the terminal value equal to the liquidating dividend as described in Equation III-7.[400]

$$Equity_t^{DD} = \sum_{t=1}^{t=\infty} \frac{DIV_t}{(1+c_e)^t}$$
III-7

where DIV_t = Dividends in year t
t = Observation year
c_e = Cost of equity

In consistence with the residual income model, we structure the discounted dividend model in two phases, with an explicit forecast period and a continuing value estimate thereafter. We calculate the intrinsic value of bank i in year t as shown in Equation III-8.

---

[400] See Damodaran (1994), p. 191. For a discussion of different versions of the discounted dividend model and issues when using the model, see Damodaran (1994), pp. 191-218.

$$IV_{it}^{DD} = \sum_{f=1}^{f=5} \frac{DIV_{i,t+f}}{(1+c_{e_{it}})^f} + \frac{\overline{DIV}_{i,t+1/t+5}}{c_{e_{it}} - g} \times \frac{1}{(1+c_{e_{it}})^5}$$ III-8

where DIV_{it} = Dividends of bank i in year t

$\overline{DIV}_{i,t+1/t+5}$ = Average DIV of bank i during the years $t+1$ and $t+5$

t = Observation year

f = Explicit forecast interval (Phase 1)

g = Growth rate, constant over banks and time

$c_{e_{it}}$ = Cost of equity of bank i in year t

In phase 1 we discount the historic dividends paid to shareholders between the years $t+1$ and $t+5$ with the cost of equity of bank i in year t. Like for the residual income model, we assume the explicit forecast period f to be five years.

Value creation in Phase 2 is measured with a continuing value assumption similar to the residual income model. We approximate the dividends paid after the explicit forecast period using the average dividends paid during Phase 1. Again, we decide to apply a conservative growth estimate in Phase 2 based on the assumption that the competitive advantage of a bank erodes over time. We therefore assume the dividends in Phase 2 to grow at the average growth rate observed in Phase 1. To be conservative we limit the growth in Phase 2 to a maximum of 3 percent and replace average growth rates that are larger than 3 percent by the upper limit of 3 percent growth. Furthermore, we assume no growth in Phase 2 if the average growth rate of the dividends in Phase 1 is negative.

We use dividends paid to shareholders as reported in DS. The cost of equity is estimated similar to the estimation in the residual income model as described in the following section.

III.3.4   Estimation of cost of equity

III.3.4.1   Use of the Capital Asset Pricing Model

As cost of equity is an opportunity cost and not a cash cost, it cannot be observed in the market and has to be estimated. The estimation of cost of equity and the usefulness of models such as the CAPM has been the subject of considerable debate.[401]

Whereas the CAPM is the preferred bank cost of equity estimate in most American and European literature,[402] there are also advocates of alternative methods such as the estimation of cost of equity via the APT, the use of an opportunity rate, or its estimation via the volatility of free cash flows for internal valuations.[403]

Rather than trying to find a theoretically correct way to estimate cost of equity, in the following we adopt a pragmatic approach. We use the CAPM, as it is the most widely used theoretical approach in empiric research.[404] The APT or any other more sophisticated method should be used only to the extent that the expected benefits of the new information exceed the cost of providing it. We opt for the CAPM, since the application of the APT is complicated and time-consuming. Furthermore, the advantages of the APT relative to the CAPM are low in the case of ex-post analysis and the study of exchange-traded companies.

"The CAPM postulates that the opportunity cost of equity is equal to the return on risk-free securities plus the company's systematic risk (beta) multiplied by the market price

---

[401] See Goedhart et al. (2002), p. 11. For an overview of the criticism of the CAPM, see Damodaran (1994), pp. 27-28; Copeland et al. (2000), pp. 224-226. Jagannathan and McGrattan (1995) give a detailed overview of the debate and empirical tests on the validity of the CAPM.

[402] See Damodaran (1994), pp. 20-26; Copeland et al. (2000), p. 435; Kirsten (2000), p. 155; Young and O'Byrne (2000), pp. 165-166.

[403] See Adolf et al. (1989), pp. 549-552; Börner and Lowis (1997), pp. 118-120. For an overview of further alternative methods, see Faust (2002), pp. 117-122.

[404] See Copeland et al. (2000), p. 214; MSDW (2001), p. 48; Pettit (2001), p. 1. For a detailed discussion of the application of CAPM to banks, see Section II.5.4.

of risk (market risk premium)."[405] The market risk premium equals the difference between the expected return on the market portfolio and the risk-free rate of return. Beta is defined as the covariance between the returns on the individual stock and the returns on the market portfolio.[406]

Given these assumptions, Equation III-9 defines the cost of equity in year t in our model as follows:

$$c_{e_{nst}} = r_{f_{nt}} + \left[E(r_m) - r_f \right]_{const} \times (beta_{st})$$
III-9

where $r_{f_{nt}}$ = Risk-free rate of return in country n in year t

$E(r_m)$ = Expected rate of return on the market portfolio m

$\left[E(r_m) - r_f \right]_{const}$ = Market risk premium constant over time and region

$beta_{st}$ = Systematic risk of the equity of regional industry s in year t

In addition to the debate concerning the CAPM itself, there is also disagreement on the estimation of the CAPM's variables. After weighing several alternative approaches, we estimate the three parameters of the cost of equity, i.e. the risk-free rate, the market risk premium, and beta, as described below.

III.3.4.2 Estimation of risk-free rate

We use the yield on benchmark indices of ten-year government bonds as reported in DS as a proxy for the risk-free rate.[407] Recent research has shown that long-term bonds are not completely risk less and their beta has varied from -0.1 to over 0.4 in the past,

---

[405] Copeland et al. (2000), p. 214.

[406] For a detailed overview of the CAPM and the underlying assumptions, see Copeland and Weston (1992), pp. 193-202; Brealey and Myers (2000), pp. 187-203.

[407] For an overview of alternative estimates of the risk-free rate, see Damodaran (1994), pp. 24-26; Copeland et al. (2000), p. 216.

with the current beta estimated at 0.25.[408] Therefore, unlevering the risk-free rate and combining the systematic equity risk of stocks and bonds into one premium is in general a reasonable adjustment. However, for the market as a whole or any stock with a beta close to 1.0 the net effect of this adjustment approximates to zero.[409] Given historic banking betas close to 1.0,[410] we do not expect this adjustment to yield an observable benefit for our analysis and we simply assume the long-term bond rate to be a proxy for the risk-free rate.

We prefer a ten-year horizon to a shorter horizon as it approximates more closely the duration of the cash flows of a company.[411] Using a ten-year horizon is also consistent with betas and market risk premiums estimated with respect to market index portfolios with a duration of approximately ten years.[412]

We use national risk-free rates, thereby taking into account the inflation risk related to investment in national market stocks.[413] DS includes benchmark indices for all the countries in the sample, except for some Asian countries.[414] For these countries, we use the Thai Government bond as an approximate value.[415]

---

[408] See Pettit (2001), p. 5.

[409] See Pettit (2001), p. 6.

[410] See for example the betas used in our analysis as described in Appendix 9, p. 251.

[411] See Faust (2002), p. 102.

[412] For a detailed discussion on the use of different time horizons, see Copeland (2000), p. 216.

[413] See Faust (2002), p. 116; Geltinger (2003), p. 68.

[414] For Malaysia, Singapore, Hong Kong, and South Korea, benchmark indices or national government bonds are not available in DS.

[415] Thai Government debt between 1989 and 2002 cannot be considered as reasonably risk-free. Therefore, the theoretically correct way of estimating the risk-free rate for these countries is to use the interest rate parity theory to convert US government rates to foreign country equivalents. See Copeland et al. (2000), pp. 387-389. Nonetheless, we do not expect the benefits of this adjustment to justify the costs related to the adjustment, as this problem relates to only 13 banks in our sample.

We use the calendar year average of the yield on benchmark indices for the years between 1989 and 2002. Using a yearly average of the risk-free rate is the theoretically correct way to calculate the capital charge in the residual income equation. When calculating a discount rate, one could also argue for the use of the long-term average or the risk-free rate expected in the future. For ease of calculation, however, we use the calendar year average for calculating capital costs as well as discounting residual incomes. Appendix 14, p. 237, gives an overview of the risk-free rates used in the model.

III.3.4.3   Estimation of market risk premium

Based on the high degree of integration of national capital markets and the globalization of the banking industry, we use a global estimate of systematic risk and a global market risk premium respectively.[416]

Generally, the market risk premium can be estimated by two broad approaches: The first approach is historical, based on past performance of stock prices. The second approach is forward looking, based on projections implied by current stock prices.[417] Using a historical approach, estimates of the market risk premium vary from 3 to almost 8 percent depending on the underlying assumptions.[418] The main assumptions

---

[416] For a detailed discussion on the advantages of the use of a global market risk premium, see Copeland et al. (2000), pp. 366-371; Pettit (2001), p. 3.

[417] See Goedhart et al. (2002), pp. 11-12. In the following, a historical approach is used. For a detailed discussion of the forward looking approach, see Copeland et al. (2000), pp. 221-223.

[418] See Copeland et al. (2000), p. 216. Most practitioners, however, use a narrower range of 3.5 to 6.0 percent. See Damodaran (1994), p. 22; Copeland et al. (2000), p. 221; Pettit (2001), p. 1; Goedhart et al. (2002), p. 11.

causing this variance regard the measurement interval of returns as well as the use of arithmetic vs. geometric averages.[419]

Our model uses a simple approach based on a forward-looking model. We follow the analysis of Goedhart et al. (2002) that results in an average inflation-adjusted cost of equity of 7 percent implied by stock market valuations from 1963 to 2001 in the US.[420] We use this estimate as a starting point and calculate a yearly market risk premium based on the cost of equity and risk-free rate in inflation-adjusted terms as shown in Appendix 15, p. 251. For the years between 1989 and 2002, we find risk premiums ranging between 2.53 and 4.81, with an average of 3.57 percent. We use this estimate for the US market as a proxy for the global risk premium, and use a constant risk premium of 3.5 percent in our model.[421]

III.3.4.4   Estimation of systematic risk

As a measure of systematic risk, we use the yearly regional industry betas between 1989 and 2002. Current research suggests using a published estimate of beta based on a multi-factor approach such as the one provided by BARRA.[422] Another option is to construct an industry average, assuming that the systematic risk of an industry applies to all firms that operate in that industry. As a rule of thumb, current research prefers industry averages to individual betas where published betas differ by more than 0.2.[423]

---

[419] For a detailed discussion on the derivation of the market risk premium, see Damodaran (1994), pp. 21-24; Copeland et al. (2000), pp. 217-221; Pettit (2001), pp. 1-5.

[420] Goedhart et al. (2002) use a standard forward-looking model, which they apply to US and UK stock market valuations of the past 40 years, and find surprisingly stable results.

[421] We discuss the sensitivity of the results when using a yearly risk premium as well as varying the constant risk premium by 0.5 percent in Section III.6.1.

[422] See Copeland et al. (2000), p. 223; MSDW (2001), p. 52.

[423] See Copeland et al. (2000), p. 224.

When comparing the individual betas reported in BARRA and DS for our sample banks in 2003, this is the case for 40 percent of the 290 banks. We therefore rely on regional industry betas. As measurement errors tend to cancel each other out, industry betas are typically more stable and reliable than individual company betas.[424]

We construct twelve regional industry betas by measuring the correlation of the return for DS regional industry indices with the return of the DS World index, as reported in Appendix 9, p. 251.[425] Analog to the estimation of a global market risk premium, we prefer a world market index as global benchmark to national benchmarks.[426]

In line with standard research, we observe monthly returns and their correlation over a period of five years.[427] Moreover, we use a three-year moving average to compensate for short-term market trends. A viable adjustment when measuring individual or industry betas is to correct for the impact of the telecommunications, media, and technology (TMT) sector share prices on the world market index during the years between 1998 and 2001.[428] As the effect on our analysis is low, we do not adjust betas by excluding the TMT sector or normalizing the TMT sector share in the world market index.[429]

---

[424] See Brealey and Myers (2000), p. 224; Annema and Goedhart (2003), p. 10.

[425] We use the DS industry indices for Banks, Investment Banks, Mortgage Finance, and Consumer Finance for North America, Europe, and Asia.

[426] See Faust (2002), pp. 114-115. For a detailed discussion of the estimation of a global beta, see Copeland et al. (2000), pp. 366-371.

[427] See Damodaran (1994), pp. 26-27; Pettit (2001), p. 8; Faust (2002), pp. 110-111.

[428] For a detailed discussion of the distortion of the measures of risk by the market bubble in the TMT sector, see Annema and Goedhart (2003).

[429] The sensitivity of the results to changes regarding this assumption is discussed in Section III.6.1.

III.4   Accuracy and explanatory value of residual income value estimates

III.4.1   Descriptive results

The key figure of our analysis is the prediction error of the value estimates, as introduced in Section III.1. The prediction error describes the relative error and is defined as MV minus IV divided by IV. Table III-3 shows the descriptive statistics of the prediction errors of the value estimates from the residual income model for the years between 1989 and 1998.

Table III-3: Descriptive statistics of prediction error

(1989 – 1998)

Statistic	Total sample	Total sample excluding Asia	Asia
N	2,900	2,090	810
Mean	0.61	0.06	2.01
Median	0.14	0.02	1.29
Standard Deviation	19.64	5.24	36.17
Minimum	-300.99	-215.16	-300.99
Maximum	940.76	45.47	940.76
Interquartile Range	1.19	0.68	2.85

Source: Own calculation

For the total sample, the mean prediction error is 0.61 and the median error is 0.14. We thus observe a bias, with observed market values being on average 61 percent higher than the value estimates from the residual income model. The median error is significantly lower than the mean error indicating positive skewness of the results and thus some extremely large values for the prediction errors.

This indication proves true when looking at the dispersion of results that shows extreme minimum and maximum values of results and a large standard deviation of 19.64. In the case of the non-symmetrical distribution of results in our sample, the interquartile range is a more representative parameter for dispersion. Yet, the interquartile range of 1.19 is still relatively high. In summary, the results for the total sample are dissatisfying in terms of accuracy.

This outcome changes when excluding the Asian subsample. As discussed in Section III.5.1, we perceive large differences in the results by region and in particular a significant bias in the value estimates for the Asian subsample. Focusing on the North American and European subsample, the average prediction error in the results from the residual income model significantly reduces. The results excluding Asia show only marginal bias with a mean prediction error of 0.06 and a median error of 0.02. The prediction errors are more closely spread about the expected error of zero and the interquartile range of 0.68 is significantly lower.

For the Asian subsample, we find an enormous bias in the results with a mean prediction error of 2.01. Also, the statistical spread of the results is large with very high extreme values. The large bias in the Asian results can be attributed to two facts. First, we conclude that the data quality of the accounting data for the Asian banks is very low. Another fact that might be responsible for the large prediction errors for the Asian subsample is the bubble in the Asian market and the subsequent crisis in the 1990s. During this period, irrational behavior lead to a systematic overvaluation of Asian stocks, which results in large prediction errors for many Asian banks in our analysis.

In summary, the results for the Asian subsample are not reliable and significantly confound the results of the remaining sample. Therefore, we exclude the observations from the Asian banks in the following analyses and focus on the results of the 209 North American and European banks resulting in 2,090 bank-year observations.

III.4.2   Residual income vs. discounted dividend value estimates

III.4.2.1   Accuracy of the value estimates

In the following section, we compare the accuracy of the value estimates from the residual income model to the corresponding value estimates from the discounted dividend model. To measure the accuracy, we look at the signed and absolute prediction errors of the value estimates from the two alternative valuation models, as displayed in Table III-4.

Table III-4: Prediction error – Residual income vs. discounted dividend model

(Total sample excluding Asia, 1989 – 1998)

Statistic	Residual Income	Discounted Dividends
Signed Prediction Error		
N	2,090	2,020
Mean	0.06	1.82
Median	0.02	0.94
Standard Deviation	5.24	4.36
Interquartile Range	0.68	1.54
Absolute Prediction Error		
N	2,090	2,020
Mean	0.83	1.87
Median	0.32	0.94
Standard Deviation	5.17	18.80
Interquartile Range	0.46	1.50
Central tendency*		
IV within 15% of MV (percent)	23.9	10.2

* The central tendency is defined as the percentage of observations with value estimates
   within 15% of observed market value

Source: Own calculation

Given gaps in the reported dividends for the 290 sample banks, the statistics for the discounted dividend model are based on only 2,796 observations. Excluding Asia, the results comprise 2,090 bank-year observations from the residual income model and 2,020 bank-year observations from the discounted dividend model.

We first look at the signed prediction errors of the value estimates. As already described in Section III.4.1, we find a mean prediction error of 0.06 and a median error of 0.02 for the value estimates from the residual income model. We thus observe a small bias with observed market values being on average 6 percent higher than the value estimates from the residual income model. For the discounted dividend model, the resulting overvaluation is significantly higher with a mean prediction error of 1.82 and a median value of 0.94. Furthermore, the results from the two valuation models differ significantly in terms of dispersion. The interquartile range of the prediction errors of the value estimates from the residual income model is 0.68, whereas the results from the discounted dividend model are significantly wider spread with an interquartile range of 1.54.

In order to get a better understanding of the accuracy of the results from both models, we next study the absolute prediction errors of the value estimates. Again, the results from the residual income model show a lower average prediction error than the results from the discounted dividend model. We observe a mean absolute prediction error for the residual income value estimates of 0.83 and a median error of 0.32. The absolute prediction errors for the results from the discounted dividend model are significantly higher with a mean error of 1.87 and a median error 0.94.

Finally, we look at the central tendency for the results from both models. For the residual income model, 23.9 percent of the value estimates are within 15 percent of the observed market value, whereas for the value estimates from the discounted dividend model this holds only for 10.2 percent of the observations. In summary, the accuracy of the results from the residual income model is significantly higher than of the results from the discounted dividend model.

III.4.2.2   Explanatory value of the value estimates

To test the explanatory value of the value estimates, we examine the ability of the value estimates to explain cross-sectional variation in the observed market values. Table III-5 reports the results of the univariate regressions of market value on the value estimates from the two valuation models as well as the results of a multivariate regression of market value on the value estimates from both alternative valuation models.

Table III-5: Regressions of market value on value estimates

(Total sample excluding Asia, 1989 – 1998, N = 2,020)

	Statistic	Residual Income	Discounted Dividend
Univariate Regression of Market Value on Value Estimates			
	OLS Coefficient	1.29**	1.55**
	OLS R^2	0.81	0.70
Multivariate Regression of Market Value on Value Estimates			
	OLS Coefficient	1.01**	0.41**
	Model OLS R^2	0.82	0.82
	Incremental OLS R^2	0.12	0.01

** Statistically significant at the 1 percent level
*   Statistically significant at the 5 percent level

Source: Stata, own calculation

The explained variability of the univariate regressions is higher for the residual income model with R^2 explaining 81 percent of the variation in market value for the residual income model compared to 70 percent for the discounted dividend model. The coefficient estimates for both models are significant. The larger coefficient for the discounted dividend model is in line with the larger bias in the results from this model. The multivariate regression reports significant coefficient estimates for both valuation models and estimates the two valuation models to jointly explain 82 percent of the variation of market values.

The reported incremental R^2 calibrates the incremental importance of each value estimate by decomposing the joint explanatory power into the portion explained by each value estimate controlling for the alternative estimate. Controlling for the effect of the discounted dividend model, the value estimates from the residual income model add 12 percent explanatory power to the regression. In contrast, the estimates from the discounted dividend model only add 1 percent explanatory power. In summary, the results of the regression analyses indicate that the residual income model dominates the discounted dividend model in terms of explanatory value.

Summarizing the results for the accuracy and explanatory value of the value estimates from the two alternative valuation models so far, we observe a superiority of the residual income model in terms of accuracy and explanatory value. To test the robustness of this outcome, we next examine the sensitivity of the results to the growth rate assumption in Phase 2.

III.4.2.3   Robustness of the results

So far we estimated the value creation in Phase 2 with a proxy for the growth rate of residual income (-10 percent) and dividends (0 to 3 percent). Instead of assigning a distinct value to the growth rate in Phase 2, we now solve the two models for the growth rate in Phase 2 under the assumption that the prediction error of the value estimates is on average zero. Then, we compare the dispersion of the resulting prediction errors about the mean value of zero to derive further conclusions on the accuracy of the value estimates from the two models.

Figure III-9 reports the descriptive statistics of the prediction errors assuming a mean of zero and solving for the growth rate in Phase 2. Assuming a mean error of zero, the residual income model results in an average growth rate of -9.90 percent, i.e. a decay rate that is very close to the initially assumed rate of -10 percent. Solving the discounted dividend model for the growth rate of the dividends in Phase 2, we find a growth rate of 8.68 percent, which is significantly larger than the growth of 0 to 3 percent assumed in our model.

Figure III-9: Dispersion of prediction error – Mean = 0

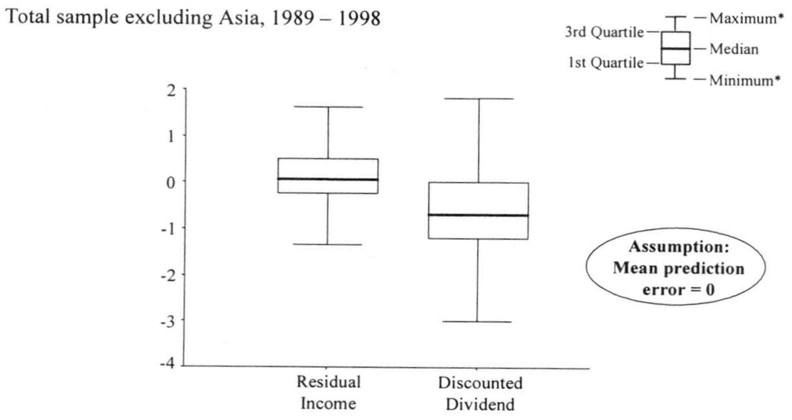

	Residual Income	Discounted Dividend
Growth rate in Phase 2 (percent)	-9.90	8.68
Median	0.05	-0.69
Interquartile Range	0.75	1.21
N	2,020	2,020

* Outliers and extremes are excluded

Source: Own calculation

The interquartile range of the prediction errors of the value estimates from the residual income model is with a value of 0.75 lower than the observed interquartile range of 1.21 for the results from the discounted dividend model. The box plots nicely illustrate the higher statistical spread of the prediction errors from the discounted dividend model compared to the residual income model. As already indicated by the interquartile ranges for both models, the variability of the results from the discounted dividend model is much higher than for the residual income value estimates.

In summary, the dispersion about the mean prediction error of zero for the discounted dividend model is wider than for the residual income model. This result is in line with the superiority of the residual income model in terms of accuracy and explanatory value observed in the Section III.4.2.1 and III.4.2.2. To calibrate these results for the banking industry with the evidence on residual income models for other industries, we next look at the empirical results provided by prior research.

III.4.3   Comparison to prior research on industrial companies

To compare the results for the banking industry to the results for other industries, we use the empirical evidence on the value estimates from alternative valuation models provided by Penman and Sougiannis (1998) and Francis et al. (2000). Penman and Sougiannis (1998) focus on industrial companies and exclude financial firms from their data set. Francis et al. (2000) base their analysis on a data set with no industry focus. Similar to the results of our study so far, the authors of both studies conclude that the residual income model dominates the discounted dividend model.

Although the structure of these studies is very similar to our model structure, some methodological differences exist. Penman and Sougiannis (1998) rely on realized attributes as we do, but calculate the value estimates on the portfolio level. Like in our model, Francis et al. (2000) calculate value estimates on the individual security level, but use forecast data in their analysis. Furthermore, the studies obviously differ in the size of the samples, sample characteristics, and the length of the observation period.

Both studies use the ratio of intrinsic value to market value as basis to calculate the prediction error of the value estimates, i.e. the reciprocal of the measure of accuracy used in our model. When comparing these results to our model results in the following, we therefore have to transform our results to this error measure.

Table III-6 shows the results found in prior research and compares it to the results for the banking industry from our study. All value estimates show a negative prediction bias. Compared to the median error of -0.07 for the residual income value estimates from the banking sample of our paper, the value estimates from the residual income models in prior research show significantly higher errors of -0.55 and -0.26. For the discounted dividend model, the bias for the banking industry is with a median error of - 0.59 again lower than for the industrial companies and for the results with no industry focus. Overall, the differences between the two models in prior research are smaller than for our results.

Table III-6: Comparison of results with prior research

(Error = IV/MV - 1, median)

Industry Focus	Author and Date	Residual Income	Discounted Dividend
Industrial companies	Penman and Sougiannis (1998)	-0.55	-0.83
No industry focus	Francis et al. (2000)	-0.26	-0.74
Banking industry	Own model	-0.07	-0.59

Source: Francis et al. (2000), Penman and Sougiannis (1998), own calculation

The differences in the data and methodology used for the three studies limit their comparability and require a careful interpretation of the above described results. While we thus cannot infer that the residual income approach does better fit the banking industry than other industries, we can at least conclude from the results that the residual income approach fits the banking industry as well as any other industry.

In summary, the higher accuracy and explanatory value found for the value estimates from the residual income model relative to the discounted dividend model, combined with the evidence found when reconciling our results with the results for other industries provided by prior research, suggest that the residual income model is an appropriate measure of shareholder value for banks.

III.5 Determinants of the prediction error

III.5.1 Hypotheses

The second part of our analysis studies the determinants of the prediction error of the value estimates from the residual income valuation model. We search for differences of the results by region, bank type, bank size, profitability, and time as potential determinants of the prediction error of the value estimates. Based on the initial hypothesis of market value having predictive power, as well as on the general principles of capital markets and corporate finance, we formulate five hypotheses concerning the characteristics of the prediction errors in relation to these potential determinants.

With respect to the results for different regional markets, we expect the predictive power of market value to be higher for more developed capital markets. The underlying rationale is that more developed markets are more efficient due to higher liquidity and lower transaction costs. We hypothesize that the more developed the market, the smaller the prediction error will be, as described in hypothesis H1.

$$H\,1\!: \left| MV_{i_{m1}t} / IV_{i_{m1}t} - 1 \right| \geq \left| MV_{i_{m2}t} / IV_{i_{m2}t} - 1 \right|$$

with market m_2 being more developed than market m_1

As far as the characteristics of the prediction errors for different bank types are concerned, we expect smaller prediction errors for bank types with more transparent business models, i.e. higher transparency concerning credit or market risks. The reason for this is that the transparency of the business model significantly eases the forecasting of future bank performance. We therefore expect the prediction error to be smaller the more transparent the business model of the bank type in question, as described in hypothesis H2.

$$H\,2\!: \left| MV_{i_{b1}t} / IV_{i_{b1}t} - 1 \right| \geq \left| MV_{i_{b2}t} / IV_{i_{b2}t} - 1 \right|$$

with business model of bank type b_2 being more transparent than b_1

Furthermore, we foresee the prediction error of the value estimates to be related to bank size and bank profitability, as potential drivers of the predictive power of the market. We expect the stock prices of banks with a high market capitalization to be on average more efficient assuming a constant free float and ownership structure. We therefore hypothesize that the prediction error for larger banks will be closer to zero than for smaller banks, as described in hypothesis H3.

$$\text{H 3:} \left| MV_{i_1t} / IV_{i_1t} - 1 \right| \geq \left| MV_{i_2t} / IV_{i_2t} - 1 \right| \text{ for } MV_{i_1t} \leq MV_{i_2t}$$

Examining the relationship between the prediction error and bank profitability, we expect the predictive power of the market for profitable banks to be higher than for banks with low profitability. The underlying rationale is that higher profitability implies both higher investor interest in a bank and higher coverage by analysts. We hypothesize the prediction error to be negatively correlated to return on equity (ROE) as a measure of bank profitability, as described in hypothesis H4.

$$\text{H 4:} \left| MV_{i_1t} / IV_{i_1t} - 1 \right| \geq \left| MV_{i_2t} / IV_{i_2t} - 1 \right| \text{ for } ROE_{i_1t} \leq ROE_{i_2t}$$

Over the last few decades, market efficiency has continuously increased due to advances in information technology and corporate governance, combined with the increasing deregulation of capital markets. Based on the recent increase in market efficiency, we expect the predictive power of the market to increase over the observation period. We hypothesize the prediction error to be smaller in the later years of our analysis, as described in hypothesis H5.

$$\text{H 5:} \left| MV_{it} / IV_{it} - 1 \right| \geq \left| MV_{i,t+x} / IV_{i, t+x} - 1 \right| \text{ for } x \geq 0$$

The following sections examine the validity of the above-formulated hypotheses based on the descriptive statistics of the model results and a regression analysis on these potential drivers of the prediction error.

III.5.2 Descriptive statistics of results

In the following, we discuss the descriptive statistics of the value estimates from the residual income model and study potential differences in the prediction error by region, bank type, bank size, profitability, and time.

Looking at the different regional subsamples shown in Figure III-10, we observe significant differences in the prediction errors for the regional subsamples.

Figure III-10: Prediction error by region

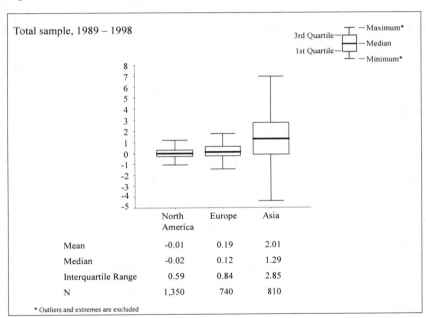

Source: Own calculation

For the North American subsample, the prediction error is relatively close to zero with a mean error of -0.01 and a median error of -0.02. The dispersion is low with an interquartile range of 0.59. Looking at the European subsample, we observe a higher bias in the value estimates, averaging at a mean error of 0.19 and a median error of 0.12. The dispersion of the prediction error is still relatively narrow, with an interquartile range of 0.84.

As already mentioned in Section III.4.1, results for the Asian subsample drastically differ from the results for the North American and European subsample. The prediction error is significantly larger with a median value of 1.29. The mean error is even higher, with a value of 2.01 indicating some extremely large prediction errors in the Asian subsample. Thus, most of the overvaluation of results for the total sample can be attributed to the highly overrated results for the Asian subsample, whereas the North American and European subsample show only small prediction errors. Compared to the North American and European subsample, the dispersion of results for the Asian subsample is wide, with an interquartile range of 2.85. Again, the Asian subsample causes most of the dispersion of results of the total sample, whereas the dispersion of the prediction errors in the North American and European subsample is relatively narrow.

The higher predictive power of the market observed for the North American and European subsamples is in line with hypothesis H1 which expects the prediction error to be smaller for more developed markets. Nonetheless, it remains unclear whether the large prediction error for the Asian market relates to rational differences in market efficiency. Other causes might be the low data quality of the Asian subsample and the irrational behavior based on the bubble in the Asian market and the subsequent crisis. Although the differences between North America and Europe are not as drastically, the prediction errors for the North American subsample are significantly smaller than the errors for the European subsample. This outcome also supports hypothesis H1 since the US market can be considered more developed and efficient than the fragmented European markets.

Given the enormous bias in the Asian subsample, we exclude Asia when looking at potential differences by bank type, bank size, profitability, and time in the following.

Looking at the descriptive statistics by bank type as shown in Figure III-11, the results do not vary as much as for the regional subsamples. Mean prediction errors range from -0.13 for Mortgage Finance to 0.17 for Consumer Finance. The median errors for the different bank types range from -0.10 to 0.15 respectively. Looking at the dispersion of the prediction errors, differences in the interquartile ranges for the bank type subsamples are not significant either.

Figure III-11: Prediction error by bank type

Total sample excluding Asia, 1989 – 1998

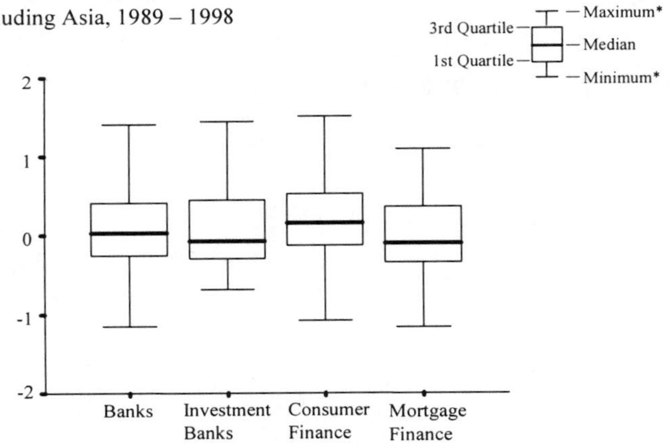

	Banks	Investment Banks	Consumer Finance	Mortgage Finance
Mean	0.06	0.14	0.17	-0.13
Median	0.03	-0.07	0.15	-0.10
Interquartile Range	0.67	0.74	0.68	0.70
N	1,800	170	60	60

* Outliers and extremes are excluded

Source: Own calculation

We observe, on average, a negative prediction error for Mortgage Finance, while the other bank types show positive prediction errors. The differences in the sign of the prediction errors might indicate that hypothesis H2 is valid to the extent that systematic differences between bank types exist. Yet, these differences are small and the economic rationale behind it is unclear. Therefore, the results might be rather driven by the regional scope and the size of the bank type subsamples. The Mortgage Finance subsample, for example, contains only six banks, five of which are located in North America. The results by bank type at a regional subsample level do not reveal systematic differences either, as shown in Appendix 17, p. 253.

As discussed in Section III.3.1.2, a more precise distinction between the sample banks in the subsample Banks would be preferable, but is not available. For the existing bank type subsamples, we reject hypothesis H2, as the results by bank type do not show systematic differences in predictive power.

To study potential differences in the prediction errors by bank size, we segment the sample banks in four subsamples according to the average market value over the observation period, as illustrated in Figure III-12.

Figure III-12: Prediction error by bank size

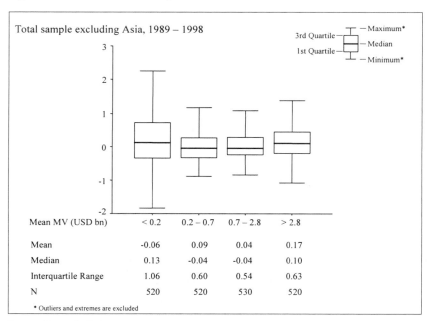

Source: Own calculation

The mean and median prediction errors for the four bank size groups do not reveal a systematic trend of the prediction error that is subject to bank size. Still, we find differences in the prediction errors comparing the results for the small banks and the large banks. For the small banks, we observe a negative mean error of -0.06 and negative skewness of results. For the large banks, we find a positive prediction error and positive skewness of results. The market seems to significantly undervalue some of the small banks and on the other hand significantly overvalue some of the large banks. In line with hypothesis H3, we observe a notably larger interquartile range for the group of small size banks than for the other three groups. As a result, descriptive statistics provide weak evidence on hypothesis H3.

Figure III-13: Prediction error by ROE

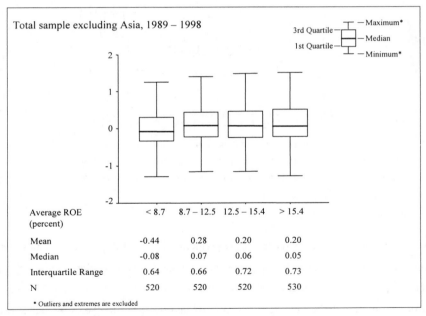

Source: Own calculation

With respect to hypothesis H4, we segment the sample banks in four subsamples according to the average ROE over the observation period. As shown in Figure III-13, we find negative prediction errors for banks with lower profitability and positive prediction errors for the groups with banks of medium and high profitability. In respect to the dispersion of results, we do not observe a systematic trend in the interquartile ranges that is determined by the profitability of the banks. Again, evidence on hypothesis H4 is only weak.

Figure III-14: Prediction error by year

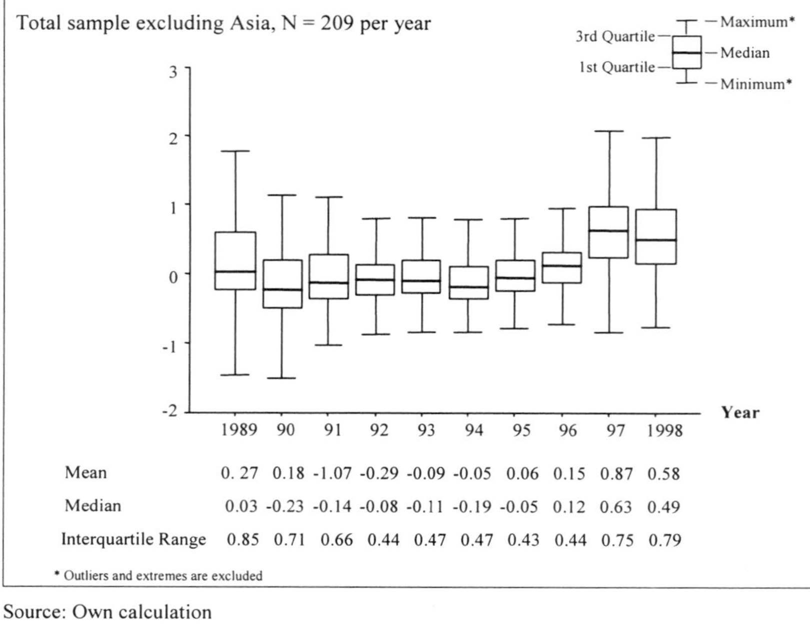

	1989	90	91	92	93	94	95	96	97	1998
Mean	0. 27	0.18	-1.07	-0.29	-0.09	-0.05	0.06	0.15	0.87	0.58
Median	0.03	-0.23	-0.14	-0.08	-0.11	-0.19	-0.05	0.12	0.63	0.49
Interquartile Range	0.85	0.71	0.66	0.44	0.47	0.47	0.43	0.44	0.75	0.79

* Outliers and extremes are excluded

Source: Own calculation

Next, we look at the development of the prediction errors of the value estimates over time, as reported in Figure III-14. The median prediction error is closer to or slightly below zero between 1989 and 1995, with medians between -0.23 and 0.03. The mean errors are more volatile ranging between -1.07 and 0.27. For the years thereafter, we observe positive mean and median prediction errors with values up to 0.87 and 0.63 respectively. Interquartile ranges decrease during the years between 1992 and 1996,

but almost double in size in 1997 and 1998. In summary, the development of the prediction errors over the observation period does not validate hypothesis H5.

If we compare the development of the prediction errors for the different regions, as
illustrated in Figure III-15, we do not observe an increase in predictive power over
time, as expected by hypothesis H5, for any of the regional subsamples. We find predictive power to be highest for the North American subsample and lowest for the Asian
subsample. Again, this adds some validity to hypothesis H1, which states that
predictive power is higher for more developed capital markets.

Figure III-15: Development of prediction error by region

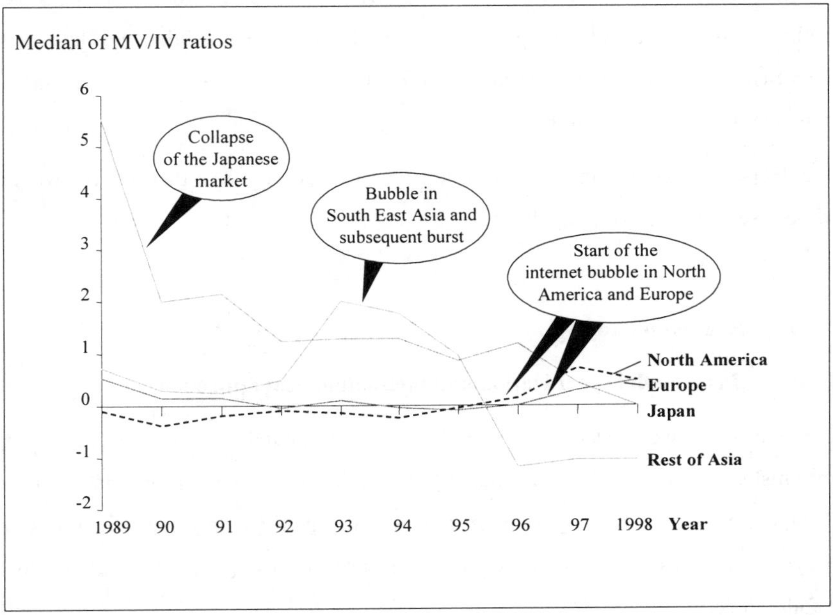

Source: Own calculation

We obtain further interesting insights, with the model results precisely mapping the
start of the internet bubble in the North American and European markets in 1995 and
1996 respectively. Isolating the results for Japan and the rest of the Asian countries, the

median prediction errors point to the collapse of the Japanese market in the early 1990s as well as to the asset bubble in the South East Asian tiger states and its subsequent burst. Thus, the model approach presents a good methodology with which to map the development of asset bubbles ex-post.

Summarizing the descriptive results of our analysis so far, we find evidence for hypothesis H1 and weak evidence for hypothesis H3 and H4. We observe smaller prediction errors for the more developed North American market as expected in hypothesis H1. The results by bank type subsample neither show significant differences for the total sample nor for the regional subsamples and this in turn suggests that hypothesis H2 should be rejected. The differences in the prediction errors when segmenting for bank size and bank profitability provide only weak evidence of hypothesis H3 and H4. Year-by-year results do not show a systematic decrease in the prediction errors over time, as proposed by hypothesis H5.

For a deeper understanding of the descriptive results discussed in this section, we next carry out several regression analyses.

III.5.3   Regression analysis

III.5.3.1   Basic model specification and methodological approach

In Section III.5.1 we discussed the validity of the formulated hypotheses using descriptive statistics. To gain further insights on the validity of our hypotheses and the potential impact of region, bank type, bank size, and profitability on the prediction errors, we specify a regression model to test the relevance of these potential determinants in the following.

Equation III-10 formulates a simple empirical model of the relevance of regional scope, bank type, size, and profitability as follows:

$$|MV / IV - 1| = \alpha + \beta_1 REG + \beta_2 IND + \beta_3 MV + \beta_4 ROE + \beta_5 YEAR + u \qquad \text{III-10}$$

We define the absolute prediction error as the dependent variable of our regression model. The independent variables are ROE as a measure of profitability and the logarithm of market value[430] as a measure of bank size as well as dummy variables for the corresponding region, bank type, and year as illustrated in Table III-7. α and β are parameters of the model, denoting the intercept and the slope coefficients respectively.

Table III-7: Overview of independent variables

Variable	Predicted Coefficient Sign	Description
REG NA	(-)	Dummy for North American subsample
IND IB	(+)	Dummy for Investment Banks subsample
IND CF	(-)	Dummy for Consumer Finance subsample
IND MF	(-)	Dummy for Mortgage Finance subsample
MV	(-)	Logarithm of market value; winsorized
ROE	(-)	Return on equity; winsorized
YEAR 1990	(-)	Dummy for year 1990
YEAR 1991	(-)	Dummy for year 1991
YEAR 1992	(-)	Dummy for year 1992
YEAR 1993	(-)	Dummy for year 1993
YEAR 1994	(-)	Dummy for year 1994
YEAR 1995	(-)	Dummy for year 1995
YEAR 1996	(-)	Dummy for year 1996
YEAR 1997	(-)	Dummy for year 1997
YEAR 1998	(-)	Dummy for year 1998

Source: Own table

As extreme results may distort the true picture of the relationship between the dependent variable and independent variables, we winsorize the dependent variable and the non-dummy independent variables, i.e. we take the lower and upper ten percent of the

---

[430] We use the logarithm of market value to account for size effects and the large number of extreme observations for market value.

observations for these variables and replace them by the next value inwards from these extreme tails. Again, we focus on the North American and European subsample given the volatility of results for the Asian subsample. As result, the sample for the regression analysis is a balanced panel composed of 209 banks and 2,090 firm-year observations over the period from 1989 to 1998. Based on the hypotheses formulated in Section III.5.1, we predict coefficient signs for the independent variables as illustrated in Table III-7.

To account for the heterogeneity across banks as well as time effects we use panel data for our analysis. We therefore slightly modify the empirical model by including subscripts to enable observations to be uniquely identified, as illustrated by Equation III-11:

$$|MV_{it} / IV_{it} - 1| = \alpha_{it} + \beta_{it_1} REG_{it} + \beta_{it_1} IND_{it} + \beta_{it_3} MV_{it} + \beta_{it_4} ROE_{it}$$
$$+ \beta_{it_5} YEAR_{it} + u_{it}$$

III-11

with $i = 1,...,290$ denoting individual banks
$t = 1,...,10$ denoting time, i.e. the observation year

The model described above allows for both time- and bank-specific slopes and intercepts. Starting from this basic model, we run four different regression models. The model specifications can be classified according to the assumptions made concerning the homogeneity of the specific parameters and the resulting parameter restrictions imposed.[431] The most restricted model is the pooled regression model that assumes all parameters and banks to be constant over time.[432] Accordingly, observations are assumed independent and are estimated using ordinary cross-sectional techniques, as described in Section III.5.3.2. Lifting some of the parameter restrictions, variable inter-

---

[431] For an overview of possible model specifications, see Greene (2002), p. 285.
[432] See Gujarati (2003), p. 641.

cept models assume constant slope coefficients but intercepts that vary over time or individuals. We conduct three panel-specific variable intercept models, referred to as between effects, fixed effects and random effects models in Section III.5.3.3, III.5.3.4, and III.5.3.5.[433]

III.5.3.2 Application of the pooled regression model and results

As noted above, the pooled regression model assumes that all coefficients are homogeneous and do not vary significantly over time or banks. Accordingly, the parameters do not contain any additional subscripts, and observations are assumed independent even within groups, as illustrated by Equation III-12:

$$\left| MV_{it} / IV_{it} - 1 \right| = \alpha + \beta_1 REG_{it} + \beta_2 IND_{it} + \beta_3 MV_{it} + \beta_4 ROE_{it} \\ + \beta_5 YEAR_{it} + u_{it} \qquad \text{III-12}$$

We estimate the regression model with ordinary least squares (OLS), assuming homogeneity of the parameters and abstracting from heteroscedasticity and autocorrelation.[434] Appendix 18, p. 254, reports the summary results for the pooled regression model.

The coefficient for the dummy variable for the North American subsample is statistically significant and negative. As expected in hypotheses H1, the prediction errors are smaller for the North American than the European subsample. With respect to the bank type variables, we do not find evidence for the validity of hypothesis H2. The coefficients for Investment Banks and Mortgage Finance are not statistically significant at sufficient confidence levels. The coefficient estimate for Consumer Finance is statisti-

---

[433] For a detailed discussion of the concepts of between effects, fixed effects, and random effects as well as the underlying assumptions, see Greene (2002), pp. 287-301.

[434] See Gujarati (2003), p. 79.

cally significant at the 10 percent confidence level, but does not show the predicted coefficient sign. The coefficient for size is statistically significant, but unlike expected, of positive sign. The results therefore reject hypotheses H3.

Unlike the descriptive statistics, the regression results strongly support the validity of hypothesis H4, as the coefficient for ROE shows statistical significance and the predictted negative coefficient. Except for the variable for 1990, dummy variables for the observation years are statistically significant. They show the predicted negative coefficient sign for the years between 1991 and 1996, but are positive in 1997 and 1998. Again, we see a decrease in the prediction errors for the first years in our observation period, but an increase in the prediction error for 1997 and 1998. Results therefore reject hypothesis H5.

The low R^2 of 0.18 implies that the independent variables only explain a small part of the variation of the dependent variable. The F-statistic is 30.17, which rejects the null hypothesis of joint insignificance of coefficients and therefore suggests that the regression model is well-specified.[435]

Still, the omission of bank-and time-variant variables in the pooled regression model might lead to a bias in the resulting estimates. In the following, we relax the restrictive assumption of parameter homogeneity and introduce heterogeneity of the intercepts to our model to gain further insights into the hypothesized relationships.

III.5.3.3   Application of the between effects model and results

The between effects model estimates the so-called between variation, i.e. the cross-sectional information reflected in the changes between subjects. We specify the fixed effects model as depicted in Equation III-13:

---

[435] See Appendix 19, p. 255.

$$\left| MV_{it} / IV_{it} - 1 \right| = \alpha + \beta_1 REG_i + \beta_2 IND_i + \beta_3 \log MV_i + \beta_4 ROE_i + c_i + u_i \qquad \text{III-13}$$

The summary results for the between effects regression are shown in Appendix 18, p. 254. The dummy variables for the observation years are dropped by the model, since only the between variation and thus bank-variant variables are examined.

Like in the pooled regression model, the coefficient for North America provides evidence for the validity of hypothesis H1. With regard to bank type variables, the resulting between estimators suggest rejecting H2 and thus do not yield new insights compared to the pooled regression results. The coefficient for bank size estimated with the between estimator is not significant at a sufficient confidence level and thus rejects H3. As a result, evidence found for H3 in the pooled and fixed effects regression is purely a result of changes of size within banks over time, but not between individual banks. H4 is supported by the significant and negative coefficient for ROE, as it is for the pooled and fixed effects estimation.

The overall R^2 is again low explaining only 6 percent of the variation of the prediction error. The R^2 for the between variation is higher as expected and explains 22 percent of the variation of the dependent between the panels. The regression model is well-specified given the F-statistic of 7.90 that soundly rejects the null hypothesis of joint insignificance of coefficients.

III.5.3.4 Application of the fixed effects model and results

The fixed effects model estimates the so-called within variation, i.e. it captures differences across units in differences in the constant term c_i.[436] The term "fixed effects"

---

[436] See Greene (2002), pp. 287-288.

indicates that the intercept may differ across individuals, but is constant over time.[437] Still, differences over time are captured in the time-variant intercept α_t by using dummy variables to account for the time effect. We specify the fixed effects model as depicted in Equation III-14:

$$\left| MV_{it} / IV_{it} - 1 \right| = \alpha_t + \beta_1 REG_i + \beta_2 IND_i + \beta_3 \log MV_{it} + \beta_4 ROE_{it} + c_i + u_{it} \quad \text{III-14}$$

The summary results for the fixed effects regression are shown in Appendix 18, p. 254. Estimation with the fixed effects model does not yield insights concerning the validity of the hypotheses H1 and H2 since the model only analyzes variation within panels and panel-invariant variables such as region and bank type are dropped.

With respect to the impact of bank size and profitability on the prediction errors, the fixed effects regression reports coefficients similar to the ones observed in the pooled regression model in Section III.5.3.2. Like for the pooled regression model, the results reject H3 and support H4. The coefficients for the dummy variables for the observation years do not show statistical significance in the years 1990, 1997, and 1998. For the remaining years, coefficients are statistically significant and negative as predicted. The results thus suggest rejecting H5.

The explained variation is low, with an accountable overall R^2 for the overall variation of 0.08 and an R^2 for the within and between group variations of 0.19 and 0.01.

As these findings might also be the result of an inefficiency bias in the fixed effects model, we conduct several specification tests on the fixed effects model in the following. We test for the homogeneity of parameters and therefore misspecification using the fixed effects model using a restricted F-test. Under the null hypothesis of strict parameter homogeneity, the pooled regression model produces consistent and efficient

---

[437] See Gujarati (2003), p. 642.

estimates, whereas the within estimator will be inefficient.[438] As shown in Appendix 20, p. 256, the resulting F-statistic is 3.84 and distributed under H_0 as $F(208, 1869)$, which is significant at the 1 percent level and leads to rejection of H_0. Thus, the intercept term is unit-variant and the fixed effects model is found to be well-specified under the assumed regression disturbances.

The fixed effects model assumes that the regression disturbances are homoscedastic with the same variance across time and individuals. Similar for pure time series analysis, this assumption might be too restrictive and lead to bias in the estimates. For this reason, we test for the existence of heteroscedasticity and serial correlation in the following.[439] We examine the normality of the residuals and find no evidence for skewness, kurtosis, or joint existence of both in the residuals. Then, we use a modified Wald test to check for groupwise heteroscedasticity in the fixed effects regression.[440] The χ^2-test statistic is 11,649.6 and rejects the null hypothesis of groupwise heteroscedasticity across panels.

To test for the existence of serial correlation, we conduct a Langrange Multiplier (LM) test.[441] The first LM statistic is 248.8 and distributed χ^2 under the null hypothesis of a first-order autoregressive process (AR1) which soundly rejects the null. Testing for the existence of a first-order moving average process (MA1) in the residuals, the resulting test statistic is 15.8 and distributed $N(0, 1)$. Again, the null hypothesis of MA1 is soundly rejected. Based on these test results, the homoscedasticity of the panels and the absence of serial correlation in the residuals assumed by the fixed effects model are valid assumptions in the case of our data set.

---

[438] See Greene (2002), p. 289.

[439] For an overview of the test statistics, see Appendix 20, p. 256.

[440] See Greene (2002), pp. 323-324.

[441] See Baltagi (2001), pp. 94-95.

III.5.3.5   Application of the random effects model

The random effects model estimates a weighted average for within and between variation, i.e. it accounts for both, time and cross-sectional effects. The regression model
can be formulated as a random effects model if the regressors are uncorrelated with the
unobserved effect.[442] The benefit of the random effects approach is increased efficiency
in the absence of effect endogeneity; however, it comes at the cost of inconsistent
estimates if the regressors are in fact correlated with c.[443]

To test for effect endogeneity we conduct a Hausman test.[444] The resulting Hausman χ^2-
test statistic of 37.45 is significant and rejects the null hypothesis of effect exogeneity.
As a result, the random effects model does not produce efficient estimates and the
fixed effects model stays the preferred estimator for our model. We therefore do not
discuss the regression results for the random effects model given in Appendix 18, p.
254.

III.5.4   Discussion

The following section summarizes the evaluation of hypotheses H1 to H5 based on the
descriptive statistics and the regression results. We assess the potential determinants of
the prediction error. Based on the empirical evidence found, we draw conclusions on
the existence of the predictive power of market values when it comes to the future
performance of banks.

---

[442] See Greene (2002), p. 293.

[443] See Greene (2002), p. 294.

[444] Under the null hypothesis of effect exogeneity, the random effects approach produces efficient and
consistent estimates; however, they are inconsistent under the alternative hypothesis of effect endogeneity. See Baltagi (2001), pp. 65-69; Greene (2002), pp. 301-303.

Figure III-16: Assessment of hypotheses

	Hypothesis	Descriptive statistics	Regression results
H1 Region	Smaller error for more developed markets	✓	✓
H3 Bank type	Smaller error for more transparent bank types	–	–
H3 Bank size	Smaller error for larger banks	(✓)	–
H4 Profitability	Smaller error for more profitable banks	(✓)	✓
H5 Time	Error decreases over time	–	–

✓ Evidence
(✓) Weak evidence
– No evidence

Source: Own graphic

Figure III-16 gives a review of the empirical evidence on the hypotheses regarding the determinants of the prediction error. Both, the descriptive statistics and the regression results provide evidence of the validity of *hypothesis H1*. We find smaller prediction errors for the North American subsample than for the European subsample. Furthermore, the prediction errors for the Asian subsample are significantly larger than for the more developed North American and European markets as expected in H1. Nevertheless, it remains unclear whether the weak predictive power observed for the Asian subsample is the result of lower data quality or of irrational investor behavior in the Asian capital markets during the bubble in the early 1990s.

With respect to *hypothesis H2*, neither the descriptive analysis nor the regression analysis reveals systematic differences between the results for the different bank types. We find no evidence for the validity of H2 and presume that existing differences are the result of differences in the regional composition of the bank type subsamples. As mentioned earlier, a more precise distinction between the sample banks in the subsample Banks would be preferable. However, further distinguishing features are not available for this subsample.

The descriptive analysis provides weak evidence on the validity of *hypothesis H3*. Looking at the regression results, however, the evidence for bank size as a determinant of the prediction error cannot be maintained. Based on these results, we reject H3.

The descriptive statistics provide weak evidence on the validity of *hypothesis H4*. The regression analysis strongly supports this evidence with a statistically significant and negative coefficient sign for ROE as predicted in H4.

When testing the validity of *hypothesis H5*, we do not observe a systematic decrease in the prediction error over the observation period. The results therefore suggest rejecting H5. On the other hand, the observation period in question might be too short for drawing any conclusions on H5 and empirical proof of H5 might require an analysis going back to earlier years with considerably lower market efficiency. Although results do not show a systematic decrease in the prediction error, they reveal significant differences over time. Looking at the results for each of the regions by year, we see that asset bubbles confound the results and account for a significant part of the bias in the prediction errors.

In summary, the results suggest that the predictive power of the market value is significantly determined by the regional scope of the bank. If this result relates to the development status of the specific market or to an asset bubble in the specific market during the observation period remains still unclear. Regarding determinants that are specific to the individual bank, results provide evidence on bank profitability as a determinant of the predictive power of the market values. For bank size and bank type as further bank-specific variables, no evidence is found.

The results of the regression analysis and the relatively low R^2 suggest that only a few of the factors affecting the predictive power of the market during the observation period are captured. Therefore, a more extended set of control variables might well reveal a more precise picture of the potential determinants of the predictive power of market value.

In summary, the findings of this study suggest that there is evidence for the predictive power of the market when it comes to the future performance of banks. Based on the empirical evidence found, we conclude that shareholder value is a relevant measure for the business performance of banks. Consequently, doubts on the empirical relevance of the shareholder value approach for the banking industry in this respect are not legitimate. The basic hypothesis underlying the concept of shareholder value, i.e. that market values reflect the future competitive advantage of a company, applies to banks. In so far, the shareholder value approach is a strategic concept that is as valid for the banking industry as it is for other industries.

III.6   Sensitivity analyses

To assess the robustness of the results we run several sensitivity analyses on the assumptions of our model. In the following section, we examine in particular those assumptions made when estimating the cost of equity, adjusting accounting variables, and constructing the residual value in Phase 2. We replicate the calculation of intrinsic value with alternative parameter specifications and examine the sensitivity of the basic model results reported in Section III.5.1 to these alternative specifications.

III.6.1   Alternative specifications of cost of equity parameters

When estimating the cost of equity we make several assumptions concerning the CAPM input parameters, the risk-free rate, the market risk premium, and beta. As already mentioned, these assumptions have long been subject to theoretical debate. Nevertheless, a theoretically correct answer often does not exist and decisions on assumptions are driven by the rationale of pragmatics. We therefore test the robustness of our model results to changes in the assumptions made.

Table III-8: Sensitivity of IV to changes in beta methodology

(1989 – 1998, percent)

	Beta calculation normalized for TMT			Beta calculation excluding TMT		
Statistic	North America	Europe	Asia	North America	Europe	Asia
N	1,350	740	810	1,350	740	810
Mean	1.00	1.00	1.00	0.97	0.99	0.98
Median	1.00	1.00	1.00	0.99	1.00	0.98
Standard Deviation	0.01	0.00	0.01	0.11	0.06	0.30
Interquartile Range	0.00	0.00	0.00	0.09	0.02	0.05

Source: Own calculation

A plausible adjustment to the calculation of beta between 1998 and 2002 is to normal-ize for the overweighting of the TMT sector in the market portfolio, as discussed in Section III.3.4.4. When accounting for the bubble of the TMT sector by normalizing for TMT or excluding TMT, beta results vary significantly for the years between 1998 and 2002, as exemplified for the beta of European banks in Appendix 21, p. 257. Nevertheless, the sensitivity of the prediction errors to changes in the beta calculation is very low, as shown in Table III-8. Given the observation period from 1989 to 1998 and an explicit forecast period of five years, our model results show no sensitivity to these changes in beta methodology except for a very low degree of sensitivity between 1996 and 1998.

As mentioned in Section III.3.4.3, the assumption with respect to the risk premium has long been a subject of debate with researchers. We therefore test the sensitivity of results to an increase in the assumed risk premium by 0.5 percent, from 3.5 percent to 4.0 percent. In addition, we examine the robustness of results when varying the risk premium by year. Table III-9 shows the descriptive statistics for the sensitivity of intrinsic value to changes in risk premium in detail.

Table III-9: Sensitivity of IV to changes in assumed risk premium

(1989 – 1998, percent)

Statistic	Risk premium of 4.0 percent			Yearly risk premium		
	North America	Europe	Asia	North America	Europe	Asia
N	1,350	740	810	1,350	740	810
Mean	0.98	0.98	0.93	0.99	0.98	0.94
Median	0.98	0.97	0.93	0.99	0.99	0.98
Standard Deviation	0.09	0.24	0.53	0.13	0.10	1.74
Interquartile Range	0.01	0.02	0.06	0.02	0.02	0.07

Source: Own calculation

For the North American and European subsamples, a change in the risk premium of 0.5 percent results in changes in intrinsic value of, on average, 2 percent. For the Asian subsample, changes in risk premium cause, on average, changes in intrinsic value of 7 percent. The sensitivity of results when using a yearly risk premium is low, with mean changes in intrinsic value of 1 and 2 percent for the North American and European subsample and 6 percent for the Asian subsample.

Overall, the robustness of the results to a change in the assumed risk premium is high. The increased accuracy when using a yearly risk premium does not lead to significant changes in intrinsic value. Use of a higher constant risk premium of 4 percent results in lower intrinsic values. For the European and Asian subsample, this adjustment further enhances the bias in the estimates.

III.6.2   Alternative adjustments of accounting variables

To correct for distortions of accounting policies, we adjust accounting variables for deferred taxes, effective average taxes, and unrecorded goodwill as discussed in Section III.3.2.2. In the following, we test the robustness of the model results to changes made to accounting variables.

Table III-10: Sensitivity of IV to accounting adjustments

(1989 – 1998, percent)

Statistic	North America	Europe	Asia
N	1,350	740	810
Mean	0.95	0.96	0.87
Median	0.99	0.98	0.93
Standard Deviation	2.14	1.40	1.34
Interquartile Range	0.11	0.17	0.16

Source: Own calculation

First, we examine the sensitivity of model results to a residual income calculation without any adjustments to accounting variables. Adjusted income equals income available to common shareholders as reported in DS Worldscope, and economic equity equals common equity. Table III-10 shows the variance of results assuming no adjustments to accounting variables. The results of the North American and European subsamples vary by a median of 1 to 2 percent. For the Asian subsample, the central tendency varies by a median of 7 percent. Mean variance is higher. The dispersion of results is small, with interquartile ranges varying from 0.11 to 0.17.

To understand to what extent individual accounting adjustments lie behind the sensitivity described above, we go on to examine sensitivity using isolated robustness tests for each accounting adjustment, as described in Appendix 22, p. 258.

First, we examine the sensitivity of results to the adjustment made for effective average taxes. We correct adjusted income and economic equity for deferred taxes alone, but do not adjust it for effective average taxes. Instead, we rely on income taxes as reported in DS Worldscope. The variance of model results averages at a median of 2 to 3 percent for the North American and European subsamples. The sensitivity of the Asian subsample is slightly higher, with a median of 7 percent.

In the next robustness test, we examine the sensitivity of model results to the adjustment for deferred taxes. In this case, adjusted income is only adjusted for effective average taxes, and economic equity equals common equity as reported in DS Worldscope. The variance of model results to this adjustment is very low for all regional subsamples, with a median of up to 1 percent.

The last robustness test concerns the adjustment for unrecorded goodwill, necessary in the case of acquisitions that are accounted for using the pooling-of-interest method. In our sample, this accounting method is only relevant for the North American subsample. The variance of model results to this adjustment is very low, with an alteration in the mean of 3 percent and no change for the median.

Summarizing the results described above, the results of our model are relatively robust when it comes to adjustments for deferred taxes and unrecorded goodwill. The variance of intrinsic values is relatively high for the Asian subsample when adjusting for effective average taxes. This might be the result of the low quality of the tax information available for most of the countries in the Asian subsample. However, not adjusting for effective average taxes in these countries would result in lower intrinsic values, and therefore even higher prediction errors for the Asian subsample.

III.6.3   Alternative specification of decay rate in Phase 2

Value creation in Phase 2 on average accounts for 43 percent of total value creation, as illustrated in Appendix 23, p. 259. Given the large share of value created in Phase 2, the assumption with respect to the value creation in the decay phase is critical. The creation of intrinsic value in Phase 2 is mainly influenced by the assumed decay rate. Table III-11 shows the sensitivity of intrinsic value to this critical assumption.

Table III-11: Sensitivity of IV to decay rate assumption

(1989 – 1998, percent)

Statistic	North America	Europe	Asia
N	1,350	740	810
Mean	1.08	1.05	0.96
Median	1.07	1.03	0.94
Standard Deviation	0.96	0.85	1.86
Interquartile Range	0.06	0.11	0.17

Source: Own calculation

We assume a constant decay rate of 10 percent for all banks in the sample. In Section III.3.2 we identify a decay rate of between 5 and 10 percent as a reasonable assumption for the decay in the banking industry. Assuming the decay rate to be 5 percent, the model results vary on average by a median of 3 to 7 percent for all regional subsamples. The interquartile ranges of these variances are low, with values ranging from 0.06 to 0.17. In summary, the robustness of results with respect to the decay rate assumption is thus considerably high. While a lower decay rate would increase the intrinsic value estimates for the North American and European subsample, it would decrease the value estimates for the Asian subsample and therefore worsen the bias of the results for the Asian subsample.

III.6.4   Discussion

Figure III-17 summarizes the results of the above described sensitivity analyses. Overall, the model results are relatively robust when it comes to changes in model assumptions.

Figure III-17: Overview of sensitivity analyses

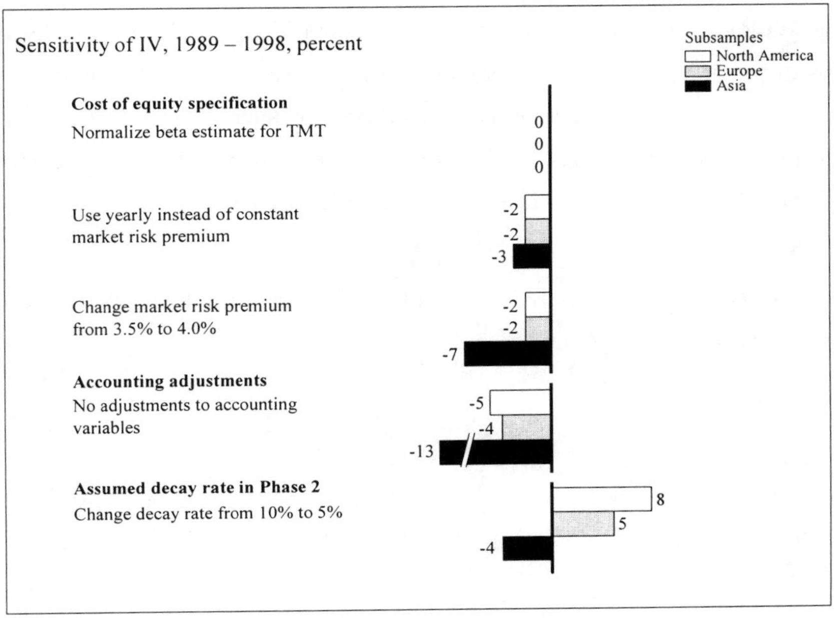

Source: Own calculation

With regard to the *cost of equity* assumptions, sensitivity is relatively low. Although beta estimates significantly deviate during 1998 and 2003 when normalizing for TMT, the sensitivity of intrinsic value estimates to these normalized betas is marginal. The sensitivity of the value estimates using a yearly risk premium is low and the higher accuracy from using yearly parameters does not lead to better results. An increase of the risk premium by 0.5 percent results in lower intrinsic values and thus enhances the existing positive prediction errors for Europe and Asia.

Sensitivity to the *accounting adjustments* is higher, in particular for the Asian subsample. The main driver of sensitivity is the adjustment for the effective average tax rate, whereas the sensitivity of intrinsic value to adjustments for deferred taxes and unrecorded goodwill is, on average, below 1 percent. The higher sensitivity of the value estimates for the Asian subsample might be the result of the low data quality for the Asian banks in the sample.

The sensitivity of intrinsic value estimates to a lower *decay rate* is relatively high as expected. A lower decay rate increases intrinsic value estimates for the North American and European subsample, whereas it reduces the value estimates for the Asian subsample given negative residual incomes for many Asian banks during the observation period. The lower decay rate thus further enhances the prediction errors for the Asian banks.

In summary, the model assumptions seem to be well-specified and balanced and the model results robust.

III.7   Conclusions

Starting from the question on the relevance of the shareholder value approach to banking, we conduct an empirical study on the existence of market value predictive power with respect to the future performance of banks. Examining this basic hypothesis of the shareholder value approach, we estimate an ex-post intrinsic value based on the historical operating performance of a sample of 290 worldwide banks and compare this ex-post intrinsic value to the market values observed between 1989 and 1998.

The initial hypothesis on the identity of market value and intrinsic value is based on two underlying assumptions, the fit of the valuation model used and the existence of market efficiency. We test the validity of the two assumptions for our sample banks successively. Our findings suggest that both assumptions are valid for our sample and that the market does have predictive power when it comes to the future performance of our sample banks.

Assessing the fit of the residual income model for banks, we find the residual income model to dominate the discounted dividend model. Reconciling the results on the accuracy of the residual income model for banks with the evidence found for other industries, we conclude that the residual income fits the banking industry at least as well as other industries if not better.

With respect to the existence of market efficiency, we look at the determinants of the prediction error. We reveal the profitability of a bank as a determinant of the prediction error of market value. This result is not specific to banks and can be explained by lower market efficiency for companies with lower profitability. Furthermore, the prediction error shows significant differences across regions and over time which can be attributed to asset bubbles overlying the developments of the corresponding regional market during the observation period. We do not find determinants of the prediction error that are specific to banks or other factors that might indicate that the predictive power for banks, unlike for non-banks, does not exist.

In summary, the empirical findings back up our theory that the market values have predictive power for the future performance of our sample banks. Given the large size and worldwide scope of our sample combined with a ten-year observation period, we conclude that this result also holds for the banking industry as a whole. Based on the evidence found, we infer that shareholder value is a relevant measure of bank perform-ance, and that, consequently, the shareholder value approach is a valid concept for banks.

The evidence found, together with the anticipated increase in the importance of share-holder value in the banking industry, suggests that further research should be carried out. After having proven the empirical relevance of shareholder value, the search for the drivers of bank shareholder value is next on the agenda. Empirical studies on the value drivers of banks constitute a starting point for further research and promise to yield important insights into the management of shareholder value of banks.

IV. Value drivers of retail banks

IV.1 Motivation and key research questions

Bank stock is 'story paper', not 'numbers paper'. This does not mean that stories are unquantifiable, only that their documentation relies on the new metrics."[445] Applying the metrics of shareholder value to banks, the objective of this paper is to quantify the story behind the shareholder value of banks and, more specifically, retail banks.

The fulfillment of performance goals set by the capital market is becoming increasingly important to banks. To meet these performance goals, bank managers need to understand the fundamental drivers of value. Contributions concerning the theoretical deviations of value drivers as well as the empirical evidence on potential drivers of shareholder value are rare. As a result, our understanding of how banks create shareholder value is limited so far. Evidence on the shareholder value creation of industrial companies is only of limited help. The business economics differ significantly between banks and non-banks. This suggests that banks have a very specific DNA of shareholder value creation that differs significantly from that of non-banks.

The original objective of shareholder value management is to permeate the organization with a philosophy of creating value through more informed, and therefore improved, decision-making and ultimately better resource allocation. In order to grow a bank's business strategically, it is critical to evaluate and understand the value metrics underlying the banking industry and the individual bank. Empirical evidence on value drivers helps to understand the metrics behind bank value and the specific DNA of shareholder value creation for banks. The implications for bank management derived from such evidence serve as a basis for value creation within banks.

---

[445] Cates (1991), p. 52.

Our study is a first step in this direction. The objective of the paper is to measure the impact of value drivers on the creation of shareholder value of retail banks. We identify the business mix, the branch structure, the cost efficiency, and the risk capabilities of a bank as potential value drivers and measure the impact of these four drivers on the value creation and the underlying financial indicators of retail banks.

In the course of this paper, we conduct an extensive regression analysis for a sample of 139 retail banks. The data set includes two important types of retail players, a sample of 33 retail units of worldwide universal banks and a sample of 106 German savings banks. For the sample banks, we study shareholder value creation and potential drivers over the observation period from 1998 to 2003. We define four regression models and relate the identified value drivers to a residual income value estimate as well as to parameters of the income, cost, and risk structure of the sample banks. In order to account for individual effects across banks and time, a panel data analysis is applied.

The banking literature has not extensively covered the area of value drivers of banks so far. The contribution of our paper is to add empirical evidence to this research area. We use a data set that is unique for two reasons. We draw on data from segment reporting that provides information on the level of (retail) business units. Combined with the savings banks data, we look at a homogeneous sample of retail players. Accordingly, we avoid the problems of limited comparability across sample banks that are typically related to bank level information provided by standard company databases. In addition, the data set includes unique information about the branch structure of banks, such as the number of customers and branches, which is not provided by standard company databases. The empirical analysis therefore promises to yield reliable and valuable insights on the value drivers of retail banks.

Section IV.2 derives a value metrics framework and links the shareholder value of a bank to strategic and operational value drivers. Section II.3 describes the data set used and the methodology employed to construct the model. Section IV.4 summarizes and discusses the empirical results. Section IV.5 concludes the paper.

IV.2   Derivation of value driver model for banks

Starting with the definition of value drivers, we consider all factors that influence the value creation of a bank as value drivers – for example, the quality o management, the customer satisfaction or the cost-income ratio (CIR), but also general economic trends, national banking practices or changes in the interest rate.

Figure IV-1: Types of value drivers and examples

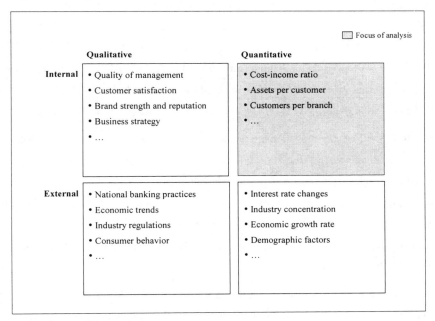

Source: Own graphic

Figure IV-1 categorizes types of value drivers for bank shareholder value along two dimensions and identifies four types of value drivers, which are illustrated with examples. One way to categorize value drivers is to make a distinction between internal and external value drivers. Internal value drivers are factors relating to the inherent performance of a bank, whereas external drivers result from the micro- and macroeconomic environment of a bank. External drivers relate to specific factors and trends in the banking industry as well as to factors concerning the general economic environment.

Second, value drivers can be categorized into qualitative and quantitative value drivers. Qualitative value drivers significantly affect the operating performance and share-holder value of banks. Unfortunately, information on these factors is typically not available and, if available, its impact on value can hardly be measured.

As our analysis aims to measure the impact of value drivers on shareholder value, we only incorporate quantitative drivers and do not consider qualitative factors in our analysis. We focus on internal drivers of shareholder value of retail banks, since these drivers are specific to the individual bank and can be influenced by bank management. We use external value drivers as control variables in our analysis only. In the course of this paper, we thus focus on internal and quantitative value drivers of retail banks.

Figure IV-2 illustrates the value metrics framework that we use to derive the potential drivers of shareholder value for retail banks. First, we approximate the shareholder value of a bank with an estimate of intrinsic value. Next, we link this value estimate to the financial indicators of the bank, such as the return on equity, the cost-income ratio or the leverage of the bank. By breaking these financial indicators down to the level of the operating performance of banks, they can be linked to the strategic and operational drivers of bank performance.

Direct measures of stock price performance and thus shareholder value, such as TRS or MVA are typically biased by short-term market reactions on exogenous effects and by potential over- or undervaluation of fundamental values in times of market bubbles and their subsequent burst. Furthermore, these direct measures of market value are neither available on the level of (retail) business units of banks nor for the German savings banks in our sample that are not exchange-listed given their affiliation to the public banking sector. We therefore approximate the shareholder value of the sample banks with an intrinsic value estimate.

Figure IV-2: Value metrics framework

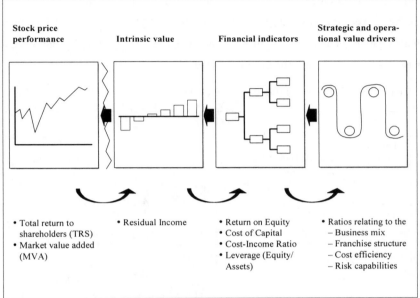

Stock price
performance

Intrinsic value

Financial indicators

Strategic and opera-
tional value drivers

- Total return to
  shareholders (TRS)
- Market value added
  (MVA)

- Residual Income

- Return on Equity
- Cost of Capital
- Cost-Income Ratio
- Leverage (Equity/
  Assets)

- Ratios relating to the
  – Business mix
  – Franchise structure
  – Cost efficiency
  – Risk capabilities

Source: Own graphic

We use residual income as a measure of intrinsic value in our analysis for several reasons. First, empirical studies have provided evidence for the superiority of residual income as a measure of shareholder value creation of companies.[446] Especially for banks, study findings suggest the superiority of residual income relative to alternative value estimates such as DCF or the discounted dividend model.[447] A pragmatic reason for the use of residual income is that it can be easily estimated with reported account-

---

[446] See Penman and Sougiannis (1998); Lee (1999); Francis et al. (2000). For a comprehensive review of the empirical evidence found, see Table III-1 in Section III.2.

[447] For large-scale evidence on a banking sample, see Section III.4. See also Uyemura et al. (1996), pp. 99-101; Matten (2000), p. 257; MSDW (2001), pp. 44-47; Fiordelisi (2002), pp. 18-27.

ing data. Typically, net income in banking includes only low levels of depreciation and accordingly shows high cash adequacy. The calculation of residual income is therefore relatively easy for banks and produces reliable results.[448] Lastly, unlike DCF or alternative valuation models, the residual income model is directly linked to the operating performance of banks and the underlying value drivers.[449]

Figure IV-3: Value driver tree for retail banks

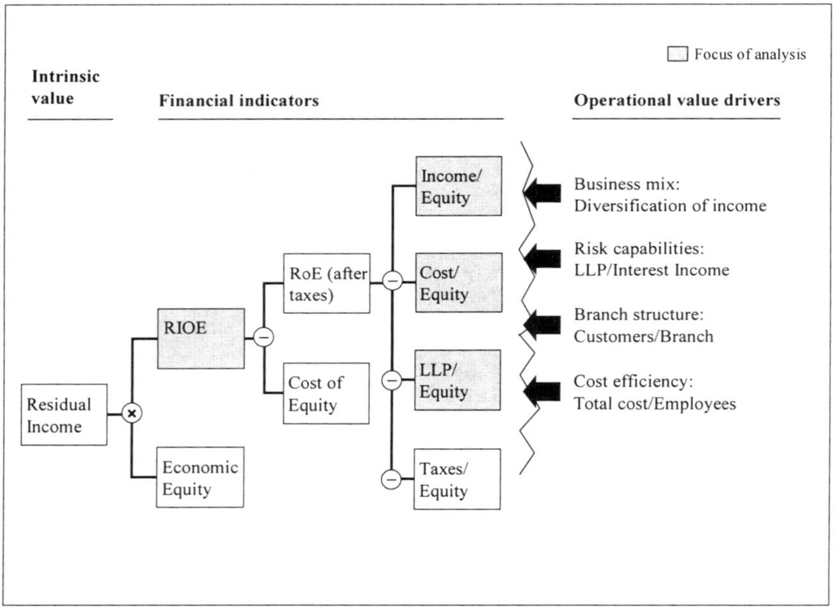

Source: Own graphic

Figure IV-3 displays a value driver tree for retail banks. We start from residual income as an initial measure of intrinsic value and break this value measure down to the level

---

[448] See Damodaran (2004), p. 27. For a detailed discussion of the calculation of residual income for banks, see Section II.5.1.2.

[449] See Copeland et al. (2000), p. 143; MSDW (2001), p. 14.

of financial indicators. Based on the underlying financials, we link the residual income on equity (*RIOE*) to three financial indicators, the *Income/Equity*, the *Cost/Equity*, and the *LLP/Equity*. These indicators relate to the income, cost, and risk structure of a bank.

Having linked the above, we identify four strategic and operational value drivers that potentially influence these financial indicators and RIOE. The *business mix* is an important strategic value driver of a bank. We use the diversification of income as an indicator for the business mix of a bank. The high or low degree of diversification implies two different strategic business models of banks. While low diversification of income represents the traditional lending-oriented business model, a higher degree of diversification is associated with a business model that focuses on fee-based, advisory-intensive banking products.

The impact of the *branch structure* on bank value has been subject to much debate in theory and practice. The question whether an optimal branch size exists in practice is still unanswered. Yet, the branch structure of banks and parameters such as the ratio of customers per branch potentially drive the value of retail banks.

Cost reduction programs characterize the restructuring efforts recently taken on by European banks. The *cost efficiency* is thus assumed critical for the value creation of banks. Our analysis will provide empirical evidence for the value impact of cost efficiency and indicators such as the Total Cost/Employee.

Finally, superior *risk capabilities* are seen as a distinct characteristic of top performers in banking and are expected to become even more important in the future. The ratio of LLP/Interest Income provides important information about the risk capabilities of a bank and is thus expected to influence bank value significantly.

IV.3   Data and methodology

IV.3.1   Data

IV.3.1.1   Data set used

The data set consists of two subsamples with different bank types, Universal Banks and Savings Banks. The Universal Banks sample consists of the retail banking units of 33 worldwide universal banks. For the Savings Banks sample, we identified the top 106 German savings banks ranked by total assets from the Bankscope database. The data for both samples covers a six-year observation period from 1998 to 2003.

The data on the bank performance and the income, cost, and branch structure was drawn from Bankscope, DSGV reporting, and the individual annual reports of the relevant banks. For the Universal Banks, data on the key financials and the branch structure was gathered manually from the segment reporting of the individual bank's annual reports. For cases in which information on the branch structure, such as the number of customers and branches, was not available in the annual reports, the data was complemented by published analyst reports.

For the Savings Banks, information on accounting variables was drawn from the Bankscope database. The information on the branch structure was gathered manually from the relevant volumes of the "Sparkassenfachbuch" published by the DSGV.[450] We use DS as source for the market data required for the estimation of cost of equity.

With respect to some banks in the Universal Banks sample, the required accounting variables are not available for all years during the observation period. Given the gaps in years, the Universal Banks sample is an unbalanced panel with 33 groups and 120

---

[450] The "Sparkassenfachbuch" is a yearbook of the association of German savings banks, Deutscher Sparkassen- und Giroverband (DSGV) that contains contact information and key statistics for the savings banks and institutions associated with the DSGV.

bank-year observations over the period from 1998 to 2003. For the Savings Banks, data for all years is available. Consequently, the Savings Banks sample presents a balanced panel with 106 groups and 636 bank-year observations. As result, we look at a total sample of 139 groups and 756 bank-year observations.

IV.3.1.2   Sample characteristics

The 139 sample banks account for a total book equity of EUR 55 bn in 1998, growing to total book equity of EUR 103 bn in 2003. Assets amount to a total of EUR 1,274 bn in 1998 and EUR 1,922 bn in 2003. Table IV-1 includes a number of descriptive statistics illustrating the key characteristics of the sample banks for the total sample.

Table IV-1: Descriptive statistics of sample characteristics – Total sample

(1998 – 2003, N=756)

Statistic	Equity (EUR mn)	Assets (EUR mn)	ROE (percent)	Customers (mn)
Mean	829	18,353	8.2	1.1
Median	170	3,841	7.0	0.3
Standard Deviation	1,988	45,749	7.6	2.4
Interquartile Range	209	4,226	6.2	0.3

Source: Own calculation

The sample banks have, on average, a book equity of EUR 829 mn with total assets of EUR 18,353 mn. The median values of equity and assets are lower, accounting for EUR 170 mn and EUR 3,841 mn and therefore indicate the existence of positive skewness and some very large banks in the sample. Average ROE is 8.2 percent, while the median value is 7.0 percent.

The skewness of the data is again shown by the number of customers per bank, for which the mean value of 1.1 mn customers is significantly higher than the median of 0.3 mn.

Figure IV-4: Sample characteristics – Universal Banks vs. Savings Banks

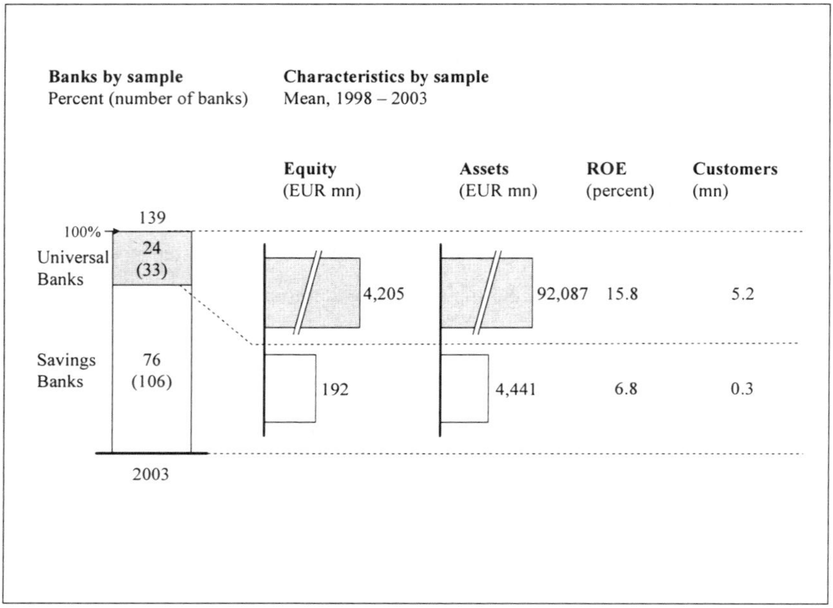

Source: Own calculation

Figure IV-4 shows the descriptive statistics for each subsample separately. The 33 retail units of the Universal Banks show a mean book equity of EUR 4,205 mn and mean assets of EUR 92,087 mn from 1998 to 2003. The Savings Banks are smaller with mean equity of EUR 192 mn and assets of EUR 4,441 mn. The profitability of the Universal Banks is, with a mean ROE of 15.8 percent, twice that of the Savings Banks. The average number of retail customers of the Universal Banks is 5.2 mn, whereas the average number of customers per Savings Bank only accounts for 0.3 mn.

Detailed descriptive statistics of the sample characteristics for the two subsamples are given in Appendix 24, p. 260. In summary, we observe significant differences in size, but also profitability when comparing the Universal Banks and the Savings Banks subsample.

With respect to the regional scope, the Universal Banks sample covers ten European countries and the US, as illustrated in Appendix 25, p. 261. In contrast, the Savings Banks are all located in Germany.

The development of the key characteristics over the observation period from 1998 to 2003 is shown in Figure IV-5.

Figure IV-5: Sample characteristics by year

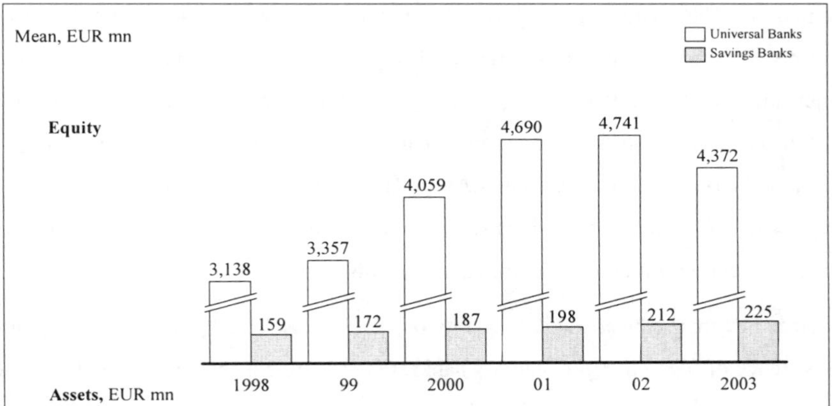

Assets, EUR mn	1998	99	2000	01	02	2003
Universal Banks	72,259	74,207	86,491	109,191	110,070	77,935
Savings Banks	3,839	4,150	4,396	4,574	4,789	4,901
ROE, percent						
Universal Banks	12.0	13.8	17.9	16.6	15.4	16.6
Savings Banks	8.6	12.2	5.6	4.2	3.2	6.9

Source: Own calculation

For the Universal Banks, we observe a continuing growth of mean equity of EUR 3,138 mn in 1998 to EUR 4,741 mn in 2002. In 2003, mean equity falls to EUR 4,372 mn. However, this dip is not a result of negative growth in the previous year, but rather of the sample composition in 2003. This is also reflected in the development of the mean assets of the Universal Banks. The mean equity of the Savings Banks grows continuously from EUR 159 mn in 1998 to EUR 225 in 2003. The same holds for the mean assets of the Savings Banks. The development of the ROE is more volatile for both subsamples. Looking at the mean ROE, the data shows a peak of 17.9 percent for the Universal Banks in 2000 and a peak of 12.4 percent for the Savings Banks in 1999.

IV.3.1.3   Representativeness of the data set

Assessing the representativeness and quality of the data set, we see the following limitations. The quality of the data is lower for the Universal Banks sample for two reasons. First, the definition of the retail segment varies across banks. Retail units might include other customer segments, e.g., small-business customers or institutional customers. In addition, some segments include the asset management business of the universal banks, while others do not. Although we tried to adjust for these inconsistencies across the retail units of banks, we could not account for all differences in the retail segment definition due to limited information outside-in.

Another fact that reduces the data quality of the Universal Banks sample is the limited consistency of segment reports across banks. One example is the definition of allocated equity, which is not clearly defined by accounting standards at the level of business segments. As a result, the total equity figure for the retail units might not be consistent across banks. The potentially lower data quality for the Universal Banks sample might bias the results of our analysis.

With respect to its regional scope, the representativeness of the Savings Banks sample, which includes only German savings banks, is obviously low. Another factor that might bias the results is the underlying assumption that savings banks are pure retail players. We assume all income positions of the savings banks to be generated with retail customers, although some of the income might be related to business with small and medium corporate customers in reality.

Still, comparability across banks is much higher for both of our subsamples relative to the usual data sets drawn from Bankscope or comparable databases since these databases do not include data at the business unit level. The information on bank perform-ance from these sources only allows comparison of pure players. The explanatory power of results for universal banks, however, is low because of the significant differ-ences in the business mix of universal banks. Given the limited universe of pure players in banking, the feasibility of analyses based on the public databases is limited.

IV.3.2   Estimation of intrinsic value

IV.3.2.1   Definition of residual income

As described in Section IV.2, we use residual income as a proxy for the shareholder value creation of our sample banks.

We estimate residual income of bank i in year t as depicted in Equation IV-1.[451]

$$RI_{it} = (ROE_{it} - c_{e_{ct}}) \times E_{i,t/t-1} \qquad\qquad \text{IV-1}$$

with RI_{it} = Residual income of bank i in year t
ROE_{it} = Return on equity of bank i in year t
$c_{e_{ct}}$ = Cost of equity of banks in country c in year t
E_{it} = Equity of bank i in year t

We use an equity approach to calculate residual income as recommended for bank valuation in literature.[452] As it is difficult to define the debt capital used for financing and assign a proper cost of capital to this debt, the equity approach is more appropriate

[451] See Stewart (1990), p. 137; Rappaport (1986), p. 121; Copeland et al. (2000), p. 143.

[452] See Copeland et al. (2000), pp. 428-429; MSDW (2001), p. 11; Damodaran (2004), p. 26.

for valuing banks.[453] Thus, we do not consider debt as capital and consider interest paid as an operating expense.

The equity of bank *i* in year *t* is defined as the equity of (the retail unit of) bank *i* in year *t*. The return on equity of bank *i* in year *t* is defined as net operating income after taxes divided by the equity of bank *i* in year *t*.

The estimation of the cost of equity and the calculation of the accounting variables are described in the following sections.

IV.3.2.2 Estimation of cost of equity

The cost of equity of our sample banks is estimated using the CAPM. We opt for CAPM, as it is the most widely used theoretical approach in empirical research and the preferred method in the context of valuing banks in most of the literature.[454] "The CAPM postulates that the opportunity cost of equity is equal to the return on risk-free securities plus the company's systematic risk (beta) multiplied by the market price of risk (market risk premium)."[455]

The market risk premium presents the difference between the expected return on the market portfolio and the risk-free rate of return. Beta is defined as the covariance between the returns on the individual stock and the market portfolio.[456]

[453] For a detailed discussion of the specifics of banks and the reasons for the use of an equity approach when valuing banks, see Section II.4.4. See also Börner and Lowis (1997), pp. 94-104; Kirsten (2000), pp. 133-135; Koch (2002), pp. 44-45; Damodaran (2004), pp. 4-7.

[454] See Kümmel (1995), p. 40; Copeland et al. (2000), p. 435; Kirsten (2000), p. 155; MSDW (2001), p. 48; Damodaran (2004), pp. 20-26.

[455] Copeland et al. (2000), p. 435.

[456] For an detailed overview of the CAPM and the underlying assumptions, see Copeland and Weston (1992), pp. 193-202; Brealey and Myers (2000), pp. 187-203; Pettit (2001).

Using CAPM the cost of equity is estimated as illustrated by Equation IV-2:

$$c_{e_{nt}} = r_{f_{nt}} + \left[E(r_m) - r_f \right]_{const} \times (beta_t)$$ IV-2

where $r_{f_{nt}}$ = Risk-free rate of return in country n in year t

$E(r_m)$ = Expected rate of return on the market portfolio m

$\left[E(r_m) - r_f \right]_{const}$ = Market risk premium constant over time and region

$beta_t$ = Systematic risk of the retail banking business in year t

The input parameters of CAPM, i.e. the risk-free rate, the market risk premium, and beta, are estimated as follows. As a proxy for the *risk-free rate,* we use the yield on benchmark indices of ten-year government bonds as reported in DS.[457] We prefer a ten-year horizon as it approximates the duration of bank cash flows and is consistent with betas and market risk premiums estimated relative to the market portfolio with a duration of approximately ten years.[458] We use national benchmark indices of our sample countries as reported in DS.[459] Furthermore, we use a calendar year average of the yield on these benchmark indices for the years between 1998 and 2003. Appendix 27, p. 263, gives an overview of the risk-free rates used in our model.

We use a global estimate of the *market risk premium* that is derived based on a simple forward-looking model approach.[460] We follow the analysis of Goedhart et al. (2002) that results in an average inflation-adjusted cost of equity of 7 percent implied by stock

---

[457] For an overview of alternative estimates of the risk-free rate, see Copeland et al. (2000), p. 216; Damodaran (1994), pp. 24-26. Recent research has shown that long-term bonds are not completely risk-less. Therefore, unlevering the risk-free rate and combining the systematic equity risk of stocks and bonds into one premium is generally a reasonable adjustment. However, for the market as a whole or any stock with a beta close to 1.0 as it is the case for banks the net effect of this adjustment approximates to zero. See Pettit (2001), pp. 5-6.

[458] See Copeland (2000), p. 216; Faust (2002), p. 102.

[459] See Faust (2002), p. 116; Geltinger (2003), p. 68.

[460] For a detailed discussion on the advantages of the use of a global risk premium, see Copeland et al. (2000), pp. 366-371; Pettit (2001), p. 3.

market valuations from 1963 to 2001 in the US.[461] We use this estimate as a starting point and calculate a yearly market risk premium based on the cost of equity and the risk-free rate in inflation-adjusted terms as shown in Appendix 28, p. 264. For the years between 1998 and 2003, we find risk premiums ranging between 3.3 percent and 5.3 percent with an average of 4.2 percent. We use these estimates for the US market as a proxy of the global market risk premium and use the three-year moving average of the risk premium reported in Appendix 28 for our model.

As a measure of *systematic risk,* we use the yearly industry betas for the banking business for each sample country between the years 1998 and 2003. We rely on industry betas as industry betas are typically more stable and reliable than individual company betas since measurement errors tend to cancel out.[462] We construct regional industry betas by measuring the correlation of the return for the national DS bank indices with the return of the DS World index on a yearly basis.[463] In line with standard research, we observe monthly returns and their correlation over a period of five years.[464] Moreover, we use a three-year moving average to compensate for short-term market trends.

A viable adjustment when measuring individual or industry betas is to correct for the impact of the TMT sector share prices on the world market index during the years between 1998 and 2001.[465] Since the effect on our analysis of studying the years 1998

---

[461] Goedhart et al. (2002) use a standard forward-looking model, which they apply to US and UK stock market valuations of the past 40 years and find surprisingly stable results. For a detailed discussion on the derivation of the market risk premium, see Damodaran (1994), pp. 21-24; Copeland et al. (2000), pp. 217-221; Pettit (2001), pp. 1-5.

[462] See Brealey and Myers (2000), p. 224; Annema and Goedhart (2003), p. 10.

[463] In line with the estimation of a global market risk premium, we prefer a worldwide market index as global benchmark to national benchmarks. See Copeland et al. (2000), pp. 366-371; Faust (2002), pp. 114-115.

[464] See Damodaran (1994), pp. 26-27; Pettit (2001), p. 8; Faust (2002), pp. 110-111.

[465] For a detailed discussion of the distortion of the measures of risk by the market bubble in the TMT sector, see Annema and Goedhart (2003).

until 2003 is significant, we adjust the beta by normalizing the TMT sector share in the world market index. Appendix 29, p. 265, reports the yearly industry betas used. The yearly cost of equity by country used in the model is shown in Appendix 30, p. 266.

IV.3.2.3 Definition of accounting variables

As a measure of equity, we use the shareholders' equity reported in Bankscope for the Savings Banks and the allocated equity as reported in the individual segment reports of the Universal Banks. For the Universal Banks sample, we adjust the equity measure on a case-by-case basis when the reported allocated equity obviously does not reflect the equity of the retail business of the relevant bank.

Table IV-2 illustrates the calculation of operating income after taxes. Total income is calculated as the sum of net interest income, fee income, and net other income as reported in Bankscope and the segment reports. Total costs are comprised of staff costs and non-staff costs including depreciation as reported in Bankscope and the segment reports. For some of the Universal Banks, administrative costs as well as loan loss provisions that pertain economically to the retail business of the bank are not allocated to the retail unit and reported at the corporate center level. When this was obvious outside-in, we reallocated these positions and included them in non-staff costs and loan loss provisions to assure consistency across sample banks.

For the Universal Banks sample, the segment reports do not show taxes at the level of retail units. To come to an after-tax measure of income, we use the effective average tax rate by country described in Appendix 26, p. 262. To calculate effective average income taxes, we multiply the pre-tax operating income defined above with the effec-

tive average tax rate estimated by Devereux et al. (2002).[466] Although taxes are reported in Bankscope, we use the above-described effective average tax rate to calculate
income taxes for the Savings Banks in order to be consistent across the two subsamples. We do not incorporate extra-ordinary or non-operating income and costs or any
other items from non-recurring events in the calculation of operating income.

Table IV-2: Calculation of operating income

Account Item	Description
Net Interest Income	Interest revenue less interest expense
+ Fee Income	Income from fees and commissions
+ Net Other Income	Other income less other expenses
Total Income	
Staff Expenses	
+ Non-Staff Expenses	Includes depreciation; possibly, corporate center costs were party reallocated to the retail units
- Total Cost	
- Loan Loss Provisions	Possibly includes reallocated corporate center loan loss provisions
- Income Taxes	Operating income before taxes multiplied by the effective average tax rate by country
= Operating Income after Taxes	

---

[466] Devereux et al. (2002) estimate an effective average tax rate for all countries in our sample except
for a number of the Asian countries. As data is missing for only 12 banks in five Asian countries,
we assume the effective average tax rate to equal the statutory tax rate in these countries. For a
definition of the effective average tax rate used, see Devereux and Griffith (2003).

IV.3.3   Model structure

IV.3.3.1   Basic model

In Section IV.2 we defined a value metrics framework that links shareholder value to the strategic and operational value drivers of a bank. To measure the impact of the identified value drivers for shareholder value, we formulate four regression models as illustrated in Figure IV-6.

Figure IV-6: Structure of regression models

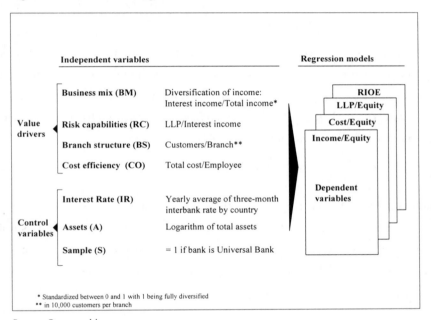

Source: Own graphic

We define the business mix (BM), the branch structure (BS), the cost efficiency (CO), and the risk capabilities (RC) as potential value drivers of a bank. With respect to the business mix, we estimate the degree of income diversification with the ratio of net interest income divided by total income. We standardize this ratio between 0 and 1 with 1 being fully diversified. Concerning the branch structure, we define the number of customers per branch, measured in 10,000 customers, as a critical parameter. As an indicator of the cost efficiency of a bank, we use the ratio of total cost per employee. At last, we estimate the risk capabilities of a bank with the ratio of LLP divided by interest income.

In addition, we include three control variables to measure the partial effect of the value drivers. We use the yearly average of the three-month interbank rate (IR) and the logarithm of total assets (A) to control for effects related to the interest rate level and bank size. A dummy variable for the sample (S) indicates differences between the Universal Banks and the Savings Banks sample.

We define four regression models to estimate the impact of these value drivers. Besides the impact on the bank's residual income, we measure the impact of the value drivers on the underlying income, cost, and risk structure as dependent variables. The first regression model estimates the impact of the value drivers on RIOE as a measure of value creation, as depicted in Equation IV-3.

$$RIOE = \alpha + \beta_1 BM + \beta_2 BS + \beta_3 CO + \beta_4 RC + \beta_5 IR + \beta_6 A + \beta_7 S + u \qquad \text{IV-3}$$

Instead of residual income, we use the RIOE as dependent variable in order to control for size effects. The independent variables are the above-described value drivers and control variables. Again, we use ratios to control for size effects and assure consistency across variables. $\beta_1, \beta_2, ..., \beta_7$ and α are parameters of the model, denoting the slope coefficient and the intercept respectively. u denotes the disturbance term.

Consistent with the model described in IV-3, we formulate three further regression models with the Income/Equity (IE), the Cost/Equity (CE), and the LLP/Equity (LE) as dependent variables. These regression models are described by the following equations.

$$IE = \alpha + \beta_1 BM + \beta_2 BS + \beta_3 CO + \beta_4 RC + \beta_5 IR + \beta_6 A + \beta_7 S + u \qquad \text{IV-4}$$

$$CE = \alpha + \beta_1 BM + \beta_2 BS + \beta_3 CO + \beta_4 RC + \beta_5 IR + \beta_6 A + \beta_7 S + u \qquad \text{IV-5}$$

$$LE = \alpha + \beta_1 BM + \beta_2 BS + \beta_3 CO + \beta_4 RC + \beta_5 IR + \beta_6 A + \beta_7 S + u \qquad \text{IV-6}$$

Extremes in the values of the dependent and independent variables might distort the true picture of the relationship between these variables. Before running the regression, we therefore winsorize the dependent and independent variables, i.e. we take the lower and upper five percent of the observations of the variables and replace them with the next value inwards from these extreme tails.

To account for heterogeneity across banks as well as time effects, we choose a panel data analysis. Panel data can provide more information on variability and efficiency as compared to conventional cross-sectional and time series data sets.[467]

Therefore, we slightly modify the empirical model by including subscripts to uniquely identify observations and reformulate Equation IV-3, as illustrated in Equation IV-7. The subscript i ($i=1, \ldots 139$) denotes the individual sample bank and subscript t ($t=1, \ldots, 6$) denotes time respectively.

$$
\begin{aligned}
RIOE_{it} = \alpha_{it} &+ \beta_{1_{it}} BM_{it} + \beta_{2_{it}} BS_{it} + \beta_{3_{it}} CO_{it} + \beta_{4_{it}} RC_{it} + \beta_{5_{it}} IR_{it} \\
&+ \beta_{6_{it}} A_{it} + \beta_{7_{it}} S_{it} + u_{it}
\end{aligned} \qquad \text{IV-7}
$$

$with\ i = 1,...,139$ denoting individual banks

$\quad t = 1,...,5$ denoting time, i.e. the observation year

According to Equation IV-7, we also reformulate Equation IV-4, IV-5, and IV-6. When discussing alternative model specifications in the next section, we focus on Equation IV-7. The model specifications for the three other models are analogous to the specifications discussed for Equation IV-7.

---

[467] For a detailed overview of the advantages of panel data analysis, see Baltagi (2001), pp. 5-7; Hsiao (2003), pp. 3-8.

IV.3.3.2 Model specification

The above-described model allows for both time- and bank-specific slopes and intercepts. Starting from this basic model, we specify four alternative model specifications.
The model specifications can be classified according to the assumptions on homogeneity of the specific parameters and the resulting parameter restrictions imposed.

The first and most restricted model is the *pooled regression model* that assumes common intercepts and common slopes for all banks and for all periods.[468] Accordingly,
observations are assumed independent and estimated using a linear model and OLS
techniques as described in Equation IV-8.[469]

$$RIOE_{it} = \alpha + \beta_1 BM_{it} + \beta_2 BS_{it} + \beta_3 CO_{it} + \beta_4 RC_{it} + \beta_5 IR_{it}$$
$$+ \beta_6 A_{it} + \beta_7 S_{it} + u_{it}$$

$$\text{IV-8}$$

The sample banks are heterogeneous in size, year of establishment and customer
branch. The model specification used in Equation IV-8 cannot reveal such firm
specific behavior. In addition, the assumption of constant intercepts and slopes across
all banks may not be reasonable for such heterogeneity. Releasing some of the
parameter restrictions, variable intercept models assume constant slope coefficients but
intercepts that vary over time or individual banks. We specify three panel-specific
variable intercept models referred to as the between effects, fixed effects, and random
effects models in the following.

The *between effects model* estimates the so-called between variation, i.e. the cross-
sectional information reflected in the changes between subjects. We specify the fixed
effects model as depicted in Equation IV-9:

---

[468] See Greene (2002), p. 285.

[469] See Gujarati (2003), p. 641.

$$RIOE_{it} = \alpha_t + \beta_1 BM_{it} + \beta_2 BS_{it} + \beta_3 CO_{it} + \beta_4 RC_{it} + \beta_5 IR_{it}$$
$$+ \beta_6 A_{it} + \beta_7 S_{it} + c_i + u_i$$

IV-9

The *fixed effects model* assumes that differences across units can be captured in differences in the constant term and introduces a group-specific constant term c_i to the regression model, as illustrated in Equation IV-10.[470]

$$RIOE_{it} = \alpha_t + \beta_1 BM_{it} + \beta_2 BS_{it} + \beta_3 CO_{it} + \beta_4 RC_{it} + \beta_5 IR_{it}$$
$$+ \beta_6 A_{it} + \beta_7 S_{it} + c_i + u_{it}$$

IV-10

Differences over time are captured by adding dummy variables to the model.[471] Limits to the fixed effects model exist when making out-of-sample predictions, since the fixed effects estimator is conditional on the sample in that c_i is not assumed to have a distribution, but is instead treated as fixed and estimable.

The *random effects model* assumes the individual specific effects as random variables that are randomly distributed across cross-sectional units like u.[472] This model is an appropriate specification if we are drawing N individuals randomly from a large population, since the individual effect is characterized as random and inference pertains to the population from which the sample was randomly drawn. The regression model can be formulated as a random effects model if regressors are uncorrelated with the unobserved effect. The approach estimates a weighted average of within and between variation, i.e. it accounts for both time and cross-sectional effects. Assuming no correlation between regressors and unobserved effects, we specify the random effects model as described in Equation IV-11.

---

[470] See Baltagi (2001), pp. 12-15; Greene (2002), pp. 287-288; Hsiao (2003), pp. 30-33.

[471] For this reason, the fixed effects approach is also referred to as the least squares dummy variable (LSDV) model. See Greene (2002), p. 287.

[472] See Baltagi (2001), pp. 15-20; Greene (2002), pp. 293-296; Hsiao (2003), pp. 34-38.

$$RIOE_{it} = \alpha + \beta_1 BM_{it} + \beta_2 BS_{it} + \beta_3 CO_{it} + \beta_4 RC_{it} + \beta_5 IR_{it}$$
$$+\beta_6 A_{it} + \beta_7 S_{it} + v_{it}$$

IV-11

$$where \ v_{it} = c_i + u_{it}$$

So which model best captures the data? The pooled regression model neglects any individual specific effects in the data. In the fixed effect model, the emphasis is on a separate intercept term for each cross-section, while in the random effect model the specific characteristic is normally distributed as a random variable. First, the choice of a specific model is based on the nature of the data. Furthermore, statistical tests can help to differentiate between the uses of the pooled regression, the fixed effects, or the random effects model.[473]

IV.3.3.3   Fit of model specifications

To test the fit of the above-discussed model specifications to our data set, we perform several tests on the fit of the model specifications and the efficiency of the coefficient estimates in the following. Based on the test results, we choose the model specification that best fits our data set and the defined model.

As described in the previous section, we conduct four different regression models with different parameter restrictions imposed. The summary results of the pooled regression, the between effects, the fixed effects, and the random effects model for the total sample are reported in Appendix 32, Appendix 33, Appendix 34, and Appendix 35, pp. 268-271.

First, we run a basic test on the fit of the specification for each of the regression models. The results of these tests are reported in Appendix 36, p. 272. Testing for potential

---

[473] See Baltagi (2001), pp. 20 and 52-69.

misspecification of the pooled regression, the between effects, and the fixed effects model, we run a basic F-test for joint parameter insignificance. The null hypothesis assumes that all parameters are jointly insignificant and thus implies, if valid, that the model is misspecified. The resulting test statistics for the pooled regression rejects the null hypothesis of joint parameter insignificance and thus does not show misspecification of the pooled regression model. The same holds for the between effects and the fixed effects model. To test the fit of the random effects model, we use a modified Wald test. The χ^2-statistic soundly rejects the null hypothesis in all cases. Like the alternative model specifications, the random effects model is well-specified and coefficient estimates are not jointly insignificant.

The reported R^2 for the four regression models and the different model specifications do not indicate the existence of multicollineartiy except for the regression on LLP/Equity. Reported R^2 are larger than 0.80 for all specifications of this regression model. Therefore, we look at the simple regressions for the independent variables. For the LLP/Interest Income, we find very high values of R^2. Since the high collinearity between LLP/Interest Income and LLP/Equity might result in statistically insignificant coefficients for the remaining regressors, we formulate an alternative regression model that excludes LLP/Interest Income. Hereafter, this model is called LLP/Equity (2).

Next, we run additional specification tests to discriminate and validate the four panel model specifications. The omission of the bank- and time-variant effects in the pooled regression model might lead to a bias in the resulting estimates. Next, we therefore test for the existence of individual effects. The results of these tests are illustrated in Appendix 37, p. 272. The pooled regression model assumes homogeneity of the parameters and only produces efficient results under this assumption. To test the validity of this restriction on the model parameters, we conduct an F-test for parameter homogeneity. Under the null hypothesis of strict parameter homogeneity the pooled regression model produces consistent and efficient estimates, whereas the within estimates will be inefficient. The resulting F-statistics soundly reject the null hypothesis of parameter homogeneity for all cases. Results therefore suggest that individual effects exist and the fixed effects model is preferred over the pooled regression model.

Finally, we conduct a Hausman test to choose between the fixed effects and the random effects model. The random effects model assumes that the unobserved effect is not correlated with the regressors and only yields increased efficiency under the absence of effect endogeneity. As reported in Appendix 38, p. 273, the Hausman statistics rejects the null hypothesis of effect exogeneity in all cases. Consequently, the fixed effects model dominates the random effects model.

Like in pure time series analysis, we also need to test for the existence of heteroscedasticity and serial correlation in the fixed effects model. The fixed effects model assumes homoscedastic regression disturbances and abstracts from serial correlation. Both assumptions might be too restrictive and lead to inefficient estimates. We therefore test for heteroscedasticity and serial correlation. We conduct an LM test to test for serial correlation in the residuals, as described in Appendix 39, p. 274. The resulting test statistics suggest rejecting the null hypothesis of the existence of both, AR1 and MA1 processes in the residuals. When running a modified Wald test for groupwise heteroscedasticity in the fixed effects model, the resulting test statistic soundly rejects the null hypothesis of groupwise heteroscedasticity in all cases, as described in Appendix 40, p. 274.

In summary, the results of the specification tests conducted suggest that the fixed effects model produces consistent and efficient coefficient estimates and dominates the pooled regression model as well as the random effects model in our case. We therefore focus on the fixed effects and between effects models in our analysis, thereby addressing different types of research questions. The fixed effects regression maximizes the explained variation within a panel group over time. For our analysis, this means that the fixed effects model looks at the drivers of the value creation of the individual sample banks over the observation period. The between effects model, in contrast, maximizes the explained variation between different panel groups, i.e. it compares the dependent variables between sample banks and examines potential variation. The between effects model thus rather presents a "competitor analysis" and, in our case, provides answers on the drivers of variations in value creation between different sample banks.

IV.4   Empirical results

IV.4.1   Descriptive statistics

The following section discusses the descriptive statistics of the dependent and independent variables of our model. We look at the RIOE ratio and the income, cost, and risk structure of our sample banks as well as the identified value drivers.

To give an impression of the size of the RIOE ratio, Table IV-3 shows the descriptive statistics of the performance spread for the Universal Banks, the Savings Banks, and the total sample.

Table IV-3: Descriptive statistics of RIOE by sample

(1998 – 2003, percent)

	Universal Banks	Savings Banks	Total Sample
N	120	636	657
Mean	7.10	-1.33	0.01
Median	5.79	-1.83	-1.36
Standard Deviation	12.83	5.31	7.69
Interquartile Range	12.68	6.55	7.36

Source: Own calculation

The mean RIOE is 0.01 percent for the total sample, with an even lower median value of -1.36 percent. Looking at each of the subsamples, the Universal Banks show a mean RIOE of 7.10 percent and thus a significantly higher performance spread than the Savings Banks with a mean RIOE of -1.33. Results for the Universal Banks sample show with a standard deviation of 12.83 a significantly wider dispersion than results for the Savings Banks sample with a standard deviation of 5.31. The same holds when looking at the interquartile ranges.

In summary, descriptive statistics indicate that the RIOE differs significantly for the two subsamples. While the RIOE of the retail units in the Universal Banks sample is on average 7.10 percent higher than the required cost of equity, the Savings Banks, on average, do not earn the cost of equity required by their shareholders.

Figure IV-7 illustrates the development of the performance spread over the observation period from 1998 to 2003. Results show a cyclical development of the RIOE with a median value ranging between 4.64 in 1999 and -4.60 in 2002. The interquartile range is relatively stable, but shows larger values in the peak years of 1999 and 2002.

Figure IV-7: Development of RIOE by year

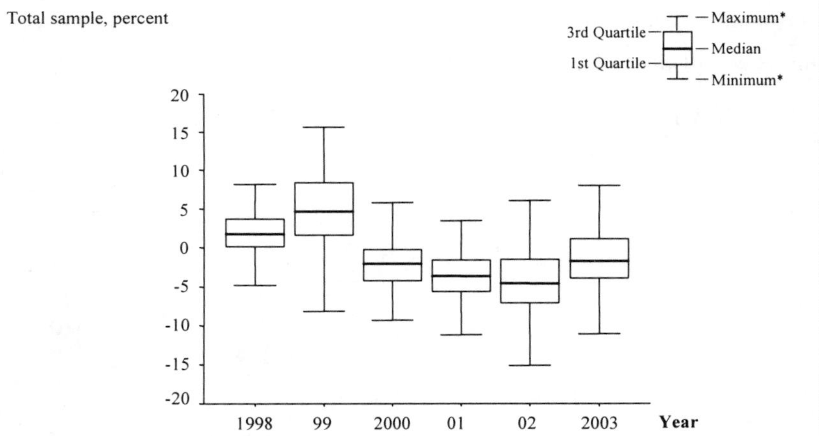

	1998	99	2000	01	02	2003
Median	1.84	4.64	-2.06	-3.68	-4.60	-1.71
Interquartile Range	3.62	6.73	4.14	4.16	5.73	5.11
N	118	121	130	131	132	124

* Outliers and extremes are excluded

Source: Own calculation

Appendix 31, p. 267, shows the development of the RIOE over time for each of the two subsamples. Both subsamples show significant volatility in the median values over the observation period. Interquartile ranges for the Savings Banks sample are again significantly lower than for the Universal Banks sample.

To give an impression of the characteristics of the variables in our model, we look at the descriptive statistics of the income, cost, and risk structure of the sample banks as well as the value drivers in the following.

Figure IV-8 illustrates the mean values of the dependent and independent variables for the Universal Banks, the Savings Banks, and the total sample. As already indicated by the performance spread for the total sample, the profitability of the Universal Banks with a mean ROE after taxes of 15.8 percent is significantly higher than the profitability of the savings banks with a mean ROE of 6.8 percent. Differences in the cost of equity are not significant and by definition only driven by regional scope because we estimate cost of equity based on industry betas by country.

Figure IV-8: Mean values of variables by sample

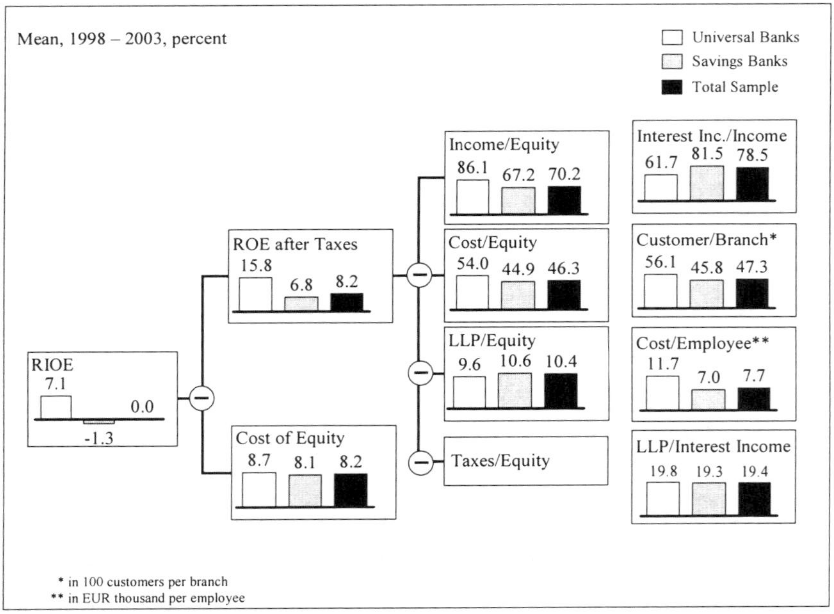

Source: Own calculation

With respect to the income structure, we observe, on average, a significantly higher ratio of income to equity of 86.1 percent for the Universal Banks compared to 67.2 percent for the Savings Banks. The retail units of Universal Banks, however, show also a higher ratio of cost to equity of 54.0 percent compared to 44.9 percent for the Savings Banks. The ratio of LLP to equity is slightly higher for the Savings Banks with 10.6 percent compared to 9.6 percent for the Universal Banks sample.

Looking at the mean values for the four value drivers, we observe significant differences in the business mix of Universal Banks and Savings Banks and a higher diversification of income for the Universal Banks. The branch structure differs between the two subsamples with, on average, 5,610 customers per branch for the Universal Banks and 4,580 customers per branch for the Savings Banks.

The cost efficiency is higher for the Savings Banks with average costs per employee of EUR 7,000 compared to EUR 11,700 for the Universal Banks. The risk capabilities do not differ significantly between the two subsamples. The ratio of LLP/Interest Income accounts, on average, for 19.8 percent for the Universal Banks and for 19.3 percent for the Savings Banks.

The mean values of the variables by year in Figure IV-9 show a decrease in the average RIOE over the observation period. The results indicate that this decrease is a combined result of a decreasing ROE after taxes and increasing cost of equity. Again, changes in cost of equity are by definition only driven by country specifics and macroeconomic trends, but not by bank individual drivers.

The decrease in the profitability is mainly the result of a reduction in the average ratio of Income/Equity from 74.3 percent in 1998 to 68.0 percent in 2003. We observe also a reduction in the Cost/Equity over time, which, however, does not compensate for the income reduction. The development of the ratio of LLP/Equity is very volatile over the observation period ranging from 4.1 percent to 15.7 percent.

The business mix measured by the degree of income diversification does not differ significantly between 1989 and 2003. The branch structure is relatively constant over time except for a sharp increase of the average number of customers per branch in 2003. However, this increase might also be the result of changes in the sample composition from 2002 to 2003.

Figure IV-9: Mean values of variables over time

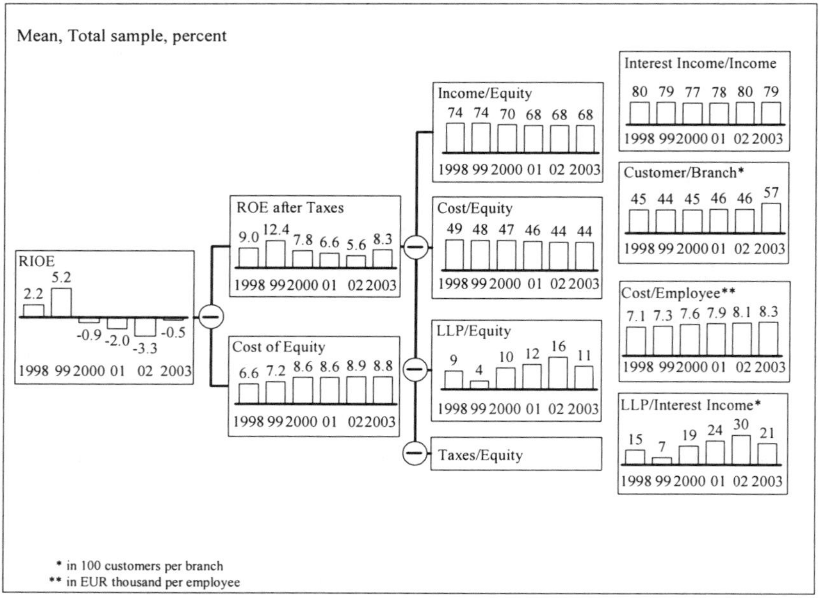

Source: Own calculation

The cost efficiency continuously worsens over the observation period with costs per employee increasing from EUR 7,100 in 1998 to EUR 8,300 in 2003. With respect to the average ratio of LLP/Interest Income, we observe high volatility ranging from 7.1 percent and 29.5 percent between 1998 and 2003.

IV.4.2   Regression results

IV.4.2.1   Business mix

As discussed in Section IV.3.3.3, we prefer the between effects and the fixed effects model to alternative model specifications in the case of our analysis. The summary results for the between effects and fixed effects model are reported in Appendix 33, p. 269, and Appendix 34, p. 270. In the following sections, we discuss the impact of the value drivers on the RIOE and the income, cost, and risk structure of our sample banks. Therefore, we look at the regression coefficients of the four regression models for each value driver separately.

Table IV-4 shows the fixed effects and between effects regression coefficients for the business mix. Looking at the results for the fixed effects regression, we analyze the impact of a diversification of income, i.e. the decrease of the interest income relative to total income, for the individual sample banks over the observation period.

Table IV-4: Regression results for business mix

(748 observations, 135 groups)

Variable	Fixed Effects		Between Effects	
	Coef.	*P>(t)*	*Coef.*	*P>(t)*
Income/Equity	-0.58	0.00	0.97	0.00
Cost/Equity	-0.20	0.00	0.89	0.00
LLP/Equity (2)	-0.39	0.00	0.11	0.04
RIOE	-0.14	0.00	-0.03	0.36

Source: Stata, own calculation

The diversification of income reduces the cost and risk of our sample banks as shown by the negative and statistically significant coefficients for Cost/Equity and LLP/Equity. This outcome is not intuitive in the first place, but might be explained by the fact that the income type that is diversified with new income types is not as cost-intensive and implies lower risks. Given the differences in the involved costs and risks between fee income and interest income, this is a valid explanation.

The coefficient for Income/Equity is negative and statistically significant. For our sample banks, a diversification of income obviously reduces total income. An explanation might be that banks are not able to fully substitute the reduced (interest) income by other income types in the short term.

The overall effect of income diversification on value creation is negative, with a coefficient for RIOE of -0.14 that is statistically significant. Thus, overall, the positive effects on costs and risk do not compensate for the negative effects on income.

For the results of the between effects model, the picture is different. We find a positive and large value for the regression coefficient of 0.97 for Income/Equity. Diversified banks thus show a higher ratio of Income/Equity than other banks, which might be driven by cross-selling effects between the income types. Yet, the higher Income/Equity ratio can also be explained by the higher share of fee income that is less equity-intensive than interest income.

Diversified banks, however, also show much higher Cost/Equity and slightly higher LLP/Equity as indicated by the statistically significant coefficients of 0.89 and 0.11 respectively. One reason for higher administrative costs might be complexity costs associated with a more diversified business mix. One explanation for the weak increase in risk might be that risk capabilities are higher for specialized players and decrease with the diversification of income.

The overall effect on RIOE is not statistically significant for the between effects regression. Adding the statistically significant effects for the income, cost, and risk structure results in a net effect of -0.03 and thus does not reveal a clear picture either. In summary, the competitive advantage of a diversified business mix does not seem to be significant for our sample banks. This outcome might be a result of the dominance of the savings banks in our sample.

For a better understanding of this outcome, we next look at the results for each of the subsamples, as shown in Table IV-5.

Table IV-5: Between effects results for business mix by subsample

Variable	Universal Banks*		Savings Banks**	
	Coef.	P>(t)	Coef.	P>(t)
Income/Equity	1.35	0.00	0.61	0.01
Cost/Equity	1.01	0.00	0.78	0.00
LLP/Equity (2)	0.23	0.01	-0.09	0.30
RIOE	0.08	0.37	-0.13	0.00

* 112 observations, 29 groups
** 636 observations, 106 groups

Source: Stata, own calculation

As for the total sample, the RIOE coefficient for the Universal Banks is not statistically significant. For the Savings Banks, we find a negative and statistically significant coefficient. In sum, the positive effects on the income structure do not compensate for the negative effects on the cost structure. A higher diversification of income thus does not translate into higher value creation for the Savings Banks. For the Universal Banks, the impact of the business mix on value creation remains unclear.

IV.4.2.2 Branch structure

Next, we look at the results for the branch structure and examine the impact of an increase in the number of customers per branch on the income, cost, and risk structure as well as on overall value creation.

The increase of customers per branch does not show a statistically significant effect on income. We thus find neither evidence for an increase in income driven by newly acquired customers nor for a decrease in income that might result from lower customer coverage for a growing number of customers per branch.

Table IV-6: Regression results for branch structure

(748 observations, 135 groups)

Variable	Fixed Effects		Between Effects	
	Coef.	P>(t)	Coef.	P>(t)
Income/Equity	-0.04	0.56	0.07	0.25
Cost/Equity	-0.05	0.06	0.04	0.36
LLP/Equity (2)	0.10	0.00	-0.02	0.31
RIOE	0.01	0.59	0.03	0.03

Source: Stata, own calculation

From an economic perspective, we expect the changes in the branch structure to significantly affect the cost structure. As expected, we find a significant and negative coefficient for the Cost/Equity ratio, which indicates the existence of scale effects. With a coefficient value of -0.05, however, the effect on the cost structure is only weak.

For the risk structure, we find evidence of a slight increase in the risk costs given the significant and positive coefficient sign for LLP/Equity. One potential explanation might be that the time spent on the assessment of the risk profile for a single customer decreases with an increasing number of customers per branch. Yet, this presumption and the underlying economic rationale are only vague.

The overall effect on value creation is not clear since we do not find a statistically significant coefficient for the RIOE. The fixed effects results for the two subsamples reported in Appendix 41, p. 275, do not show statistically significant results either.

The between effects results do not reveal differences in the income, cost, or risk structure for banks with differing branch structure. None of the coefficients for Income/Equity, Cost/Equity, and LLP/Equity is statistically significant. Surprisingly, we find evidence for a positive effect on value creation with a statistically significant coefficient for RIOE of 0.03. Looking at the between effects results for each of the subsamples shown in Appendix 42, p. 276, we find neither statistical significance for the effect on RIOE nor for the effects on the income, cost, and risk structure.

The above-described results for the fixed effects and between effects model do not provide evidence for the impact of the branch structure, measured by the ratio of Customers/Branch, on the value creation of our sample banks. To test the robustness of this result, we conduct further regression analyses using alternative parameters of the branch structure of banks.

First, we use the squared ratio of Customer/Branch as a value driver in our analysis. If an optimal branch size exists, the square of this ratio will better describe the relationship between the branch structure and value. As described in Appendix 43, p. 277, the regression results using the squared variable do not provide any evidence for the impact of the branch structure on value.

Furthermore, we approximate the branch structure of banks with alternative measures such as the employees per branch, the customers per employee, and the assets per customers. The regression results do not show statistical or economical significance for any of these potential drivers, as reported in Appendix 43. These alternative measures thus do not provide evidence for the impact of the branch structure on the value creation of banks either.

In summary, we do not find evidence for a correlation between the branch structure and the value creation of banks. The results therefore suggest that a direct impact of the branch structure on value does not exist and that potential implications for the value creation of banks are driven by the interdependence of the branch structure and other value drivers.

IV.4.2.3   Cost efficiency

Table IV-7 summarizes the results for the impact of cost efficiency on the value creation of our sample banks and the underlying financial indicators.

Table IV-7: Regression results for cost efficiency

(748 observations, 135 groups)

Variable	Fixed Effects		Between Effects	
	Coef.	*P>(t)*	*Coef.*	*P>(t)*
Income/Equity	-1.44	0.00	0.86	0.41
Cost/Equity	0.49	0.07	2.58	0.00
LLP/Equity (2)	0.55	0.12	0.21	0.56
RIOE	-1.30	0.00	-0.96	0.00

Source: Stata, own calculation

As expected, an increase in the costs per employee has a negative effect on the Cost/Equity ratio with a significant and positive coefficient. However, the value of the coefficient and its statistical significance are not as high as one might expect.

On the other hand, we find a highly negative and significant coefficient for the ratio of Income/Equity. The economic reason for this strong impact of the cost efficiency on the income structure is unclear. Looking at the impact of cost efficiency on risk, the coefficients for LLP/Equity do not show statistical significance.

Overall, we find a strong impact of the cost efficiency on the RIOE with a significant coefficient of -1.30. As expected, the increase in the costs per employee destroys value. This outcome seems to be robust, since the results for the Universal Banks and Savings Banks subsamples do not differ significantly from the above-discussed results for the total sample, as shown in Appendix 41, p. 275, and Appendix 42, p. 276.

The results for the between effects regression reveal a different picture. Differences in the cost efficiency explain variations in the cost structure between banks, as indicated by the significant coefficient for Cost/Equity of 2.58. We thus find banks with higher costs per employee to have a significantly higher ratio of Cost/Equity. For the income and risk structure, the coefficient results are not statistically significant. This outcome is intuitive from an economical standpoint since we do not expect differences in the cost efficiency to explain variations in the income or risk structure across banks.

Table IV-8: Between effects results for cost efficiency by subsample

Variable	Universal Banks*		Savings Banks**	
	Coef.	P>(t)	Coef.	P>(t)
Income/Equity	-1.65	0.34	4.11	0.00
Cost/Equity	0.89	0.52	4.66	0.00
LLP/Equity (2)	-0.24	0.69	0.30	0.55
RIOE	-1.43	0.03	-0.66	0.01

* 112 observations, 29 groups
** 636 observations, 106 groups

Source: Stata, own calculation

Overall, the coefficient for RIOE is significant and negative with a value of -0.96. The findings suggest that banks with higher cost efficiency create more value than other banks. This also holds when looking at the between effects results for the Universal Banks and Savings Banks subsample shown in Table IV-8.

However, differences between the two subsamples exist concerning the impact of cost efficiency on the income, cost, and risk structure between the Universal Banks and the Savings Banks. The effects of cost efficiency on the cost, income, and risk structure of the Universal Banks are not statistically significant. For the Savings Banks, the effects on the Income/Equity and the Cost/Equity ratio are both significant and very strong. The strong effect on the cost structure is economically intuitive, while the effect on the income structure is not. The positive effect on income indicates the existence of interdependences between higher cost per employee and other factors that affect the income structure.

To get a better understanding of these factors, we next look at the staff and non-staff costs per employee and their impact on value separately, as reported in Table IV-9.

Table IV-9: Regression results for cost efficiency – Staff vs. Non-staff costs

(727 observations, 131 groups)

	Fixed Effects				Between Effects			
	Staff Cost/ Employee		Non-staff Cost/ Employee		Staff Cost/ Employee		Non-staff Cost/ Employee	
Variable	*Coef.*	*P>(t)*	*Coef.*	*P>(t)*	*Coef.*	*P>(t)*	*Coef.*	*P>(t)*
Income/Equity	-3.86	0.00	1.66	0.06	-3.61	0.08	4.18	0.01
Cost/Equity	-2.29	0.00	4.21	0.00	0.18	0.91	3.52	0.01
LLP/Equity (2)	0.34	0.67	1.62	0.04	-1.35	0.06	0.60	0.30
RIOE	-1.08	0.01	-1.74	0.00	-2.01	0.00	0.90	0.04

Source: Stata, own calculation

One economic rationale that might explain the positive effect of the cost efficiency on the income structure relates to the staff costs. An increase of the staff costs per employee is potentially associated with an increase in the staff quality and thus results in growing income. Looking at the results for the staff cost per employee, however, we do not find evidence for this hypothesis. Moreover, the results suggest a laterally reversed interrelation between Staff Cost/Employee and Income/Equity. In addition, the results for the fixed effects and the between effects model suggest that a higher ratio of Non-staff Cost/Employee increases income. From an economic perspective, this outcome is not intuitive at all. An isolated analysis of the staff and non-staff costs accordingly does not provide an economic explanation for the observed impact on income.

With respect to RIOE, both models suggest that a higher Staff Cost/Employee ratio reduces the value creation of banks. This outcome is contrary to economic theory, which expects the value creation in a service business such as banking to increase with higher quality of staff. As expected, the fixed effects results provide evidence for a negative effect of higher Non-staff Cost/Employee on value. The between effects, however, show a positive effect and thus suggest that higher Non-staff Cost/Employee create value. In summary, the evidence found for the staff vs. non-staff costs is for large parts inconsistent with economic theory. One reason for the controversial results might be the limited reliability of the data on the staff and non-staff costs reported in the segment reporting and Bankscope.

IV.4.2.4   Risk capabilities

Table IV-10 shows the regression results for the impact of the risk capabilities on value creation and the underlying income, cost, and risk structure of our sample banks.

As expected, the coefficient for LLP/Equity is significant and of positive sign. This outcome is economically intuitive and suggests that an increase in the ratio of LLP/Interest Income increases the LLP/Equity of our sample banks. As discussed in Section IV.3.3.3, the results for the univariate regressions of LLP/Interest Income on LLP/Equity report the LLP/Interest Income to explain more than 80 percent of the variation of LLP/Equity for all model specifications and thus support this result.

The coefficient for Income/Equity is not statistically significant and suggests that changes in the risk capabilities do not affect the income structure of our sample banks. Unexpectedly, the regression results show a significant coefficient for Cost/Equity. The ratio of Cost/Equity for our sample banks decreases with an increase in the LLP/Interest Income. This outcome, however, does not necessarily result from an eco-nomic impact of the risk capabilities on the cost structure. One potential explanation of this effect is the use of the loan loss provisions to smooth earnings in a given year. To smooth out earnings over time, a bank might report higher LLP for years with lower costs and vice versa. Smoothing effects thus can explain the regression coefficient for Cost/Equity.

Table IV-10: Regression results for risk capabilities

(748 observations, 135 groups)

Variable	Fixed Effects		Between Effects	
	Coef.	P>(t)	Coef.	P>(t)
Income/Equity	-0.01	0.56	0.01	0.93
Cost/Equity	-0.08	0.00	-0.15	0.20
LLP/Equity (1)	0.52	0.00	0.49	0.00
RIOE	-0.28	0.00	-0.16	0.00

Source: Stata, own calculation

Overall, the regression coefficient for RIOE is negative and statistically significant. In summary, an increase in the risk capabilities of a bank, measured by the ratio of LLP/Interest Income, creates value.

The results of the between effects regression provide further evidence for this outcome. As expected, the regression coefficients for Income/Equity and Cost/Equity are not statistically significant. The regression coefficient for LLP/Equity is significant and positive. Therefore, differing risk capabilities across banks can explain differences in the risk structure of these banks. The overall effect on value creation is also significant, i.e. banks with higher risk capabilities create more value than other banks.

The regression results for each of the two subsamples do not differ significantly from the results for the total sample, as shown for the fixed effects model in Appendix 41, p. 275, and for the between effects model in Appendix 42, p. 276.

IV.4.3   Discussion

The following section summarizes the assessment of the four potential value drivers of bank shareholder value. Figure IV-10 gives a review of the empirical evidence found concerning the impact of the business mix, the branch structure, the cost efficiency, and the risk capabilities on value.

Figure IV-10: Overview of regression results

		Coefficient
		(+) Positive sign
		(-) Negative sign
		~ Not stat. significant

	Variable	Fixed Effects / Between Effects results				Impact on value
		Income	Cost	Risk	RIOE	
Business mix	Diversification of income	(-) / (+)	(-) / (+)	(-) / (+)	(-) / ~	?
Branch Structure	Customers/Branch	~ / ~	(-) / ~	(+) / ~	~ / (+)	(✓)
Cost Efficiency	Cost/Employee	(-) / ~	(+) / (+)	~ / ~	(-) / (-)	✓
Risk Capabilities	LLP/Interest Income	~ / ~	(-) / ~	(+) / (+)	(-) / (-)	✓

Source: Own graphic

The study findings on the *business mix* as a driver of bank value are controversial. The results of the fixed effects regression suggest that a diversification of income reduces value creation at least in the short-term. The between effects regression does not provide a clear picture of the impact of the business mix on value. While the coefficient for RIOE is statistically insignificant, we find significant coefficient values for the income, cost, and risk structure of the sample banks. Results suggest that a diversified business mix increases income, but also increases the costs and risks of a bank. To summarize, the sign of the overall effect on value creation remains unclear.

The results of the between effects model suggest that the *branch structure* is an important factor to explain variations in the value creation across banks. In contrast, the fixed effects regression does not provide any evidence that changes in the branch structure of the sample banks have an impact on their value creation. We do find, however, evidence of cost reductions for an increasing number of customers per branch, which indicates the existence of scale effects. To test the robustness of this outcome, we look at alternative parameters of the branch structure of banks and investigate their impact on value. The regression results for these parameters do not provide any evidence of the impact of the branch structure on value either. Consequently, the study findings suggest that the branch structure has no direct impact on value.

The impact of the *cost efficiency* on the value creation of the sample banks is more obvious. We find a statistically significant and negative coefficient sign for the RIOE for both, the fixed effects and the between effects model. The results therefore strongly suggest that an increase in cost efficiency creates value for our sample banks. In addition, both specification models show a significant impact of cost efficiency on the cost structure. Isolated analyses of the impact of staff cost vs. non-staff cost does not yield valuable insights, which might be a result of low data quality for these variables.

For the *risk capabilities*, we find a strong impact on RIOE for the fixed effects and the between effects results. Both models also provide evidence for a strong effect of the risk capabilities on the risk structure as expected. To sum up, the results suggest that improvements in the risk capabilities of a bank create value.

In summary, we find strong evidence for the cost efficiency and risk capabilities as drivers of bank shareholder value. For the business mix and the branch structure, results are ambiguous. The regression coefficients either do not show statistical signifi-cance or do not make sense from an economic standpoint. For that reason, the data set used in our analysis does not allow a conclusion to be drawn about the impact of the business mix and the branch structure on value. Further research is therefore required into these potential drivers of bank shareholder value.

IV.5   Conclusions

This paper provides empirical evidence on the drivers of shareholder value of retail banks. We look at a sample of 139 retail players over the observation period between 1998 and 2003 and use a unique set of accounting information and structural data of these banks to study the drivers of bank value. We identify the business mix, the branch structure, the cost efficiency, and the risk capabilities as potential value drivers and apply a panel data analysis to examine their impact on the value creation as well as the underlying income, cost, and risk structure.

The study findings suggest that the cost efficiency and the risk capabilities of a bank are relevant drivers of shareholder value for our sample banks. Concerning the business mix and the branch structure, the empirical evidence for our sample banks is ambiguous.

Contrary to expectations, the regression results for the business mix imply that a diversification of income of an individual sample bank destroys value, at least in the short-term. In addition, differing business mixes do not explain variations in the value creation across banks. Regression results for the underlying income, cost, and risk structure of the banks are controversial as well. Therefore, we cannot draw a conclusion about the value creation potential of the business mix of a bank based on our bank sample.

The empirical evidence on the branch structure indicates that differences in the branch structure explain variations in the value creation of our sample banks. Yet, we do not find evidence for the value impact of changes in the branch structure of individual sample banks over time. Therefore, we conclude that the branch structure of a bank has no direct impact on value and that potential value implications are rather driven by the interdependence of the branch structure and other value drivers.

The study is a first step towards a better understanding of the empirical drivers of shareholder value in banking. However, the complete decryption of the DNA of shareholder value creation of banks will require further research in the future. The scope of our study thus might be extended in several dimensions.

One dimension is to break down the value drivers studied in this paper to a more operational level. Such a research design, however, must draw on internal bank data. While it is unrealistic to perform alike studies across competing banks, the comparison of value drivers across bank branches of a single bank would be a possible research design that promises interesting insights into the bottom-level drivers of shareholder value. Based on the empirical evidence provided by such studies, implications for bank management can be derived and transformed into actionable and thus valuable advice for bank managers.

References

Adolf, Rüdiger, Cramer, Jürgen, and Ollmann, Michael (1989): Die Bewertung von Kreditinstituten – ein Modell zur Ermittlung des Ertragswertes I/II, in: Die Bank, Vol. 28, Iss. 9/10, pp. 485-492 and 546-554.

Amely, Tobias (1997): Shareholder Value als strategisches Steuerungsinstrument?, in: Sparkasse, Vol. 114, Iss. 6, pp. 227-281.

Annema, André and Goedhart, Marc H. (2003): Better Betas, in: McKinsey on Finance Iss. 6, pp. 10-13.

Arnsfeld, Torsten (1998): Deduktion einer grenzkostenorientierten Eigenkapital-kostenkalkulation für Banken, Frankfurt am Main.

Arnsfeld, Torsten and Gehrke, Norman (2001): Unternehmenswertsteuerung in dyna-mischen Lebenszyklen von Banken, in: Die Bank, Vol. 40, Iss. 7, pp. 492-496.

Baltagi, Badi H. (2001): Econometric Analysis of Panel Data, 2nd edition, Chichester.

Barfield, Richard (1998a): Putting on a Performance, in: The Banker, Vol. 148, Iss. 864, pp. 66-68.

Barfield, Richard (1998b): The True Test of Performance, in: The Banker, Vol. 148, Iss. 869, pp. 26-27.

Becker, Dirk (1999): Bewertung von Bankakquisitionen unter Einbeziehung von Zu-sammenschlusseffekten, Berlin.

Becker, Gernot M. (1996): Shareholder-Value-Analysis gewinnt an Bedeutung, in: Bankmagazin, Vol. 44, Iss. 2, pp. 22-27.

Becker, Gernot M. (1997): Implikationen des Shareholder-Value-Managements für das Kreditgeschäft, in: Die Bank, Vol. 36, Iss. 2, pp. 106-111.

Behm, Ulrich (1994): Shareholder-value und Eigenkapitalkosten von Banken, Bern et al.

Bernard, Victor L. (1995): The Feltham-Ohlson Framework: Implications for Empiricists, in: Contemporary Accounting Research, Vol. 11, Iss. 2, pp. 733-747.

Berndt, Holger (2002): Eckpunkte für die Weiterentwicklung der Sparkassen und Landesbanken, in: Zeitschrift für das gesamte Kreditwesen, Vol. 55, Iss. 15, pp. 730-734.

Biddle, Gary C., Bowen, Robert M., and Wallace, James S. (1997): Does EVA Beat Earnings? Evidence on Associations with Stock Returns and Firm Values, in: Journal of Accounting and Economics, Vol. 24, Iss. 3, pp. 301-336.

Bodmer, Adriana (2001): Value based management für Banken, Bern, Stuttgart, and Vienna.

Brealey, Richard A. and Myers, Stewart C. (2000): Principles of Corporate Finance, 6th edition, Boston et al.

Bremke, Kirsten and Bußmann, Johannes (2000): Ansätze zur risikobasierten Gesamtbanksteuerung, in: Die Bank, Vol. 39, Iss. 2, pp. 128-133.

Brunner, Christoph (1996): Value based management – zentrale Herausforderung der Bankführung, in: Geiger, Hans (Ed.): Schweizerisches Bankwesen im Umbruch, Bern, Stuttgart, and Vienna, pp. 81-96.

Brüning, Jan-Bernd and Hoffjan, Andreas (1997): Gesamtbanksteuerung mit Risk-Return-Kennzahlen, in: Die Bank, Vol. 36, Iss. 6, pp. 362-369.

Buba (2002a): Bankenstatistik Februar 2002, Deutsche Bundesbank, Statistisches Beiheft zum Monatsbericht 1, pp. 1-112.

Buba (2002b): Rechnungslegungsstandards für Kreditinstitute im Wandel, Deutsche Bundesbank, Monatsbericht, June 2002, pp. 41-57.

Buba (2003a): Die Ertragslage der deutschen Kreditinstitute im Jahr 2002, Deutsche Bundesbank, Monatsbericht, September 2003, pp. 15-43.

Buba (2003b): Ertragslage und Finanzierungsverhältnisse deutscher Unternehmen im Jahr 2001, Deutsche Bundesbank, Monatsbericht, April 2003, pp. 49-71.

Böhme, Markus (1997): Die Zukunft der Universalbank: Strategie, Organisation und Shareholder Value im Informationszeitalter, Wiesbaden.

Börner, Christoph J. and Lowis, Stephan (1997): Ein Rahmenmodell für die Umsetzung des Shareholder-value-Konzepts bei Banken, in: Mitteilungen und Berichte, Institut für Bankwirtschaft und Bankrecht an der Universität zu Köln, Vol. 28, Iss. 77, pp. 87-133.

Büschgen, Hans E. (1998): Bankbetriebslehre: Bankgeschäfte und Bankmanagement, 5th revised and extended edition, Wiesbaden.

Cates, David C. (1991): Performance Measurement: Welcome to the Revolution, in: Banking Strategies, Vol. 73, Iss. 3, pp. 51-56.

Coenenberg, Adolf G. and Salfeld, Rainer (2003): Wertorientierte Unternehmensführung: Vom Strategieentwurf zur Implementierung, Stuttgart.

Copeland, Thomas E., Koller, Timothy M., and Murrin, Jack (1990): Valuation: Measuring and Managing the Value of Companies, 1st edition, New York.

Copeland, Thomas E., Koller, Timothy M., and Murrin, Jack (2000): Valuation: Measuring and Managing the Value of Companies, 3rd edition, New York.

Copeland, Thomas E. and Weston, Fred J. (1992): Financial Theory and Corporate Policy, 3rd edition, Reading et al.

Courteau, Lucie, Kao, Jennifer, and Richardson, Gordon D. (2000): The Equivalence of Dividend, Cash Flows and Residual Earnings Approaches to Equity Valuation Employing Ideal Terminal Value Expressions, Working Paper, February 3, 2000.

Damodaran, Aswath (1994): Damodaran on Valuation: Security Analysis for Investment and Corporate Finance, New York.

Damodaran, Aswath (2004): Valuing Financial Service Firms, Stern Business School, New York Univ., http://pages.stern.nyu.edu/~adamodar/New_Home_Page/papers.

Dechow, Patricia M., Hutton, Amy P., and Sloan, Richard G. (1999): An Empirical Assessment of the Residual Income Valuation Model, in: Journal of Accounting and Economics, Vol. 26, Iss. 1, pp. 1-34.

Devereux, Michael P. and Griffith, Rachel (2003): Evaluating Tax Policy for Location Decisions, in: International Tax and Public Finance, Vol. 10, Iss. 2, pp. 107-126.

Devereux, Michael P., Griffith, Rachel, and Klemm, Alexander (2002): Corporate Income Tax Reforms and International Tax Competition, in: Economic Policy, Vol. 35, Iss. 10, pp. 451-495.

Dombret, Andreas and Bender, Oliver (2001): Kapitalmarktorientierte Bewertung von Banken in der Praxis, in: Hummel, Detlev and Breuer, Rolf E. (Eds.): Handbuch Europäischer Kapitalmarkt, Wiesbaden, pp. 323-332.

Drukarczyk, Jochen (1995): DCF-Methode und Ertragswertmethode – einige klärende Anmerkungen, in: Die Wirtschaftsprüfung, Vol. 48, Iss. 10, pp. 329-334.

Fama, Eugene F. (1970): Efficient Capital Markets: A Review of Theory and Empirical Work, in: Journal of Finance, Vol. 25, Iss. 2, pp. 383-417.

Fama, Eugene F. (1991): Efficient Capital Markets II, in: Journal of Finance, Vol. 46, Iss. 5, pp. 1575-1617.

Faust, Martin (2002): Bestimmung der Eigenkapitalkosten im Rahmen der wertorientierten Unternehmenssteuerung von Kreditinstituten, Marburg.

Feltham, Gerald A. and Ohlson, James A. (1995): Valuation and Clean Surplus Accounting for Operating and Financial Activities, in: Contemporary Accounting Research, Vol. 11, Iss. 2, pp. 689-731.

Fernández, Pablo (2002): Valuation Methods and Shareholder Value Creation, San Diego.

Fiordelisi, Franco (2002): Shareholder Value and the Clash in Performance Measurement: Are Banks Special?, Working Paper at the University of Wales Bangor.

Flannery, Marc J. and James, Christopher M. (1984): The Effect of Interest Rate Changes on the Common Stock Returns of Financial Institutions, in: Journal of Finance, Vol. 39, Iss. 4, pp. 1141-1153.

Francis, Jennifer, Olsson, Per, and Oswald, Dennis R. (2000): Comparing the Accuracy and Explainability of Dividend, Free Cash Flow, and Abnormal Earnings Equity Value Estimates, in: Journal of Accounting Research, Vol. 38, Iss. 1, pp. 45-70.

Frankel, Richard and Lee, Charles M. C. (1998): Accounting Valuation, Market Expectation, and Cross-sectional Stock Returns, in: Journal of Accounting and Economics, Vol. 25, Iss. 3, pp. 283-319.

Gebhardt, Günther and Daske, Holger (2004): Zukunftsorientierte Bestimmung von Kapitalkosten für die Unternehmensbewertung, Working Paper Series: Finance & Accounting, Goethe-Universität, Frankfurt am Main, No. 132, September 2004.

Gebhardt, Günther, Reichardt, Rolf, and Wittenbrink, Carsten (2002): Accounting for Financial Instruments in the Banking Industry, Working Paper Series: Finance & Accounting, Goethe-Universität, Frankfurt am Main, No. 95, November 2002.

Geltinger, Andreas (2003): Unternehmensbewertung: allgemeine Grundsätze und Besonderheiten bei der Bewertung und wertorientierten Steuerung von Banken, Stuttgart.

Goedhart, Marc H., Koller, Timothy M., and Williams, Zane D. (2002): The Real Cost of Equity, McKinsey on Finance, Iss. 5, pp. 11-15.

Goldman Sachs (2001): The Changing Structure of Banking in Germany: Ripples from the Public Sector, Goldman Sachs, Equity and Fixed Income Research Europe.

Greene, William H. (2002): Econometric Analysis, 5th edition, New Jersey.

Gujarati, Damodar N. (2003): Basic Econometrics, 4th edition, New York.

Hamoir, Olivier et al. (2002): Europe's Banks: Verging on merging, in: The McKinsey Quarterly, Vol. 39, Iss. 3, pp. 117-125.

Henzler, Herbert (2003): Werte von Innen, Financial Times Deutschland, July 16, 2003, p. 30.

Hiller, Christian von and Fehr, Benedikt (2005): Werben um die Gunst der Finanzmärkte, Frankfurter Allgemeine Zeitung, Iss. 16, January 20, 2005, p. 18.

Hsiao, Cheng (2003): Analysis of Panel Data, 2nd edition, Cambridge.

Höhmann, Kai (1998): Shareholder-Value von Banken, Wiesbaden.

Hörter, Steffen (1996): Das Shareholder-Value-Konzept: ein Steuerungsinstrument für Banken?, in: Zeitschrift für das gesamte Kreditwesen, Vol. 49, Iss. 4, pp. 146-148.

Hörter, Steffen (1998): Shareholder Value-orientiertes Bank-Controlling, Sternenfels and Berlin.

Hörter, Steffen (2000): Shareholder Value: Changing the Face of the European Financial Industry, in: Schuster, Leo (Ed.): Shareholder Value Management in Banks, New York, pp. 13-35.

Jagannathan, Ravi and McGrattan, Zhenyu (1995): The CAPM Debate, in: Federal Reserve Bank of Minneapolis: Quarterly Review, Vol. 19, Iss. 4, pp. 2-17.

Johnson, Hazel J. (1996): The Bank Valuation Handbook: A Market-based Approach to Valuing a Bank, 2nd edition, Chicago, London, and Singapore.

Kendall, Maurice G. (1953): The Analysis of Economic Time Series, Part I: Prices, in: Journal of the Royal Statistical Society, Vol. 116, Iss. 1, pp. 11-34.

Kennedy, Christopher (1999): Shareholder Value in europäischen Banken, in: Die Bank, Vol. 38, Iss. 4, pp. 224-227.

Kirsten, Dirk W. (1995): Value-based-management – Schlüssel zum strategischen Erfolg, in: Die Bank, Vol. 34, Iss. 11, pp. 672-676.

Kirsten, Dirk W. (2000): Das bankspezifische Shareholder-Value-Konzept: Anwendbarkeit und Konkretisierung für deutsche Kreditinstitute, Wiesbaden.

Koch, Thorsten (2002): Bewertung von Bankakquisitionen, Frankfurt am Main.

Krag, Joachim (1988): Die Bewertungsprivilegien der Kreditinstitute, in: Zeitschrift für das gesamte Kreditwesen, Vol. 41, Iss. 9, pp. 18-19.

Krumnow, Jürgen (2001): Externe Rechnungslegung von Banken – internationale Standards für den europäischen Kapitalmarkt, in: Hummel, Detlev and Breuer, Rolf E. (Eds.): Handbuch Europäischer Kapitalmarkt, Wiesbaden, pp. 175-205.

Kunowski, Stefan (2002): Bewertung von Kreditinstituten, Munich.

Kümmel, Axel Tibor (1995): Bewertung von Kreditinstituten nach dem Shareholder-Value-Ansatz: unter besonderer Berücksichtigung des Zinsänderungsrisikos, Berlin.

Lee, Charles M. C. (1999): Accounting-based Valuation: Impact on Business Practices and Research, in: Accounting Horizons, Vol. 13, Iss. 4, pp. 413-423.

Leemputte, Patrick J. (1989): Maximizing Shareholder Value, in: Bank Administration, Vol. 65, Iss. 6, pp. 16-22.

Lehar, Alfred et al. (1998): Risikoadjustierte Performancemessung in Banken: Konzepte zur Risiko-Erfolgssteuerung, in: Österreichisches Bankenarchiv, Vol. 46, Iss. 11 and 12, pp. 857-869 and 949-955.

Liebich, Kim (1995): How to Value a Bank, in: ABA Banking Journal, Vol. 87, Iss. 8, pp. 21-23.

Lottner, Jens (1997): Wertorientierte Steuerung von Kreditinstituten, Dresden.

Matten, Chris (2000): Managing Bank Capital: Capital Allocation and Performance Measurement, 2nd edition, Chichester et al.

Mercer, Z. Christopher (1992): Valuing Financial Institutions, Homewood.

Merkle, Thomas (2001): Bereichsbewertung der Universalbank, Frankfurt am Main.

Merrill Lynch (2005): Pan-European Banks: European Banks & IAS – A Refresher, Merill Lynch, Global Securities Research & Economics Group.

MOW (2003): State of the Financial Services Industry 2003, MOW Report, Mercer Oliver Wyman.

MSDW (2001): Valuing Financial Stocks with Residual Income, Morgan Stanley Dean Witter, Equity Research North America.

Müller, Horst (1994): Bewertung von Kreditinstituten, in: Albach, Horst (Ed.): Werte und Unternehmensziele im Wandel der Zeit, Wiesbaden, pp. 85-95.

O'Byrne, Steven F. (1996): EVA and Market Value, in: Journal of Applied Corporate Finance, Vol. 9, Iss. 1, pp. 116-125.

OECD (2004): The Performance of Financial Groups in the Recent Difficult Environment, in: Organisation for Economic Co-operation and Development (Ed.): Financial Market Trends, No. 86, March 2004, pp. 63-81.

Penman, Steven H. and Sougiannis, Theodore (1998): A Comparison of Dividend, Cash Flow, and Earnings Approaches to Equity Valuation, in: Contemporary Accounting Research, Vol. 15, Iss. 3, pp. 343-383.

Pettit, Justin M. (2001): The Equity Risk Measurement Handbook, in: EVAluation, Vol. 3, Iss. 3, pp. 1-12.

Prangenberg, Arno (2000): Konzernabschluß International: Grundlagen und Einführung in die Bilanzierung nach HGB, IAS and US-GAAP, Stuttgart.

Rappaport, Alfred (1986): Creating Shareholder Value: The New Standard for Business Performance, New York.

Rezaee, Zabihollah (2001): Financial Institutions, Valuations, Mergers, and Acquisitions: The Fair Value Approach, 2nd edition, New York et al.

Schell, Gerhard R. (1988): Die Ertragsermittlung für Bankbewertungen, Frankfurt am Main.

Schierenbeck, Henner (1991): Ertragsorientiertes Bankmanagement: Controlling in Kreditinstituten, 3rd revised and extended edition, Wiesbaden.

Schierenbeck, Henner (1997): Ertragsorientiertes Bankmanagement im Visier des Shareholder Value-Konzeptes, in: Basler Bankenvereinigung (Ed.): Shareholder Value-Konzepte in Banken: Tagungsband zum 4. Basler Bankentag, 27. November 1996, Bern, Stuttgart, and Vienna, pp. 3-48.

Schierenbeck, Henner (1998): Shareholder Value-Management im Konzept ertragsorientierter Banksteuerung, in: Die Bank, Vol. 37, Iss. 1, pp. 13-17.

Schlund, Marc (2001): Das Product Life Cycle Management — Eine kritische Würdigung anhand des Beziehungsmarketing, Diplomarbeit, European Business School, Schloß Reichartshausen am Rhein.

Schmidt, Reinhart and Wilhelm, W. (1988): Rendite-Sicherheit-Wachstum: 52 Finanzdienstleister unter der Lupe, in: Manager Magazin Iss. 2, pp. 137-141.

Schmittmann, Stefan, Penzel, Hans-Gert, and Gehrke, Norman (1996): Integration des Shareholder Value in die Gesamtbanksteuerung, in: Die Bank, Vol. 35, Iss. 11, pp. 648-653.

Schroeck, Gerhard (2002): Risk Management and Value Creation in Financial Institutions, Hoboken.

Schuster, Leo (2000): The Shareholder Value and Stakeholder Discussion: An International Overview, in: Schuster, Leo (Ed.): Shareholder Value Management in Banks, New York, pp. 3-12.

Seidel, Stephan (2000): Der Shareholder-value-Ansatz zur Integration von Rentabilitäts- und Risikomanagement im ertragsorientierten Wertmanagementkonzept für Banken, Göttingen.

Shaw, Ray (2000): Shareholder Value or Stakeholder Value? That is the Question, in: Schuster, Leo (Ed.): Shareholder Value Management in Banks, New York, pp. 36-52.

Sinn, Walter, Dayal, Ranu, and Pitman, David (2003): Creating Value in Banking 2003, BCG Report, The Boston Consulting Group.

Sinn, Walter et al. (2004): Winners in the Age of Titans, Creating Value in Banking 2004, BCG Report, The Boston Consulting Group.

Sonntag, Alexander (2001): Bewertung von Banken. Ein Discounted Cashflow-Ansatz für Commercial Banks unter Einbeziehung der Marktzinsmethode, Wiesbaden and Leipzig.

Steevens, Carsten (2005): Fünfundzwanzig, Börsen-Zeitung, Iss. 21, February 1st, 2005, p. 8.

Stewart, G. Bennett (1990): The Quest for Value: a Guide for Senior Managers, New York.

Stickney, Clyde P. and Weil, Roman L. (1997): Financial Accounting: An Introduction to Concepts, Methods, and Uses, 8th edition, Fort Worth et al.

Strutz, Eric (1993): Wertmanagement bei Banken, Bern, Stuttgart, and Vienna.

Subrahmanyan, K. R. and Venkatachalam, M. (2004): Earnings, Cash Flows and Ex post Intrinsic Value of Equity, Working Paper, Duke University and University of Southern California.

Süchting, Joachim (1996): Unternehmenssteuerung in Banken nach dem Shareholder-Value-Konzept, in: International Bankers Forum e.V. (Ed.): Die Banken auf dem Weg ins 21. Jahrhundert: Strategien und Konzept, Wiesbaden, pp. 407-418.

Uyemura, Dennis G., Kantor, Charles C., and Pettit, Justin M. (1996): EVA for Banks: Value Creation, Risk Management and Profitability Measurement, in: Journal of Applied Corporate Finance, Vol. 9, Iss. 3, pp. 94-112.

Vettiger, Thomas (1996): Wertorientiertes Bankcontrolling, Bern, Stuttgart, and Vienna.

Wariboko, Nimi (1994): Principles and Practice of Bank Analysis and Valuation, Ibadan et al.

Weaver, Samuel C. (2001): Measuring Economic Value Added: A Survey of the Practices of EVA Proponents, in: Journal of Applied Finance, Vol. 11, Iss. 2, pp. 7-17.

Wilde, Klaus D. (1982): Langfristige Bankmarktprognosen durch quantitative Risikoanalyse, in: Die Bank, Vol. 21, Iss. 10, pp. 465-470.

Wildgruber, Jörg (1998): Das Prognoseproblem bei der Ermittlung des Entscheidungswertes von Kreditinstituten, Frankfurt am Main.

Wittkowski, Bernd (2005): Feindbild Deutsche Bank, Börsen-Zeitung, Iss. 31, February 15, 2005, p. 8.

Young, S. David and O'Byrne, Steven F. (2000): EVA and Value-Based Management: a Practical Guide to Implementation, New York et al.

Zessin, Axel (1982): Unternehmensbewertung von Kreditinstituten, Göttingen.

Zimmer, Steven A. and McCauley, Robert N. (1991): Bank Cost of Capital and International Competition, in: Federal Reserve Bank of New York Quarterly Review, Vol. 15, Iss. 3/4, pp. 33-59.

Zimmermann, Gebhard and Jöhnk, Thorsten (1998): Shareholder-Value oder Stakeholder-Ansatz als Zielkonzeption für öffentlich-rechtliche Kreditinstitute?, in: Zeitschrift für das gesamte Kreditwesen, Vol. 51, Iss. 6, pp. 31-34.

Zimmermann, Heinz (1995): Fristentransformation und Eigenkapitalkosten von Banken, in: Thommen, Jean-Paul (Ed.): Management-Kompetenz: die Gestaltungsansätze des Executive MBA der Hochschule St. Gallen, Wiesbaden, pp. 589-608.

Zimmermann, Heinz and Oertmann, Peter (1996): Über die Kapitalkosten von Grossbanken bei integrierten Kapitalmärkten, in: Geiger, Hans (Ed.): Schweizerisches Bankwesen im Umbruch, Bern, Stuttgart, and Vienna, pp. 273-287.

List of Appendices

Appendix 1: Overview of forecast horizons used in bank valuation

Years	Source
3 years	Hörter (1998), p. 156
	Matten (2000), p. 277
3 to 6 years	Börner and Lowis (1997), p. 100
	Kirsten (1995), p. 674
	Vettiger (1996), p. 131
4 years	Zessin (1982), p. 64
3 to 10 years	Adolf et al. (1989b), p. 488
	Behm (1994), p. 60
5 years	MSDW (2001), p. 24
	Damodaran (2004), p. 29
5 to 7 years	Becker (1999), p. 63
	Kümmel (1995), p. 55
	Merkle (2001), p. 226
	Wilde (1982), p. 467
5 to 10 years	Faust (2002), p. 75
	Kunowski (2002), p. 70
	Mercer (1992), p. 259
	Rezaee (2001), p. 187
	Strutz (1993), p. 86
	Wariboko (1994), p. 94
10 years	Höhmann (1998), p. 92

Source: Own graphic

Appendix 2: Forecast horizon for banks using a residual income approach

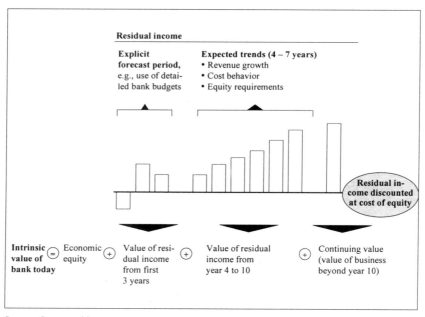

Source: Own graphic

Appendix 3: Methods for forecasting future bank performance

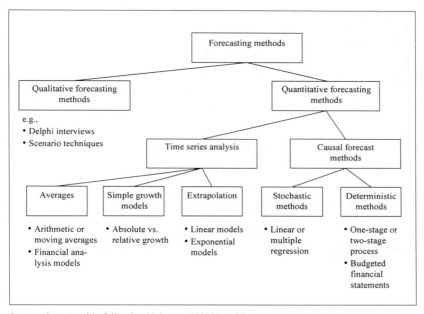

Source: Own graphic following Höhmann (1998), p. 94

Appendix 4: Overview of growth rates assumed in literature

Growth assumption	Source
g = 0	Becker (1999), p. 120
	Faust (2002), p. 80
	Geltinger (2003), p. 65 and p. 196
	Merkle (2001), p. 230
	Strutz (1993), p. 95
	Vettiger (1996), p. 126
g = inflation rate	Adolf et al. (1989a), p. 548
	Kümmel (1995), p. 42
g as value driver	Behm (1994), p. 60
	Börner and Lowis (1997), p. 122

Source: Own graphic

Appendix 5: Overview of industry betas for banks by country

Year	Canada	France	Germany	Ireland	Italy	Netherlands	Scandinavia	Spain	Switzerland	UK	USA	Europe	World
							Industry betas for banks (normalized for TMT sector)						
1989	0.65	N/a	0.94	0.84	0.74	0.69	0.65	N/a	0.76	0.99	0.80	0.86	1.20
1990	0.61	N/a	0.94	0.86	0.68	0.74	0.74	N/a	0.82	1.07	0.77	0.88	1.19
1991	0.62	N/a	0.90	0.93	0.66	0.71	0.79	N/a	0.80	1.07	0.69	0.85	1.18
1992	0.61	N/a	0.89	1.05	0.66	0.72	0.86	N/a	0.77	1.06	0.65	0.85	1.13
1993	0.58	N/a	0.88	1.22	0.70	0.69	0.94	N/a	0.74	1.07	0.58	0.86	1.08
1994	0.57	0.78	0.86	1.32	0.74	0.65	1.07	N/a	0.74	1.09	0.55	0.88	1.05
1995	0.55	0.82	0.79	1.37	0.75	0.58	1.19	1.05	0.71	1.08	0.50	0.88	1.08
1996	0.55	0.82	0.66	1.30	0.71	0.55	1.32	1.10	0.67	1.09	0.48	0.86	1.11
1997	0.59	0.83	0.54	1.21	0.67	0.58	1.40	1.09	0.58	1.07	0.46	0.83	1.14
1998	0.76	0.93	0.52	1.11	0.71	0.70	1.38	1.13	0.63	1.08	0.59	0.86	1.18
1999	0.99	1.16	0.66	1.06	0.78	0.87	1.21	1.17	0.84	1.05	0.83	0.93	1.21
2000	1.12	1.34	0.82	1.04	0.85	1.01	1.01	1.22	1.12	1.06	1.05	1.01	1.23
2001	1.10	1.36	0.95	1.00	0.87	1.10	0.89	1.21	1.30	1.02	1.14	1.04	1.19
2002	0.98	1.29	1.03	1.01	0.92	1.16	0.86	1.23	1.35	1.01	1.10	1.06	1.13
2003	0.86	1.27	1.18	0.99	0.97	1.27	0.87	1.25	1.39	1.02	1.05	1.09	1.07
Average	0.97	1.23	0.86	1.04	0.85	1.02	1.20	1.10	1.10	1.04	0.96	1.00	1.17

Source: DS, own calculations

Appendix 6: Overview of exemplary banking betas from public sources

As of December 2003

Bank	BARRA	Bloomberg	Datastream
Deutsche Bank	0.94	1.11	0.97
Commerzbank	1.11	1.28	1.69
Citigroup	1.27	1.13	1.43
Societe Generale	1.08	1.31	1.2
Barclays	1.27	N/a	1.4
Bank of America	0.72	0.63	0.6

Source: BARRA, Bloomberg, Datastream

Appendix 7: Overview of industry betas by bank type and region

Year	North America				Europe				Asia		
	Banks	Investment Banks	Consumer Finance	Mortgage Finance	Banks	Investment Banks	Consumer Finance	Mortgage Finance	Banks	Investment Banks	Consumer Finance
1989	0.77	1.55	1.20	1.14	0.86	1.02	1.01	1.27	1.45	2.06	1.08
1990	0.74	1.33	1.08	0.97	0.88	0.99	1.02	1.31	1.44	2.06	1.08
1991	0.68	1.17	0.91	0.83	0.85	0.90	0.98	1.25	1.43	2.00	1.19
1992	0.65	1.08	0.77	0.82	0.85	0.81	0.90	1.14	1.34	1.89	1.36
1993	0.58	1.01	0.62	0.76	0.86	0.79	0.86	1.12	1.27	1.82	1.52
1994	0.55	0.96	0.55	0.77	0.88	0.84	0.91	1.13	1.24	1.86	1.63
1995	0.50	0.88	0.47	0.75	0.88	0.91	1.00	1.16	1.31	1.97	1.67
1996	0.48	0.92	0.49	0.85	0.86	0.96	1.14	0.98	1.41	2.17	1.60
1997	0.48	1.00	0.55	0.87	0.83	1.01	1.16	0.50	1.49	2.31	1.54
1998	0.61	1.22	0.76	0.92	0.86	1.06	1.09	0.05	1.54	2.26	1.37
1999	0.84	1.53	1.03	0.91	0.93	1.12	0.85	-0.13	1.53	2.04	1.20
2000	1.00	1.85	1.21	0.85	0.98	1.12	0.65	-0.02	1.45	1.78	0.93
2001	1.02	2.02	1.20	0.63	0.97	1.11	0.48	0.11	1.33	1.62	0.77
2002	0.93	2.05	1.10	0.39	0.96	1.12	0.40	0.24	1.16	1.45	0.63
Average	0.70	1.33	0.85	0.82	0.89	0.98	0.89	0.72	1.38	1.95	1.26

Source: DS, own calculation

Appendix 8: Allocation of interest income using a matched-opportunity rate

Consolidated balance sheet

		Liabilities and equity	
	120	Deposits	1,000
	933	Equity	53
	1,053		053

Lending operations

	933	Debt to treasury	880
		Equity	53
	933		933

Deposit operations

Cash reserves	120	Deposits	1,000
Loans to treasury	880		
	1,000		1,000

Treasury

Loans to lending	880	Debt to deposits	880
	880		880

Income statement

Interest income (12% x 933)	111.96
Interest expense (5% x 1,000)	-50.00
Net interest income	61.96

Calculation of income using a matched-opportunity rate (MOR)

Spread on loans	32.76
(12% x 933 – 9% x 880 – 0% x 53)	
or (12%-9%) x 933 + 9% x 53)	
(+) Spread on deposits	11.60
(7% x 880 + 0% x 120-5% x 1,000)	
or (7%-5%) x 1,000 – 7% x 120)	
(+) Mismatch profits	17.60
(9% x 880-7% x 880)	
(=) Net interest income	61.96

Assumptions

Yield on 3-year loans	12%
MOR on 3-year loans	9%
Rates on 1-year deposits	5%
MOR on 1-year deposits	7%

Source: Own exemplary calculation

Appendix 9: Overview of key adjustments to valuation models

	Model used			Adjustments					
Author and year	Discounted income	DCF	Residual income	Use of equity approach	Cash flow derivation	Consideration of required retention	Forecast horizon (Years)	Growth assumption in terminal value	Cost of equity estimate
Adolf et al. (1989a)	x			yes	n/a	yes	3 – 10	g = inflation	OR**
Becker, D. (1999)	x	x		yes	indirect	yes	5 – 7	g = 0	CAPM
Behm (1994)		x		yes	indirect	no	3 – 10	g = value driver	CAPM/Other
Bodmer (2001)		x	x	yes	indirect	yes	casewise*	casewise*	CAPM
Börner and Lowis (1997)		x		yes	indirect	yes	3 – 6	g = value driver	APT
Copeland et al. (2000)		x	(x)	yes	indirect	yes	N/a***	casewise*	CAPM
Damodaran (2004)		x	x	yes	indirect	yes	5	n/a	CAPM
Faust (2001)		x		yes	indirect	n/a	5 – 10	g = 0	CAPM
Geltinger (2003)	x	x		yes	indirect	yes	n/a	g = 0	CAPM
Höhmann (1998)		x	x	yes	indirect	yes	10	casewise*	CAPM
Hörter (1998)		x	x	yes	indirect	yes	3	casewise*	CAPM
Kirsten (2000)		x	x	yes	indirect	yes	casewise*	casewise*	CFV/OR**
Koch (2002)		x		yes	indirect	yes	n/a	n/a	CAPM/APT
Kümmel (1995)		x		yes	direct	yes	5 – 7	g = inflation	CAPM
Kunowski (2002)	x	x		yes	indirect	yes	5 – 10	n/a	CAPM
Matten (2000)		x	x	yes	indirect	yes	3	n/a	CAPM
Mercer (2002)	x	x		(yes)	n/a	n/a	5 – 10	n/a	CAPM
Merkle (2001)	(x)	x	x	yes	indirect	yes	3 – 10	g = 0	CAPM
MSDW (2001)			x	yes	n/a	n/a	5	g < 0	CAPM
Rezaee (2001)		x	(x)	yes	indirect	yes	5 – 10	n/a	CAPM
Strutz (1993)		x		yes	indirect	yes	5 – 10	g = 0	CAPM/APT
Uyemura et al. (1997)			x	yes	indirect	n/a	n/a	n/a	CAPM
Vettiger (1996)		x	x	yes	direct	yes	3 – 6	g = 0	CAPM/APT
Zessin (1982)	x			yes	n/a	n/a	4	n/a	OR**

* Parameter to be defined casewise based of the specifics of the individual bank

** Opportunity rate

*** General forecasting horizon of 5 - 10 years, bank-specific length of forecast horizon not defined

Source: Own table

Appendix 10: Sample characteristics by year

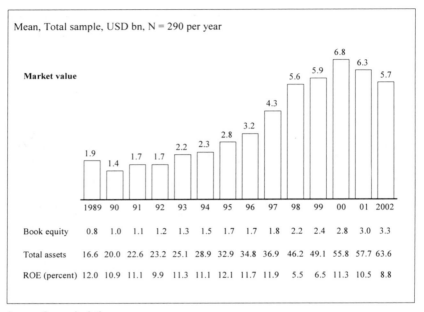

Mean, Total sample, USD bn, N = 290 per year

	1989	90	91	92	93	94	95	96	97	98	99	00	01	2002
Book equity	0.8	1.0	1.1	1.2	1.3	1.5	1.7	1.7	1.8	2.2	2.4	2.8	3.0	3.3
Total assets	16.6	20.0	22.6	23.2	25.1	28.9	32.9	34.8	36.9	46.2	49.1	55.8	57.7	63.6
ROE (percent)	12.0	10.9	11.1	9.9	11.3	11.1	12.1	11.7	11.9	5.5	6.5	11.3	10.5	8.8

Source: Own calculation

Appendix 11: Distribution of sample banks by country

(2002)

Country	Number of banks	Market value (USD bn)	Share (percent)
Canada	8	82.4	7.8
United States	127	970.3	92.2
North America – Subtotal	135	1,052.7	100.0
Austria	3	1	0.2
Belgium	1	10	2.2
Denmark	7	14.2	3.1
Finland	1	0.1	0.0
France	5	27.3	6.0
Germany	6	45.6	10.0
Greece	3	6.8	1.5
Ireland	2	22.4	4.9
Italy	12	57.7	12.7
Netherlands	3	1.1	0.2
Portugal	2	7.3	1.6
Spain	10	82.1	18.1
Sweden	2	14.3	3.1
Switzerland	7	33.3	7.3
United Kingdom	10	130.5	28.8
Europe – Subtotal	74	453.5	100.0
			0.0
Hong Kong	1	0.2	0.1
Japan	69	111.1	79.5
Malaysia	3	10.3	7.3
Singapore	1	9.3	6.7
South Korea	2	5.1	3.6
Thailand	5	3.9	2.8
Asia – Subtotal	81	139.9	100.0
Grand Total	290	1,646.1	

Source: Own calculation

Appendix 12: Distribution by bank type per region

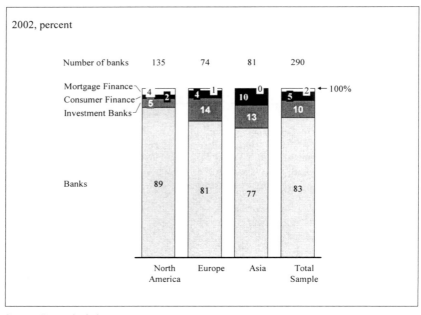

Source: Own calculation

Appendix 13: Sample coverage of DS banking indices by year

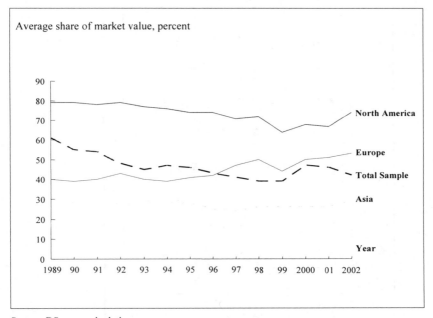

Source: DS, own calculation

Appendix 14: Overview of risk–free rate by country

(Clean Price Index, USD, percent)

Risk-free rate – DS Benchmark 10-year Government Bond Index

Year	Austria	Belgium	Canada	Den-mark	Finland	France	Ger-many	Greece	Ireland	Italy	Japan	Nether-lands	Por-tugal	Spain	Sweden	Switzer-land	UK	USA
1989	7.19	8.72	9.79	9.77	11.30	8.79	6.90	10.00	9.17	13.10	5.16	7.21	10.00	13.50	11.20	5.13	10.11	8.50
1990	8.77	9.99	10.79	10.60	11.30	9.92	8.66	10.00	10.34	13.10	6.90	8.92	10.00	13.82	13.14	6.41	11.56	8.55
1991	8.54	9.25	9.49	9.27	11.30	9.03	8.42	10.00	9.42	13.14	6.40	8.74	10.00	12.09	10.72	6.23	10.08	7.86
1992	8.15	8.61	8.07	8.89	12.01	8.57	7.80	10.00	9.21	13.29	5.24	8.10	10.00	11.71	9.90	6.52	9.09	7.00
1993	6.71	7.22	7.24	7.29	8.78	6.75	6.47	10.00	7.69	11.23	4.18	6.36	9.59	10.23	8.54	4.61	7.40	5.86
1994	7.03	7.76	8.38	7.85	9.03	7.21	6.86	10.00	7.95	10.56	4.20	6.87	10.45	10.02	9.58	4.99	8.01	7.08
1995	7.13	7.49	8.15	8.26	8.76	7.53	6.82	10.00	8.25	12.22	3.39	6.90	11.45	11.29	10.26	4.68	8.16	6.57
1996	6.31	6.49	7.21	7.19	7.03	6.32	6.21	7.00	7.29	9.43	3.03	6.15	8.57	8.74	8.04	4.16	7.79	6.43
1997	5.67	5.76	6.13	6.23	5.93	5.56	5.65	7.00	6.29	6.84	2.34	5.58	6.36	6.39	6.64	3.53	7.02	6.34
1998	4.72	4.75	5.28	4.93	4.78	4.65	4.57	6.40	4.79	4.90	1.49	4.63	4.83	4.83	5.01	2.88	5.52	5.26
1999	4.69	4.76	5.55	4.92	4.73	4.61	4.50	6.37	4.65	4.76	1.75	4.64	4.80	4.75	4.98	2.87	4.98	5.64
2000	5.55	5.59	5.92	5.64	5.46	5.42	5.26	6.09	5.43	5.60	1.77	5.40	5.60	5.53	5.35	3.80	5.26	6.04
2001	5.06	5.12	5.48	5.09	5.04	4.96	4.81	5.27	4.94	5.19	1.33	4.96	5.16	5.12	5.09	3.28	4.91	5.02
2002	4.95	4.97	5.30	5.02	4.89	4.88	4.79	5.10	4.91	5.03	1.25	4.89	5.02	4.95	5.27	3.02	4.86	4.59
Average	6.46	6.89	7.34	7.21	7.88	6.73	6.27	8.09	7.17	9.17	3.46	6.38	7.99	8.78	8.12	4.44	7.48	6.48

Source: DS

Appendix 15: Estimation of market risk premium

(percent)

Year	(1) US risk-free rate*	(2) US inflation rate/ CPI**	(3) =(1) - (2) Inflation adjusted risk-free rate	(4) = 7*** - (3) Market risk premium
1989	8.50	4.60	3.90	3.10
1990	8.55	6.10	2.45	4.55
1991	7.86	3.10	4.76	2.24
1992	7.00	2.90	4.10	2.90
1993	5.86	2.70	3.16	3.84
1994	7.08	2.70	4.38	2.62
1995	6.57	2.50	4.07	2.93
1996	6.43	3.30	3.13	3.87
1997	6.34	1.70	4.64	2.36
1998	5.26	1.60	3.66	3.34
1999	5.64	2.70	2.94	4.06
2000	6.04	3.40	2.64	4.37
2001	5.02	1.60	3.42	3.58
2002	4.59	2.40	2.19	4.81
Average	6.48	2.95	3.53	3.47

* DS Benchmark 10-year US Government Bond Index, calendar year average of Clean Price Index
** Consumer Price Index
*** Average real cost of equity in the past 40 years assumed to be 7 percent. See Goedhart, Koller, and Williams (2002)

Source: DS, US Bureau of Labor and Statistics, Goedhart, Koller, and Williams (2002)

Appendix 16: Overview of yearly regional industry betas

Year	North America				Europe				Asia		
	Banks	Investment Banks	Consumer Finance	Mortgage Finance	Banks	Investment Banks	Consumer Finance	Mortgage Finance	Banks	Investment Banks	Consumer Finance
1989	0.77	1.55	1.20	1.14	0.86	1.02	1.01	1.27	1.45	2.06	1.08
1990	0.74	1.33	1.08	0.97	0.88	0.99	1.02	1.31	1.44	2.06	1.08
1991	0.68	1.17	0.91	0.83	0.85	0.90	0.98	1.25	1.43	2.00	1.19
1992	0.65	1.08	0.77	0.82	0.85	0.81	0.90	1.14	1.34	1.89	1.36
1993	0.58	1.01	0.62	0.76	0.86	0.79	0.86	1.12	1.27	1.82	1.52
1994	0.55	0.96	0.55	0.77	0.88	0.84	0.91	1.13	1.24	1.86	1.63
1995	0.50	0.88	0.47	0.75	0.88	0.91	1.00	1.16	1.31	1.97	1.67
1996	0.48	0.92	0.49	0.85	0.86	0.96	1.14	0.98	1.41	2.17	1.60
1997	0.48	1.00	0.55	0.87	0.83	1.01	1.16	0.50	1.49	2.31	1.54
1998	0.61	1.22	0.76	0.92	0.86	1.06	1.09	0.05	1.54	2.26	1.37
1999	0.84	1.53	1.03	0.91	0.93	1.12	0.85	-0.13	1.53	2.04	1.20
2000	1.00	1.85	1.21	0.85	0.98	1.12	0.65	-0.02	1.45	1.78	0.93
2001	1.02	2.02	1.20	0.63	0.97	1.11	0.48	0.11	1.33	1.62	0.77
2002	0.93	2.05	1.10	0.39	0.96	1.12	0.40	0.24	1.16	1.45	0.63
Average	0.70	1.33	0.85	0.82	0.89	0.98	0.89	0.72	1.38	1.95	1.26

Source: DS, own calculation

Appendix 17: Dispersion of the prediction errors by region and bank type

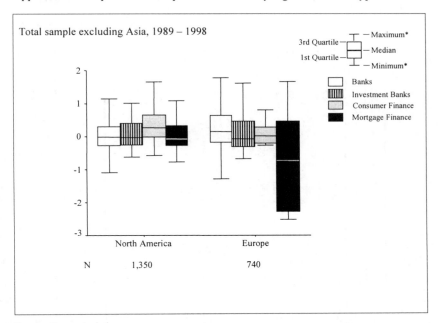

Source: Own calculation

Appendix 18: Summary statistics for regression models

2,090 observations, 209 groups

Variable	Predicted Coefficient Sign	Pooled OLS		Between Effects		Fixed Effects		Random Effects	
		Coef.	P>(t)	Coef.	P>(t)	Coef.	P>(t)	Coef.	P>(z)
REG NA	(-)	-0.098	0.00	-0.093	0.00	drop		-0.097	0.00
IND IB	(+)	0.031	0.27	0.038	0.43	drop		0.033	0.49
IND CF	(-)	0.115	0.01	0.137	0.08	drop		0.098	0.20
IND MF	(-)	0.078	0.08	0.102	0.19	drop		0.050	0.52
MV	(-)	0.010	0.04	0.005	0.61	0.105	0.00	0.025	0.00
ROE	(-)	-0.016	0.00	-0.02	0.00	-0.014	0.00	-0.014	0.00
YEAR 1990	(-)	-0.045	0.17	drop		-0.034	0.25	-0.042	0.15
YEAR 1991	(-)	-0.112	0.00	drop		-0.123	0.00	-0.113	0.00
YEAR 1992	(-)	-0.199	0.00	drop		-0.223	0.00	-0.202	0.00
YEAR 1993	(-)	-0.162	0.00	drop		-0.210	0.00	-0.171	0.00
YEAR 1994	(-)	-0.190	0.00	drop		-0.241	0.00	-0.199	0.00
YEAR 1995	(-)	-0.242	0.00	drop		-0.320	0.00	-0.256	0.00
YEAR 1996	(-)	-0.153	0.00	drop		-0.250	0.00	-0.171	0.00
YEAR 1997	(-)	0.155	0.00	drop		-0.021	0.55	0.130	0.00
YEAR 1998	(-)	0.093	0.00	drop		-0.048	0.19	0.066	0.04
Constant	N/a	0.655	0.00	0.712	0.00	-0.627	0.00	0.439	0.00
R-square within				0.01		0.19		0.17	
R-square between				0.22		0.01		0.17	
R-square overall		0.18		0.06		0.08		0.17	

Source: Stata, own calculation

Appendix 19: F-test for joint insignificance of coefficient estimates

(H₀: coefficients are jointly insignificant => model is misspecified)

Regression model	Distribution	Test statistic	Degrees of freedom		p value*
			Num.	Denum.	
Pooled Regression	F	30.17	15	2,073	**0.000**
Between Effects	F	7.90	7	201	**0.000**
Fixed Effects	F	38.69	11	1,869	**0.000**
Random Effects	χ^2	436.72	15		**0.000**

* According to the corresponding distribution with *Num.* and *Denum.* degrees of freedom; bold *p* value suggests rejecting H₀.

Source: Stata, own calculation

Appendix 20: Specification tests for fixed effects model

Specification test	Null hypothesis	Test statistic	Distribution	df	p value*
F-test for fixed effects	Parameter homogeneity	3.84	F	(208, 1869)	**0.000**
Hausman test for effect homogeneity	Effect heterogeneity	37.45	χ^2	11	**0.000**
Test for normality of residuals	Skewness of residuals				**0.000**
	Kurtosis of residuals				**0.001**
	Joint skewness and kurtosis	49.14	χ^2	2	**0.000**
Modified Wald test for heteroskedasticity	Groupwise heteroskedasticity across panels	11,649.60	χ^2	209	**0.000**
LM test for serial correlation	H₀: residuals are AR1	248.82	χ^2	1	**0.000**
	H₀: residuals are MA1	15.77	N	(0, 1)	**0.000**

* According to the corresponding distribution with df degrees of freedom; bold p value suggests rejecting H₀.

Source: Stata, own calculation

Appendix 21: Comparison of beta methodologies – European banks

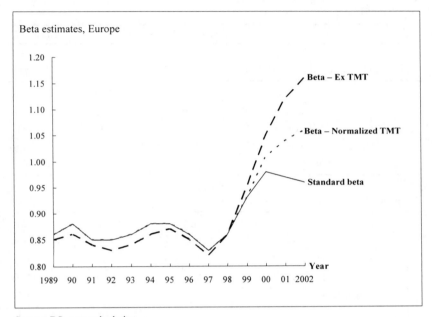

Source: DS, own calculation

Appendix 22: Sensitivity of IV to isolated accounting adjustments

(1989 – 1998, percent)

Statistic	North America	Europe	Asia
Sensitivity of IV to adjustments for effective average taxes			
N	1,350	740	810
Mean	0.90	1.00	0.99
Median	0.97	1.02	0.93
Standard Deviation	2.14	1.43	2.56
Interquartile Range	0.15	0.28	0.17
Sensitivity of IV to adjustments for deferred taxes			
N	1,350	740	810
Mean	0.90	1.00	0.99
Median	1.00	1.00	1.00
Standard Deviation	0.26	0.09	1.41
Interquartile Range	0.02	0.01	0.00
Sensitivity of IV to adjustments for unrecorded goodwill			
N	1,350	740	810
Mean	1.03	N/a	N/a
Median	1.00	N/a	N/a
Standard Deviation	0.21	N/a	N/a
Interquartile Range	0.00	N/a	N/a

Source: Own calculation

Appendix 23: Average value creation by phase

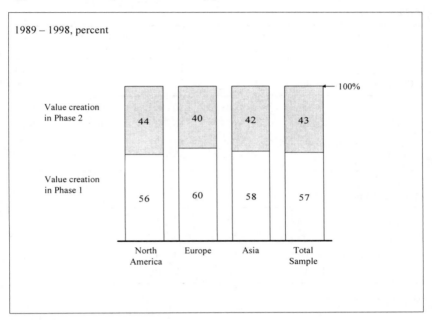

1989 – 1998, percent

Value creation
in Phase 2

Value creation
in Phase 1

	North America	Europe	Asia	Total Sample
Value creation in Phase 2	44	40	42	43
Value creation in Phase 1	56	60	58	57

100%

Source: Own calculation

Appendix 24: Descriptive statistics of characteristics by subsample

(1998 – 2003)

Statistic	Equity (EUR mn)	Assets (EUR mn)	ROE (percent)	Customers (mn)
Universal Banks (N=120)				
Mean	4,205	92,087	15.8	5.2
Median	3,014	63,933	14.5	4.0
Standard Deviation	3,365	81,919	13.1	4.2
Interquartile Range	3,651	62,409	13.4	4.3
Savings Banks (N=636)				
Mean	192	4,441	6.8	0.3
Median	147	3,309	6.5	0.2
Standard Deviation	131	3,104	4.8	0.2
Interquartile Range	109	2,560	5.3	0.2

Source: Own calculation

Appendix 25: Distribution of Universal Banks by country

(1998 – 2003)

Country	Number of banks	Equity (EUR bn)	Share (percent)
Belgium	2	22.5	4
France	1	12.6	2
Germany	5	61.0	11
Italy	6	101.7	19
Netherlands	2	45.6	8
Portugal	3	36.2	7
Spain	5	54.8	10
Sweden	3	69.2	13
Switzerland	3	73.3	14
UK	2	9.8	2
USA	1	52.5	10
Total	33	539.1	100

Source: Own calculation

Appendix 26: Overview of tax rates by country

(percent)

Year	Belgium	France	Ger-many	Italy	Nether-lands	Por-tugal	Spain	Sweden	Switzer-land	UK	USA
					Effective Average Tax Rate						
1998	0.35	0.35	0.48	0.29	0.30	0.31	0.28	0.23	0.28	0.27	0.33
1999	0.35	0.33	0.44	0.29	0.30	0.31	0.28	0.23	0.28	0.26	0.33
2000	0.35	0.31	0.44	0.28	0.30	0.29	0.29	0.23	0.28	0.26	0.33
2001	0.35	0.30	0.34	0.27	0.30	0.29	0.29	0.23	0.28	0.26	0.33
2002	0.35	0.29	0.34	0.27	0.30	0.27	0.29	0.23	0.28	0.26	0.33
2003	0.29	0.29	0.35	0.31	0.30	0.27	0.29	0.23	0.28	0.26	0.33
Average	0.34	0.31	0.40	0.28	0.30	0.29	0.28	0.23	0.28	0.26	0.33

Source: Devereux, Griffith, and Klemm (2002)

Appendix 27: Overview of risk-free rates by country

(Clean Price Index, USD, percent)

Year	Belgium	France	Germany	Italy	Netherlands	Portugal	Spain	Sweden	Switzerland	UK	USA
				Risk-free rate – DS Benchmark 10-year Government Bond Index							
1998	4.75	4.65	4.57	4.90	4.63	4.83	4.83	5.01	2.88	5.52	5.26
1999	4.76	4.61	4.50	4.76	4.64	4.80	4.75	4.98	2.87	4.98	5.64
2000	5.59	5.42	5.26	5.60	5.40	5.60	5.53	5.35	3.80	5.26	6.04
2001	5.12	4.96	4.81	5.19	4.96	5.16	5.12	5.09	3.28	4.91	5.02
2002	4.97	4.88	4.79	5.03	4.89	5.02	4.95	5.27	3.02	4.86	4.59
2003	4.14	4.13	4.09	4.24	4.13	4.16	4.10	4.57	2.47	4.47	3.99
Average	4.89	4.78	4.67	4.95	4.77	4.93	4.88	5.04	3.05	5.00	5.09

Source: DS

Appendix 28: Estimation of market risk premium

(percent)

Year	(1) US risk-free rate*	(2) US inflation rate**	(3) =(1) - (2) Inflation adjusted risk-free rate	(4) = 7*** - (3) Market risk premium	3-year moving average
1997	6.34	2.34	4.64	2.36	
1998	5.26	1.55	3.66	3.34	3.25
1999	5.64	2.19	2.94	4.06	3.92
2000	6.04	3.38	2.64	4.37	4.00
2001	5.02	2.83	3.42	3.58	4.25
2002	4.59	1.59	2.19	4.81	4.56
2003	3.99	2.27	1.72	5.28	3.36
2004	4.26	2.68	1.58	5.42	
Average 98 – 03	**5.09**	**2.30**	**2.76**	**4.24**	**3.89**

* US Benchmark 10-year US Government Bond Index, calendar year average of Clean Price Index

** Change in US CPI (Consumer Price Index)

*** Assumption: Average real cost of equity in the past 40 years of 7 percent.

Source: DS, Goedhart, Koller, and Williams (2002)

Appendix 29: Overview of yearly banking betas by country

Year	Beta normalized for TMT sector										
	Belgium	France	Ger-many	Italy	Nether-lands	Por-tugal	Spain	Sweden	Switzer-land	UK	USA
1998	0.42	0.93	0.52	0.71	0.70	0.57	1.13	1.95	0.63	1.08	0.59
1999	0.44	1.16	0.66	0.78	0.87	0.65	1.17	1.68	0.84	1.05	0.83
2000	0.50	1.34	0.82	0.85	1.01	0.74	1.22	1.31	1.12	1.06	1.05
2001	0.53	1.36	0.95	0.87	1.10	0.69	1.21	1.08	1.30	1.02	1.14
2002	0.57	1.29	1.03	0.92	1.16	0.66	1.23	1.04	1.35	1.01	1.10
2003	0.69	1.27	1.18	0.97	1.27	0.62	1.25	1.04	1.39	1.02	1.05
Average	0.53	1.23	0.86	0.85	1.02	0.65	1.20	1.35	1.10	1.04	0.96

Source: DS, own calculations

Appendix 30: Overview of cost of equity by country

(percent)

Year	Belgium	France	Germany	Italy	Netherlands	Portugal	Spain	Sweden	Switzerland	UK	USA
					Estimated cost of equity						
1998	6.44	8.38	6.63	7.75	7.41	7.12	9.35	12.79	5.38	9.85	7.61
1999	6.51	9.27	7.16	7.89	8.12	7.40	9.42	11.69	6.23	9.20	8.94
2000	7.60	10.78	8.56	8.99	9.46	8.54	10.42	10.58	8.26	9.50	10.24
2001	7.26	10.39	8.60	8.68	9.35	7.94	9.95	9.40	8.48	9.00	9.56
2002	7.26	10.06	8.91	8.70	9.52	7.65	9.86	9.44	8.44	8.92	9.01
2003	6.89	9.21	8.82	8.11	9.21	6.64	9.11	8.74	8.04	8.54	8.19
Average	6.99	9.68	8.11	8.35	8.85	7.55	9.69	10.44	7.47	9.17	8.92

Source: DS, own calculation

Appendix 31: Development of RIOE by sample

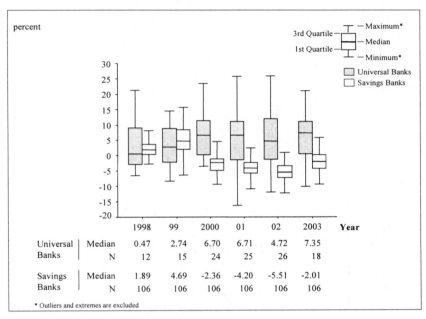

		1998	99	2000	01	02	2003	**Year**
Universal Banks	Median	0.47	2.74	6.70	6.71	4.72	7.35	
	N	12	15	24	25	26	18	
Savings Banks	Median	1.89	4.69	-2.36	-4.20	-5.51	-2.01	
	N	106	106	106	106	106	106	

* Outliers and extremes are excluded

Source: Own calculation

Appendix 32: Summary results for the pooled regression – Total sample

(748 observations, 135 groups)

Variable	RIOE		Income/Equity		Cost/Equity		LLP/Equity (1)		LLP/Equity (2)	
	Coef.	P>(t)	Coef.	P>(t)	Coef.	P>(t)	Coef.	P>(t)	Coef.	P>(t)
Interest Income/Income (BM)	-0.09	0.00	0.66	0.00	0.71	0.00	0.05	0.00	0.01	0.67
Customer/Branch (FS)	0.03	0.00	0.05	0.11	0.02	0.34	0.01	0.06	-0.02	0.12
Total Cost/Employee (CO)	-1.04	0.00	0.62	0.18	2.30	0.00	-0.06	0.47	0.52	0.02
LLP/Interest Income (RC)	-0.26	0.00	0.01	0.88	-0.09	0.00	0.52	0.00	–	
Interest Rate (IR)	-0.87	0.00	-0.04	0.96	0.92	0.06	0.14	0.28	0.62	0.06
Log Assets (A)	0.00	0.21	-0.04	0.00	-0.04	0.00	0.00	0.16	0.01	0.19
Sample (S)	0.12	0.00	0.05	0.18	-0.08	0.00	-0.01	0.04	-0.05	0.00
Constant	0.18	0.00	0.73	0.00	0.38	0.00	0.00	0.77	0.00	0.96
R^2	0.55		0.17		0.29		0.85		0.02	

Source: Stata, own calculation

Appendix 33: Summary results for the between effects model – Total sample

(748 observations, 135 groups)

Variable	RIOE		Income/Equity		Cost/Equity		LLP/Equity (1)		LLP/Equity (2)	
	Coef.	P>(t)	Coef.	P>(t)	Coef.	P>(t)	Coef.	P>(t)	Coef.	P>(t)
Interest Income/Income (BM)	-0.03	0.36	0.97	0.00	0.89	0.00	0.09	0.00	0.11	0.04
Customer/Branch (FS)	0.03	0.03	0.07	0.25	0.04	0.36	0.02	0.10	-0.02	0.31
Total Cost/Employee (CO)	-0.96	0.00	0.86	0.41	2.58	0.00	-0.16	0.42	0.21	0.56
LLP/Interest Income (RC)	-0.16	0.00	0.01	0.93	-0.15	0.20	0.49	0.00	–	
Interest Rate (IR)	-0.57	0.44	-0.09	0.98	-0.50	0.83	-0.45	0.42	-2.27	0.03
Log Assets (A)	0.00	0.76	-0.04	0.08	-0.04	0.01	0.00	0.70	0.00	0.75
Sample	0.11	0.00	-0.04	0.59	-0.14	0.01	-0.02	0.10	-0.05	0.06
Constant	0.11	0.02	0.55	0.01	0.32	0.04	0.01	0.80	0.12	0.08
R^2 within	0.67		0.12		0.00		0.91		0.02	
R^2 between	0.49		0.32		0.41		0.73		0.08	
R^2 overall	0.51		0.16		0.28		0.84		0.00	

Source: Stata, own calculation

Appendix 34: Summary results for the fixed effects model – Total sample

(748 observations, 135 groups)

Variable	RIOE		Income/Equity		Cost/Equity		LLP/Equity (1)		LLP/Equity (2)	
	Coef.	P>(t)	Coef.	P>(t)	Coef.	P>(t)	Coef.	P>(t)	Coef.	P>(t)
Interest Income/Total Income	-0.14	0.00	-0.58	0.00	-0.20	0.00	-0.13	0.00	-0.39	0.00
Customer/Branch	0.01	0.59	-0.04	0.29	-0.05	0.06	0.02	0.07	0.10	0.00
Total Cost/Employee	-1.30	0.00	-1.44	0.00	0.49	0.07	-0.15	0.14	0.55	0.12
LLP/Interest Income	-0.28	0.00	-0.01	0.56	-0.08	0.00	0.52	0.00	–	
Interest Rate	-1.33	0.00	-0.14	0.69	1.25	0.00	0.27	0.00	1.89	0.00
Log Assets	-0.06	0.00	-0.14	0.00	-0.04	0.02	-0.01	0.10	0.14	0.00
Constant	0.77	0.00	2.22	0.00	0.80	0.00	0.13	0.01	-1.08	0.00
R^2 within	0.70		0.22		0.12		0.93		0.15	
R^2 between	0.16		0.12		0.06		0.50		0.01	
R^2 overall	0.00		0.05		0.02		0.76		0.00	

*** Statistically significant at the 1 percent level
** Statistically significant at the 5 percent level
* Statistically significant at the 10 percent level

Source: Stata, own calculation

Appendix 35: Summary results for the random effects model – Total sample

(748 observations, 135 groups)

Variable	RIOE		Income/ Equity		Cost/ Equity		LLP/ Equity (1)		LLP/ Equity (2)	
	Coef.	P>(t)	Coef.	P>(t)	Coef.	P>(t)	Coef.	P>(t)	Coef.	P>(t)
Interest Income/Income (BM)	-0.12	0.00	-0.31	0.00	-0.02	0.63	-0.07	0.00	-0.07	0.09
Customer/Branch (FS)	0.03	0.02	0.01	0.74	-0.02	0.48	0.02	0.01	0.00	0.85
Total Cost/Employee (CO)	-1.30	0.00	-1.29	0.00	0.74	0.01	-0.16	0.08	0.73	0.01
LLP/Interest Income (RC)	-0.29	0.00	-0.04	0.17	-0.08	0.00	0.52	0.00	–	
Interest Rate (IR)	-1.17	0.00	-0.12	0.75	1.18	0.00	0.21	0.01	0.96	0.00
Log Assets (A)	-0.01	0.00	-0.07	0.00	-0.03	0.00	0.00	0.29	0.02	0.01
Sample (S)	0.17	0.00	0.41	0.00	0.11	0.00	0.02	0.14	-0.07	0.00
Constant	0.32	0.00	1.47	0.00	0.66	0.00	0.05	0.05	-0.09	0.11
R^2 within	0.69		0.21		0.10		0.93		0.08	
R^2 between	0.42		0.00		0.03		0.66		0.00	
R^2 overall	0.54		0.00		0.04		0.83		0.01	

Source: Stata, own calculation

Appendix 36: Specification tests of regression models

(Ho: coefficients are jointly insignificant => model is misspecified)

Regression model	Distribution	Test statistic	p value*
Pooled regression			
RIOE	$F(6, 741)$	96.05	**0.00**
Income/Equity	$F(6, 741)$	24.38	**0.00**
Cost/Equity	$F(6, 741)$	48.20	**0.00**
LLP/Equity (1)	$F(6, 741)$	688.91	**0.00**
LLP/Equity (2)	$F(5, 742)$	1.04	0.39
Fixed Effects			
RIOE	$F(6, 607)$	239.59	**0.00**
Income/Equity	$F(6, 607)$	28.52	**0.00**
Cost/Equity	$F(6, 607)$	14.18	**0.00**
LLP/Equity (1)	$F(6, 607)$	1,309.35	**0.00**
LLP/Equity (2)	$F(5, 608)$	20.97	**0.00**
Between Effects			
RIOE	$F(6, 128)$	11.00	**0.00**
Income/Equity	$F(6, 128)$	10.19	**0.00**
Cost/Equity	$F(6, 128)$	13.30	**0.00**
LLP/Equity (1)	$F(6, 128)$	55.08	**0.00**
LLP/Equity (2)	$F(5, 129)$	1.58	0.17
Random Effects			
RIOE	$\chi^2(6)$	1,089.46	**0.00**
Income/Equity	$\chi^2(6)$	22.41	**0.00**
Cost/Equity	$\chi^2(6)$	58.25	**0.00**
LLP/Equity (1)	$\chi^2(6)$	7,750.66	**0.00**
LLP/Equity (2)	$\chi^2(5)$	15.43	**0.01**

* According to the corresponding distribution with degrees
of freedom as stated in parentheses; bold p value suggests rejecting Ho.

Source: Stata, own calculation

Appendix 37: Test for significance of fixed effects

(Ho: parameter homogeneity => fixed effects model is misspecified)

Regression model	F-statistic	Num.	Denum.	p value*
		Degrees of freedom		
RIOE	10.57	134	607	**0.00**
Income/Equity	23.62	134	607	**0.00**
Cost/Equity	29.70	134	607	**0.00**
LLP/Equity (1)	11.66	134	607	**0.00**
LLP/Equity (2)	4.15	134	608	**0.00**

* According to the F distribution with *Num.* and *Denum.* degrees of freedom; bold p value suggests rejecting Ho.

Source: Stata, own calculation

Appendix 38: Hausman test for effect endogeneity

(Ho: regressors not correlated with c => random effects)

	χ^2-statistic	df	p value*
RIOE	176.96	6	**0.00**
Income/Equity	634.77	6	**0.00**
Cost/Equity	236.19	6	**0.00**
LLP/Equity (1)	43.49	6	**0.00**
LLP/Equity (2)	87.79	5	**0.00**

* According to the χ^2 distribution with df degrees of freedom; bold p value suggests rejecting Ho

Source: Stata, own calculations

Appendix 39: LM test for serial correlation

(Ho is either that rho=0 if residuals are AR1 or that lamda=0 if residuals are MA1)

Regression model	Test statistic	Distributed as	p value*
(Ho: residual are AR1)			
RIOE	2.08	$N(0,1)$	0.15
Income/Equity	6.32	$N(0,1)$	**0.01**
Cost/Equity	25.22	$N(0,1)$	**0.00**
LLP/Equity (1)	16.20	$N(0,1)$	**0.00**
LLP/Equity (2)	1.44	$N(0,1)$	0.23
(Ho: residual are MA1)			
RIOE	1.44	$\chi^2(1)$	**0.07**
Income/Equity	2.51	$\chi^2(1)$	**0.01**
Cost/Equity	5.02	$\chi^2(1)$	**0.00**
LLP/Equity (1)	4.03	$\chi^2(1)$	**0.00**
LLP/Equity (2)	1.20	$\chi^2(1)$	0.11

* According to the corresponding distribution with *Num.* and *Denum.* degrees of freedom; bold p value suggests rejecting Ho.

Source: Stata, own calculation

Appendix 40: Modified Wald test for groupwise heteroscedasticity

(Ho: groupwise heteroskedasticity across panels)

Regression model	Test statistic	Df	p value*
RIOE	13,523.39	135	**0.00**
Income/Equity	19,759.60	135	**0.00**
Cost/Equity	1.20E+32	135	**0.00**
LLP/Equity (1)	95,184.77	135	**0.00**
LLP/Equity (2)	120,000.00	135	**0.00**

* According to the χ^2 distribution with *Df* degrees of freedom; bold p value suggests rejecting Ho.

Source: Stata, own calculation

Appendix 41: Summary results for the fixed effects model by sample

Variable	RIOE		Income/Equity		Cost/Equity		LLP/Equity (1)		LLP/Equity (2)	
	Coef.	P>(t)	Coef.	P>(t)	Coef.	P>(t)	Coef.	P>(t)	Coef.	P>(t)
Universal Banks (112 observations, 29 groups)										
Interest Income/Total Income	0.06	0.50	-0.26	0.28	-0.32	0.10	-0.14	0.03	-0.20	0.03
Customer/Branch	0.15	0.00	0.11	0.40	0.03	0.75	0.07	0.05	0.03	0.54
Total Cost/Employee	-1.06	0.00	-2.69	0.01	-1.32	0.11	-0.61	0.02	-1.05	0.01
LLP/Interest Income	-0.04	0.42	0.11	0.41	-0.01	0.95	0.32	0.00	–	
Interest Rate	0.35	0.42	4.13	0.00	3.21	0.00	0.77	0.02	0.00	0.99
Log Assets	-0.02	0.48	-0.03	0.57	0.01	0.86	-0.01	0.49	-0.01	0.81
Constant	0.22	0.37	1.36	0.05	0.58	0.30	0.24	0.20	0.35	0.16
R² overall	0.26		0.00		0.19		0.22		0.08	
Savings Banks (636 observations, 106 groups)										
Interest Income/Income (BM)	-0.17	0.00	-0.67	0.00	-0.20	0.00	-0.12	0.00	-0.52	0.00
Customer/Branch (FS)	-0.01	0.47	-0.08	0.03	-0.08	0.00	0.00	0.69	0.10	0.01
Total Cost/Employee (CO)	-1.15	0.00	-0.59	0.20	1.45	0.00	-0.17	0.10	1.50	0.00
LLP/Interest Income (RC)	-0.29	0.00	0.00	0.89	-0.08	0.00	0.54	0.00	–	
Interest Rate (IR)	-1.51	0.00	-0.80	0.28	1.09	0.00	-0.02	0.08	2.57	0.00
Log Assets (A)	-0.07	0.00	-0.17	0.00	-0.06	0.00	-0.01	0.01	0.17	0.00
Constant	0.83	0.00	2.44	0.00	0.92	0.00	0.18	0.00	-1.35	0.00
R² overall	0.32		0.00		0.02		0.90		0.02	

Source: Stata, own calculation

Appendix 42: Summary results for the between effects model by sample

Variable	RIOE		Income/Equity		Cost/Equity		LLP/Equity (1)		LLP/Equity (2)	
	Coef.	P(t)	Coef	P(t)	Coef	P(t)	Coef	P(t)	Coef	P(t)
Universal Banks (112 observations, 29 groups)										
Interest Income/Total Income	0.08	0.37	1.35	0.00	1.01	0.00	0.17	0.01	0.23	0.01
Customer/Branch	0.08	0.13	0.29	0.04	0.22	0.05	0.08	0.02	0.04	0.36
Total Cost/Employee	-1.43	0.03	-1.65	0.34	0.89	0.52	-0.69	0.09	-0.24	0.69
LLP/Interest Income	-0.24	0.02	-0.49	0.08	-0.29	0.20	0.36	0.00	–	
Interest Rate	-1.20	0.38	-3.12	0.42	-1.20	0.69	-1.03	0.25	-2.43	0.07
Log Assets	-0.02	0.20	-0.05	0.25	-0.02	0.52	0.00	0.87	-0.01	0.69
Constant	0.45	0.04	0.87	0.13	0.09	0.84	-0.02	0.90	0.13	0.52
R² overall	0.38		0.52		0.54		0.60		0.20	
Savings Banks (636 observations, 106 groups)										
Interest Income/Total Income	-0.13	0.00	0.61	0.01	0.78	0.00	0.02	0.58	-0.09	0.30
Customer/Branch	0.00	0.90	-0.03	0.69	-0.03	0.56	0.00	0.62	-0.05	0.04
Total Cost/Employee	-0.66	0.01	4.11	0.00	4.66	0.00	0.56	0.00	0.30	0.55
LLP/Interest Income	-0.13	0.00	0.41	0.02	0.00	0.98	0.60	0.00	–	
Interest Rate	*drop*		*drop*		*drop*		*drop*		*drop*	
Log Assets	0.01	0.05	-0.05	0.04	-0.06	0.01	-0.01	0.04	0.01	0.26
Constant	0.03	0.31	0.51	0.01	0.32	0.04	0.00	0.88	0.06	0.39
R² overall	0.55		0.02		0.17		0.92		0.03	

Source: Stata, own calculation

Appendix 43: Regression results for alternative branch structure parameters

(748 observations, 135 groups)

Variable	(Customer/Branch)²		Employee/Branch		Customer/Employee*		Assets/Customers	
	Coef.	P>(t)	Coef.	P>(t)	Coef.	P>(t)	Coef.	P>(t)
Fixed Effects regression								
Income/Equity	0.00	0.88	0.00	0.84	-0.02	0.05	0.00	0.64
Cost/Equity	-0.02	0.29	0.00	0.47	-0.04	0.00	0.00	0.02
LLP/Equity (1)	0.02	0.01	0.00	0.16	0.00	0.57	0.00	0.59
LLP/Equity (2)	0.10	0.00	0.00	0.00	-0.01	0.55	0.00	0.00
RIOE	0.01	0.35	0.00	0.23	0.01	0.05	0.00	0.87
Between Effects regression								
Income/Equity	0.00	0.88	0.00	0.84	-0.02	0.05	0.00	0.64
Cost/Equity	-0.02	0.29	0.00	0.47	-0.04	0.00	0.00	0.02
LLP/Equity (1)	0.02	0.01	0.00	0.16	0.00	0.57	0.00	0.59
LLP/Equity (2)	0.10	0.00	0.00	0.00	-0.01	0.55	0.00	0.00
RIOE	0.01	0.35	0.00	0.23	0.01	0.05	0.00	0.87

* in 100 customer per employee

Source: Stata, own calculation